The Book of Daniel

LA MONTAÑA ~ The Movie

Based on a true story.

Watch for Free
on YouTube

DVD Available
by Donation
SOM International

DVD Available
on Amazon

https://www.youtube.com/watch?v=elKostRbNOw

The Book of Daniel

and other related prophecies

RUSSELL M. STENDAL

RANSOM PRESS INTERNATIONAL

RANSOM PRESS INTERNATIONAL

CONTENTS

Foreword I

PART I

The Prophecy of Daniel

CHAPTER ONE
God is the Judge 1

CHAPTER TWO
Being Understood in Heaven.................................11

CHAPTER THREE
True Liberty 27

CHAPTER FOUR
Seven Times Over The Beast 43

CHAPTER FIVE
The Writing on the Wall..55

CHAPTER SIX
Perfection Is a State of the Heart.......................73

CHAPTER SEVEN
The Sum of the Matters 89

CHAPTER EIGHT
Walking in the Light..109

CHAPTER NINE
Confirming the Covenant......................................131

CHAPTER TEN
The Time of Fulfillment 153

CHAPTER ELEVEN
Kings of the South and North.............................167

CHAPTER TWELVE
A Time of Trouble 181

Part II
Prophecies of David, Haggai, Zephaniah, and Zachariah

CHAPTER THIRTEEN
The Morning Star and a Prophecy of David 197

CHAPTER FOURTEEN
The Time Is When the Lord Says: Haggai's Prophecy... 221

CHAPTER FIFTEEN
The Prophet Haggai on Placing
the Right Foundation 239

CHAPTER SIXTEEN
God's House Restored: Prophecy
of Zephaniah and Haggai 245

CHAPTER SEVENTEEN
City of Truth and Mountain
of Holiness: Zechariah's Prophecy 269

APPENDIX
Simple Timeline According
to Scripture 275

Foreword

As I was working on the edits of this book, a good friend said to me, "I've been thinking a lot about you because you are beginning your productive years. It's time to work and support your family according to what is established in the system. What do you think about what is happening in the world around us? What do you think you are doing?"

I do not doubt that he had good intentions in our chat. I tried to justify my situation in the same way he did when he spoke of his life. In the conversation, our convictions were clear to both of us, even though neither of us knew how to express them at that moment. How could I summarize my passion for working for the Lord in a way that he would understand, since it wasn't logical by the standards of the world?

In a time when the purity and simplicity of the Word have become a great feast or great bondage, so much effort and dedication to a job that began as an impulse placed by the Lord can only be explained with the reaction that our Lord Jesus had when he saw the state of the temple: The zeal of thy house has consumed me (Psalm 69:9; John 2:17). The work to which God has called me has consumed me.

Several weeks passed after the encounter with my friend, but to my surprise, the answers to his questions kept coming little by little. The One who motivated me to begin this project is the same One who began answering my questions. I found the summary of his responses in the last chapter of this book in Scripture:

> *Thus speaketh the LORD of the hosts, saying, This people say, The time is not yet come, the time to build the house of the LORD. Then came the word of the LORD by the hand of Haggai the prophet, saying, Do you have time, all of you, to dwell in your panelled houses, and this house is deserted? Now therefore thus hath the LORD of the hosts said; Consider your ways.* (Haggai 1:2–5)

It is foolishness in the eyes of the world to spend so much time dedicated to the Lord's work; others consider a person who walks against this world's system as "unemployed." However, when I read these verses, I ask myself, "If we truly do not have the time that we think we have, and this is evident in my life, what is more foolish? Is it more foolish to go against the system or to go against the zeal that has been placed in my heart by the Lord, the zeal for the truth?"

Remaining faithful to a calling (if this is the right word) is not easy; recognizing work produced by the zeal of the Lord as a "real job" isn't easy. Only the Lord can work beforehand so we don't deviate from his path that has been laid out. So in the end we can say, like David, that if this is foolishness to the world, then we will yet be more vile…" (2 Samuel 6:14–22).

Many, consciously or unconsciously, will speak of the woman who, out of her own free will (just like the true sacrifices for the Lord were done), broke the alabaster box and then poured the ointment of great price upon the Lord's head. They will say, "What foolishness, what waste; that perfume could have been sold at a great price and given to the poor." In the same manner, the Lord will tell them:

> *But Jesus said, Let her alone; why trouble ye her? She has wrought a good work on me. For ye have the poor with you always, and whenever ye will, ye may do them good; but me ye have not always. She has done what she could, for she has anticipated anointing my body for the burial. Verily I say unto you, Wherever this gospel shall be preached throughout the whole world, this also that she has done shall be spoken of for a memorial of her. (Mark 14:6–9)*

All those who have decided to pour out their lives before the Lord out of their own free will, with sincerity and honesty of heart and against what is common in the eyes of men, comprise this woman.

The book you're holding came about as I had described: against the current. It was produced as part of a series of unpremeditated, spontaneous messages in an auditorium, recorded and destined for some radio stations situated in high-risk zones in Colombia with the purpose of spreading the gospel through radio waves.

The book contains part of a series of one hundred messages, called "A Different Kingdom," and is completed with three more messages: "The Prophecy of David in Psalm 22" and "The Prophecy of Haggai" that are part of another series of one hundred messages called "Peace Be with You."

The messages in both audio and written format fulfill the same purpose. Before they went to the public, they were written in the tablets of the hearts of the people who feel a fervent zeal for the house of the Lord, just like their Master. The circumstances in which each one of these people have found themselves is as indescribable as knowing that the Lord has a master plan.

People such as Russell Stendal and his family have been the voices, the ambassadors of the Lord from the embassy of the Lord to Colombia – a country whose best personification could be the demon-possessed Gergesenes that Scripture describes (Matthew 8:28–34; Mark 5:1–20; Luke 8:26–39).

The message these faithful people have been preaching is linked to the beginning of the book of Daniel and the end of the book of Haggai: purity of heart that is united with holiness. Daniel purposed in his heart – stood by his conviction – that he would not defile himself with the portion of the king's food or wine. The end of the book of Haggai says, Consider now in your heart from this day forth . . . from the day that the foundation of the LORD'S temple was laid, put your heart into it (Haggai 2:18).

If this book and the trials each of us has experienced can serve as a guide to lead us to a personal and direct encounter with the Lord without intermediaries, following our Master and older Brother, the Lord Jesus, it will be gratifying. Even more than that, it will be indescribable if what the apostle described in Galatians 2:20 is fulfilled in us.

> *I am crucified with Christ; nevertheless I live; yet not I, but Christ lives in me, and the life which I now live in the flesh I live by the faith of the Son of God, who loved me and gave himself for me.* (Galatians 2:20)

All things considered, what a privilege it is to dedicate my productive years to the service of the Lord! The latter years will definitely be better than the former.

Samuel David Hernández G., Editor

Part I

The Prophecy of Daniel

Chapter One

God is the Judge

Full of supernatural wonders, this book is a record of the life and revelations given to Daniel as a captive Jew in Babylon, and to David, Haggai, and Zechariah. It is a course in history and Israel's relationship to it. Jerusalem was in ruins, and many Israelites were captive in Babylon.

Beginning with four boys in a pagan land ruled by a prideful king, and ending with the king's recognition of the presence of God in these four, the Lord used this king to reveal an outline of his plan. He revealed the human empires, where they are going to end, and how the true kingdom of God will come forth. We find all of this in twelve brief chapters.

Later in the Gospels, the Lord Jesus said he did not come to judge us, but if he did judge us, his judgment would be true.

> *Ye judge after the flesh, but I judge no one. And yet if I judge, my judgment is true, for I am not alone, but I and the Father that sent me.* (John 8:15–16)

God is My Judge

The Lord Jesus did not come to do his own will or to speak his own words. He came to do the will of his Father and speak his Father's words.

1. The foundation is in the Gospels where we learn that Jesus is the fulfillment of the word "Daniel," which means "God is (the) judge." Jesus was filled with his Father's life and presence. When Scripture refers to him as a judge, it's because the Father's judgement flows through him, which we will cover more in chapter (John 8:26, 9:39, 12:47-49).

2. The Father has seen fit to confer great authority on the Lord Jesus Christ (Acts 10:42, 2 Corinthians 5:10, John 5:22).

Jesus said he was the temple of God,[1] and his plan is to have a greater temple where he is the cornerstone[2] and we are the living stones;[3] he is the older brother,[4] the head of the body.[5] In that temple we, as believers, are partakers of his nature – meaning he works in us to bring forth his characteristics in us – because he lives in us and he is the beginning and the end. Whereby are given unto us exceeding great and precious promises, that by these ye might be made participants of the divine nature, having fled the corruption that is in the world through lust (2 Peter 1:4).

When the meaning of the word "Daniel" is fulfilled in us, we will stop judging by our own criteria. We will not judge according to appearances, and we will not judge on our own. If we live with the presence of our Lord in us, we will fulfill his will, do his work, and express his words; then the judgment of God will flow through us.

This same judgment is what Daniel illustrates to both Israel and the Gentile nations with his God-given interpretations of visions and dreams.

Daniel 1

> [1] *In the third year of the reign of Jehoiakim king of Judah Nebuchadnezzar king of Babylon came unto Jerusalem and besieged it.*
>
> [2] *And the Lord gave Jehoiakim king of Judah into his hand with part of the vessels of the house of God which he carried into the land of Shinar to the house of his god, and he brought the vessels into the treasure house of his god.*

Who gave the king of the people of God into the hands of a pagan king? Clearly, the Lord did. If the Lord is judge, he has the right to do anything he wants. He spoke through his prophet Jeremiah telling the Israelites it was better for them to go into captivity than to fight against the Babylonians. That is why they called Jeremiah a traitor to their country; even so, it was still the word of God.

During this time, the Lord spoke through the mouth of Jeremiah that if just one righteous man could be found, the city would be spared; but there weren't any found. Under the law, it wasn't possible for fallen

---

1 John 2:19-21
2 See Matthew 21:42; Mark 12:10; Luke 20:17.
3 1 Peter 2:3–5
4 Romans 8:29
5 Colossians 1:18

man to be righteous because no one can fulfill the law of God in his or her own life or in their own strength.

Babylon

Babylon symbolizes confusion, and this is what man comes to when he implements his own plans in his own way. Another name for Babylon is "the land of Chaldea," or "of the Chaldeans," which means "spiritualist." This second definition has to do with this kind of spiritualism: when man follows his own way, he falls into the hands of other spirits. The third identifies this place as "the land of Shinar," or "land of two rivers."

Babylon was in the midst of two natural rivers: the Euphrates and the Tigris. However, one river of Babylon was a man-made river called Chebar. Similar to how Babylon confused its own religious, economic, and political systems, men today have tried to construct their own river, their own source, and their own sustenance.

In the world's economy, people always want to produce money out of nowhere. Sooner or later, those economies will fall, and printing money leads into the economic business cycles of the world.

In politics, man in his own wisdom has concluded that the source of authority and power proceeds from the people. This produces oscillations that go back and forth. Politics yo-yo from left to right and back again; what is done by some in power is later undone by others.

In religion, when man attempts to be his own source (of wisdom, doctrine, philosophy, etc), a kind of spiritual homosexuality is created. Many countries are now approving laws for homosexuals and lesbians to marry, but even if some governments allow it, they will never be able to reproduce life. It's impossible. Likewise, everything becomes sterile when we receive our ideas and plans from man instead from God. In the same manner, such a church cannot beget life. The only thing it can do is try to make our stay on earth a little better.

When the church gets deeply involved in humanism, thinking that the center of everything is their own happiness, people lose their way. This not only happened to the people of God, but they also became worse than the pagans! Because of this, the Lord sent Nebuchadnezzar to destroy Jerusalem and take the best of it to Babylon.

> *³ And the king spoke unto Ashpenaz the prince of his eunuchs, that he should bring certain of the sons of Israel of the royal lineage of the princes,*
> *⁴ young men in whom there was no blemish whatsoever but*

*who were good looking and taught in all wisdom and wise in
knowledge and of good understanding, and that had strength
in them to stand in the king's palace, that they might be taught
the letters and speech of the Chaldeans.*

The king sent his men to bring in the best: the noblemen of Judah and
Jerusalem. In the Old Testament, one was either born a slave or a free
man (or in other words, a man of noble birth). In Revelation 12:5 a Man
of noble birth is born.[6]

God uses all these examples (including some of the great injustices
of history) to show us we are all born as slaves to our own desires. This
causes us to become enslaved to the prince of this world, which is the
devil himself. God also shows us that we have the opportunity of being
born a second time through our Lord Jesus. Scripture says that when the
Son of God sets someone free, then they are truly free (John 8:36), and
there is liberty wherever the Spirit of the Lord is (2 Corinthians 3:17).
God wants to give us his Spirit because he wants us to be the temple of
the Holy Spirit.

These young men, who had no blemish and were the best of the people of God, were taken captive to Babylon to be taught the writing and
language of the Chaldeans. In the original, "Chaldean" means "spiritualist." Therefore, the king's men gave the young men a course on spiritualism so they could learn the teachings of the magi, astrologers, and wise
men of that time who were spiritualists. The man who was in charge was
the chief of the eunuchs. A "eunuch" is a man who has been castrated.
The king would not allow the man in charge of that part of the palace to
have children. Therefore, we can deduce that this prince, and most likely
everyone under his care, would be castrated to avoid any potential usur-
per to the throne who might want to create his own dynasty.[7]

*[5] And the king appointed them a daily provision of the king's
food and of the wine which he drank, so nourishing them three
years, that at the end thereof they might stand before the king.*

Daniel and His Friends

If the king chose the best and wisest of all the nations he conquered; if he

---

6   And she brought forth a man child, who was to rule all the Gentiles with a rod of
iron; and her child was caught up unto God and to his throne. (Revelation 12:5)

7   The word, eunuch, is used 44 times in the JB translation. A careful study of the use
of this word in Scripture will help anyone who is struggling to understand the back-
ground and definition of this term.

then castrated them and submitted them to three years of intense study in the writings and language of the Chaldeans, this would have included many strange tenets. The Chaldean spiritualists, like some of their pagan counterparts that continue even into "modern" times (such as some members of the tribal groups I have had the opportunity to live among and also among the modern spiritualists and "santeros" so common in Latin America), believed there was a spirit behind everything, and they needed to get permission from all the spirits in order to be able to act. If anything went wrong, these spirits had to be placated . . . even with human blood. Imagine what kind of courses Daniel and his friends were required to study!

> *6 Now among these of the sons of Judah were Daniel, Hananiah, Mishael, and Azariah:*

Daniel and his friends were taken captive along with the vessels of the temple of God (v. 2). The vessels symbolize the true servants of God, like Daniel, his friends, and others. Compared to the rest of the people of God, Daniel and his friends were the cream of the crop. The Lord's commandment was that they had to go to Babylon in captivity as a result of a collective sin of all the people of God. We don't know of any wrong that Daniel and his friends might have done individually before their captivity. But they found themselves in an unfortunate situation, in the midst of those who supposedly were the people of God.

But God is the judge. Not only does "Daniel" mean "God is the judge," but the meanings of names of his friends express the goodness, the mercy, and the benevolence of God. The Chaldeans, however, changed the names of these Israelites:

> *7 unto whom the prince of the eunuchs gave names: for he gave unto Daniel the name of Belteshazzar . . .*

Bel was one of the Babylonians main gods, similar to Baal. Belteshazzar means "Bel preserves his life." So instead of having a name that means "God is the judge," they changed it to "Baal preserves his life."

> *7 . . . and to Hananiah, of Shadrach; and to Mishael, of Meshach; and to Azariah, of Abednego.*

All these names had to do with the supposed goodness of pagan gods.

> *8 And Daniel purposed in his heart that he would not defile himself with the portion of the king's food, nor with the wine*

which he drank; therefore he requested of the prince of the eu-
nuchs that he might not defile himself.

Daniel didn't feel contaminated because he still wanted to work in harmony with the authority placed by God, not his own will. God sent the pagans to destroy Jerusalem and capture the inhabitants. Even after such a disaster, Daniel did not curse them or lament his situation or have a bad attitude toward them like many Christians claiming to represent God might do. Instead, he simply requested that he not contaminate himself with the food and drink of the king.

There are two kinds of wine: the first symbolizes the life of the natural man, and the second symbolizes the life of God. Daniel didn't want to nourish the life of the natural man; he wanted to feed the life of God in him. Daniel could have mixed the two as many priests and Levites did in Israel until they harvested a tremendous problem. Daniel could have entered into complete apostasy. However, his decision was to not defile himself. Daniel recognized that God was the judge; he had given the Babylonians authority, and if they obligated him to eat or drink something, he would have to do it. But if they gave him permission, he would abstain himself.

> [9] *(And God brought Daniel into grace and mercy with the prince of the eunuchs.)*

Daniel found grace in the eyes of the man who was placed in authority in this pagan university.

> [10] *And the prince of the eunuchs said unto Daniel, I fear my lord the king, who has appointed your food and your drink; for when he shall see your faces more downcast than the other young men who are like unto you, then ye shall condemn my head before the king.*

Some governments demand results, and King Nebuchadnezzar was like this to an extreme. A person who did not produce what the king wanted would be immediately condemned. The director of the Chaldean university feared that if the king saw one of these young men downcast, he, the director, could be executed.

> [11] *Then Daniel said to Melzar, whom the prince of the eunuchs had set over Daniel, Hananiah, Mishael, and Azariah,*
> [12] *Prove, now, with thy servants ten days, and let them give us vegetables to eat and water to drink.*

13 Then let our countenances be looked upon before thee, and the countenances of the young men that eat of the portion of the king's food; and as thou seest, deal with thy servants.

Daniel was willing to be realistic. He essentially said to the prince, "We are going to do things God's way, and you can judge for yourself in ten days."

14 So he consented to them in this matter and proved them ten days.

15 And at the end of ten days their countenances appeared fairer and fatter in flesh than the young men who ate the portion of the king's food.

This still happens in our time. People decide whether they are going to spiritually feed themselves from what the world offers or from God. Sometimes what comes from God seems like vegetables and water; but Scripture says that man will not live by bread alone, but by every word that proceeds from the mouth of God! (Deuteronomy 8:3).

In Scripture, God's word is sometimes symbolized as "water" and other times as "green pastures" (vegetables). Daniel and his friends chose to receive only what God provided, and they did better than those who received a banquet with the best of the kingdom of Babylon.

16 Thus Melzar took the portion of their food and the wine that they should drink and gave them vegetables.

It went well for Melzar because he received the expensive wine and food and gave these young men vegetables and water!

17 And unto these four young men, God gave them knowledge and intelligence in all letters and science; furthermore Daniel had understanding in all visions and dreams.

The interpretation of dreams and visions was an important thing to the ancient pagans and the Chaldeans.[8] Their science dealt with determining the times with astrology.[9]

On several occasions, there were kings who had dreams that no one could interpret. These dreams can come from at least three sources. Someone can have a dream that comes from God, they can have dreams from the devil, or sometimes one can have a dream about the beans they ate the night before. Imagine being in a course of spiritualism and having

---

8   Genesis 41:1–10; Daniel 2
9   Matthew 2:1–10

to interpret every crazy dream that anyone had!

So, in the middle of a course meant to teach them the knowledge and the letters of the Chaldeans and spiritualists, Daniel initiated a suspension of the king's food. They nourished themselves with what came from God. Instead of receiving the secrets of the Chaldeans and learning to act like the astrologers and magicians, these four boys received knowledge and intelligence in all letters and science from God. Furthermore, Daniel gained understanding in all visions and dreams. In the middle of this, God gave them an even greater course – one that came from the very nature of God.

> [18] *Now at the end of the days after which the king had said he should bring them in, the prince of the eunuchs brought them in before Nebuchadnezzar.*
>
> [19] *And the king communed with them, and none among them all was found like Daniel, Hananiah, Mishael, and Azariah; and therefore they stood before the king.*

From God's point of view, they remained with their true names that were given them as sons of God and not the pagan names.

Even when they were in Babylon, in the very heart of all the paganism of the time and enrolled in the highest course available, they did not let themselves become defiled. This pagan instruction was filled with many perversions and mysteries. Men had to be initiated in occult practices in order to understand these mysteries. Much of this involved worshipping pagan goddesses such as Ashtoreth[10] through sexual acts. The fact that the four men were most likely castrated may have been a major blessing because it prevented them from participating in the deep rituals and sexual activity in the pagan temples of Babylon. Many times, what seems like a curse turns out to be a blessing.

> [20] *And in all matters of wisdom and intelligence, that the king enquired of them, he found them ten times better than all the magicians and astrologers that were in all his realm.*
>
> [21] *And Daniel continued even unto the first year of King Cyrus.*

When Daniel and his friends arrived in Babylon, they had decided not to contaminate themselves. This led to many tests during their time there. Because of God's goodness and the fact that they did not contaminate themselves, the king found them ten times greater in wisdom and intelligence.

---

10   1 Kings 11:5, 33; 2 Kings 23:13

This chapter is like a summary of Daniel's life because at the end, it implies that he outlived all these magicians and astrologers and even several pagan kings. When Babylon ended, Daniel continued.

God didn't place Daniel and his three friends in Babylon to claim it for himself. God wasn't interested capturing Babylon; he wasn't interested in what these pagan magicians, Chaldeans, or kings were doing. He wasn't trying to control the world. That wasn't his plan. His plan was to show that he could take of his people who desired to be clean and keep them undefiled in the midst of the very worst system of Babylon.

Furthermore, the authority of God was always going to be higher than the authority of the pagans. This was true even when God allowed the ultimate consequences of each person's will to be fulfilled. God is still doing this today. Look at what God says near the end of the book:

> *Many shall be purified and made white and purged, but the wicked shall get worse; and none of the wicked shall understand, but the wise shall understand.*[11] (Daniel 12:10)

Daniel received understanding and wisdom from God, but he was also understood by God. We will soon see that when Daniel asked for an explanation, God responded immediately and sent Gabriel to explain it to him (Daniel 8:16; 9:21). Michael, one of the main princes, had to spend twenty-one days fighting alongside Gabriel so that Daniel could receive the response. Likewise, Gabriel said that from the first day Daniel gave his heart to understand, his words were heard (Daniel 10:12–13).

When Daniel spoke with God, God understood him. Sadly, there are many who spend much time in prayer and little or nothing is understood about them in heaven; it's all confusion and repetition of vain words. These people do not receive and cannot receive the response that the prayers of Daniel received.

Let us pray:

Lord, let us as individuals and as a people be clean like Daniel was in the midst of so much adversity, in the middle of so much temptation and corruption. Let us be clean, purged, and understood as he was. Lord show us the meaning of the verse, the wise shall understand. Let us be wise and understood in the heavenly realm. Amen.

---

11   In the Spanish version of the Jubilee Bible, the verse "the wise shall understand" is translated, as "the understood shall understand."

CHAPTER TWO

Being Understood in Heaven

Daniel 2

¹ *And in the second year of the reign of Nebuchadnezzar, Nebuchadnezzar dreamed dreams, with which his spirit was troubled, and his sleep fled from him.*
² *Then the king commanded to call magicians, astrologers, enchanters, and Chaldeans, that they might show the king his dreams. So they came and presented themselves before the king.*

Magicians, Astrologers, and Spiritualists

This second chapter began before the first chapter ended because it makes reference to the second year of the reign of Nebuchadnezzar, and the time frame of the first chapter is a period of three years. So, this chapter develops in the middle of the witchcraft and spiritualist course with all the pagan practices.

> ³ *And the king said unto them, I have dreamed a dream, and my spirit was troubled to know the dream.*

In one sense, all men have an unfulfilled "dream" inside that they cannot remember – they feel it in their soul and know in their mind when things are not right. Emptiness and longing exists in each person born in Adam's nature. People want to know the interpretation, and they look for it in different places hoping someone might give them an explanation.

> ⁴ *Then the Chaldeans spoke to the king in Syriack, O king, live for ever; tell thy servants the dream, and we will show the interpretation.*

> *5 The king answered and said to the Chaldeans, The thing is gone from my memory; if ye will not make known unto me the dream with its interpretation, ye shall be cut in pieces, and your houses shall be made a dunghill.*

We might think that some modern governments and authoritarian leaders are difficult because they place high demands on people, but in the time of the kings of Babylon, rulers demanded results immediately, and if these weren't produced, the king had the power to kill people.

> *6 But if ye show the dream and its interpretation, ye shall receive of me gifts and rewards and great honour: therefore show me the dream, and its interpretation.*
> *7 They answered the second time and said, Let the king tell his servants the dream, and we will show the interpretation of it.*

Perhaps they spoke in Syriack so the court wouldn't realize they weren't as smart as they made themselves out to be or didn't have the power they pretended to have.

> *8 The king answered and said, I know of certainty that ye would gain time because ye see the thing is gone from my memory.*
> *9 But if ye will not make known unto me the dream, there is but one decree for you for ye certainly prepare lying and corrupt words to speak before me, until the time is changed; therefore tell me the dream, and I shall know that ye can show me its interpretation.*

For the king, it was better to have forgotten the dream. He knew that if the Chaldeans told him the dream, he would remember it; if they couldn't tell him, he suspected they didn't have the wisdom to declare its true significance. In the same manner, those who pretend to give declarations of things invisible to the human race cannot do it, much less give an interpretation.

Notice the attitude of Daniel and his friends. They didn't come to Babylon with words of condemnation for the king; they did not talk bad about him; they didn't bad-mouth Babylon's army; and they didn't speak against Babylon. They accepted God's judgment on them and their people, but they also found a way to receive nourishment with clean food and to remain pure in the midst of a completely contaminated environment.

> *10 The Chaldeans answered before the king, and said, There is not a man upon the earth that can show the king's matter;*

> *furthermore there is no king, prince, nor lord that asked such*
> *a thing of any magician or astrologer or Chaldean.*
> ¹¹ *Finally, the thing that the king requires is singular, and there*
> *is no one that can show it before the king except the angels of*
> *God, whose dwelling is not with flesh.*

Even in the midst of their paganism, the Chaldeans knew that angels of God existed who had the wisdom to declare these events. They also knew they had no contact with them.

The word "angel" can speak of the heavenly hosts, but that isn't its exclusive use. "Angel" is the word "Malachi" in Hebrew, which simply means "my messenger." Anyone who is a messenger of God – anyone who receives a charge from God or is sent by God to do something special – is an angel of God. The word "angel" can refer to flesh and blood people like us or God's heavenly hosts. This is why Scripture says that some, having entertained angels, were kept (Hebrews 13:2).

The spiritualists, the magicians, and the astrologers knew there were angels of God who understood these things, but they also knew they dwell among humans. Similarly, in his first letter, John speaks of the antichrist. He says the spirit of antichrist is whatever does not confess that Jesus Christ is come in flesh (1 John 4:3). Notice it doesn't say whoever "does not confess that Jesus Christ has come in flesh." It is a present continuous verb.

Jesus Christ came two thousand years ago, and the antichrist has no problem with that; it has no problem with the Lord being far away and not having anything to do with us, just like the magicians and astrologers had no problem with the angels in whose dwelling is not with flesh. But when we begin to speak of a people of God who have his presence and his wisdom and a continuous open access to him, these people begin to say it isn't true; they say it's impossible.

> ¹² *For this cause the king was angry and very furious and com-*
> *manded to destroy all the wise men of Babylon.*
> ¹³ *And the decree went forth, and the wise men were taken to*
> *be slain, and they sought Daniel and his fellows to kill them.*

All these characters, the so-called wise men of this world, cannot tell the human race its true history, the real meaning of life. If they can't even tell us how we got here, how can we trust what they have to say about the future? They can't do it. The king got mad and decided to kill all of them. The only problem was that Daniel and his three friends were also attending the Chaldean university.

Today, it takes a long time for a government to implement a decree; but in those days, the king's orders were fulfilled instantly. This had its advantages and disadvantages.

> *¹⁴ Then Daniel spoke with counsel and wisdom to Arioch the captain of the king's guard, who was gone forth to slay the wise men of Babylon.*
> *¹⁵ He spoke and said to Arioch the king's captain, What is the reason for which this decree has gone forth from the king with such haste? Then Arioch made the thing known to Daniel.*

Arioch told Daniel the king had discovered that the wise men, the magi, the spiritualists, and the witches were nothing but a bunch of liars and that it was better to kill them all. How many "wise" people in the universities and colleges and positions of power in this day and age are, in reality, only liars?

> *¹⁶ And Daniel went in, and asked the king that he give him time and that he would show the king the interpretation.*

Daniel is an example and a shadow of Jesus who also came as a slave, respecting God's judgment and saying, I can of my own self do nothing; as I hear, I judge, and my judgment is just because I seek not my own will, but the will of the Father who has sent me (John 5:30). Jesus said he did not come to do his own will or to say his own words. Any judgment that came out of his mouth would be his Father's judgment flowing through him.

What did the Lord Jesus do with the Samaritan woman he found near the well who'd had five husbands and was living with one that was not her husband? He gave her life, he treated her with dignity, and she came away filled with joy and ready to convince everyone, even the religious Jews, about his truth.

The Lord Jesus spoke to them about the Good Samaritan, but they didn't understand. They brought him the woman caught in adultery, but the Lord didn't even accuse her.[12] He sent her forth with a word that probably remained engraved in her heart and mind for the rest of her life: go and sin no more (John 8:11).

If we depend on what God says, then what he says can be fulfilled in

---

12   Under the law, only a free woman could be sentenced to death for adultery. This woman was a slave to sin (like many others under law) but a direct, personal word from the Lord set her free! (See Leviticus 19:20.)

us. If that woman truly believed the word that God gave her, it was possible for her to go and sin no more. If it hadn't been possible, he wouldn't have spoken it.

Daniel had the same attitude as the Lord Jesus. He didn't judge the Babylonians, even though he was in the midst of a terrible and perverse situation. He took everything with a good attitude. He desired good for the pagan king and not evil. Deep down, the king knew that the magicians, the Chaldeans, and the professors at the university were not as wise as they made themselves out to be. Even with their occult sciences, they couldn't tell him the dream he had the night before.

> *[17] Then Daniel went to his house and made the thing known to Hananiah, Mishael, and Azariah, his companions,*

These men had been given pagan names, as mentioned before. Daniel, which means "God is the judge," was replaced with Belteshazzar, which means "Baal will preserve his life." Daniel's three friends had also received different names, but the Bible keeps referring to them with their Hebrew names.

> *[18] to petition mercies of the God of heaven concerning this mystery and that Daniel and his fellows should not perish with the rest of the wise men of Babylon.*
> *[19] Then the mystery was revealed unto Daniel in a night vision for which Daniel blessed the God of heaven.*
> *[20] And Daniel spoke and said, Blessed be the name of God from age to age for wisdom and might are his;*
> *[21] and it is he that changes the times and the opportunities; he removes kings and sets up kings; he gives wisdom unto the wise and knowledge unto those that know understanding:*

Being Understood

Verse 21 says God gives wisdom to the wise and knowledge to those that know understanding. This word "understanding" appears frequently throughout the Word of God. Who are the ones that know understanding? It's one thing when God enlightens us and opens our minds and hearts so we can understand something. But there are those who pass beyond that realm and "know understanding," because God understands them and knows them.

When they say something or when they ask him something, it makes sense to God. The clean remnant are purged of all contamination and, like Daniel, have decided to do everything possible to not contaminate themselves.

Daniel remained undefiled by eating only vegetables and drinking water. We can remain undefiled by rejecting the river of humanism with its "production" and "agriculture." We can decide to receive everything that comes from God, our clean source. The man-made river was constructed to cultivate grapes, fatten cows, and make the pagan cult function. The king's food came from those sacrifices and offerings. The river of Chebar, which was a canal made by man, provided all of this.

"Euphrates" means "double fruitfulness." This is what happens when things are done God's way. On the other hand, the river of humanism produces fornication and homosexuality. It produces the union of humanity with other spirits that are not of God. It also creates the illusion that man in union with man can reproduce life.

This isn't true. In the United States and Europe, there is much talk about human and homosexual rights. True, we all have rights. Fornicators also have rights because they are also citizens. The same law applies to everyone. Some Christians, by trying to clean the nation on their own, propose a kind of inquisition to end homosexuality. This may sound good, but it isn't God's way, for he makes his sun to rise on the evil and on the good and sends rain on the just and on the unjust (Matthew 5:45). However, at the end of the season, judgment will take place based on the fruit.

Before the Babylonians took over Jerusalem and before king Jehoiakim, Josiah was the king who lost control of Israel. Scripture says that Josiah made some of the greatest reforms in the history of Israel. He attempted tremendous reform to rid the nation of evil. He tore down the pagan altars that no one dared to tear down because Solomon had made them. He took the pagan priests, killed them, and burned their bones on top of their own altars. He killed witches and spiritualists; he reformed everything by brute force.

Josiah was so sure he had God's approval that when the king of Egypt came against the king of Babylon, he went to the battle, even though God had not told him to do so. In the end, he was so scared that Scripture says he took off his kingly suit of chain mail that covered him completely. He put on a common captain's breastplate to disguise himself. It had leather joints at the sides to join the front and back, and an arrow pierced him through the unprotected side. Josiah's glory and reform ended.

If God's life is in us, we will not have to impose our values on others by brute force. People who sin know they lack fullness and satisfaction. Can we really blame them if they haven't seen anything better, if the people of God have never shown them what works better?

The goal and the challenge we have is the same one Daniel and his three friends had. They came to Babylon, captured by the same spiritualists that King Josiah had spent his whole life trying to destroy. All the bad that the enemy tried to do to them turned into good. If they were castrated, this would have removed them from a realm of temptation, but it's clear they realized that the decision to remain clean and uncontaminated depended on them.

God began to intervene when they decided not to contaminate themselves. The same God who had declared the judgment now declared that they would find grace with their captors. He began to work in a way that the king of the pagans himself would have to acknowledge God as the only true God, and all those other spirits were good for nothing.

Daniel was conscious that he was in Babylon because God declared it; he is the judge, and for some reason God decided to allow this. Daniel knew that science and wisdom came from God.

On the other hand, the word "understanding" is interesting. God gives wisdom to the wise, but knowledge (which is the essence and explanation for how everything functions and what things are) is given to those who know understanding. We think that God can give us understanding, but it is one thing to say we understand God and quite another when God understands us and when we are understood before his throne in heaven.

How many of us keep on repeating endless prayers, sounding like the confusion of Babylon before the throne of God? These prayers have little or no significance in heaven because true knowledge is given to those that know understanding, to those that speak God's language because it flows from a clean heart.

The phrase "those that know understanding" has been erased from many translations of the Bible simply because they didn't know what to do with it. If we want to obtain true knowledge (vision; the ability to see things for what they are and how they work, where they come from, and where they are going), we need to be understood by God. It's necessary that the way we live here is coherent in heaven.

I fear that many of the prayers that come from some of those who claim to represent God are just as confusing as the prayers of the astrologers, magicians, and Chaldeans of Babylon. They try to use God for their own personal gain and want everyone to revolve around them; when they do not know the answer, they begin talking in "Syriack" so no one will realize their falseness. They praise their own capacity while hiding their lack of understanding.

How many times have we heard a person give us scientific explanations with impressive words, but in the end, they haven't said anything? Daniel, on the other hand, received an answer from God, and it was not due to some hidden ability of his own.

> 21.*. . it is he that changes the times and the opportunities . . .*

There are times and opportunities. Where are we in God's timetable? What are the opportunities that the Lord has for us further on? We will never know if we are not understood in heaven. The opportunities can come and go without us even realizing it. Many are blind because seeing they do not see.[13]

> 21 *. . . he removes kings and sets up kings . . .*

In Latin America and around the world, people are concerned and even troubled about things such as the president's re-election or what's happening in the United States of America; or they worry about changes in the Vatican, etc. God says we need to pray for those who are in power, in spite of what we think of them, because he allowed them to be in that position.

> 22 *He reveals that which is deep and hidden; he knows what is in darkness, and the light dwells with him.*

There is no light outside of God. What we think is light is not light because outside of him, there is only darkness.[14]

> 23 *Unto thee, O God of my fathers, do I confess and give thee praise that thou hast given me wisdom and might and now hast shown me what we asked of thee, for thou hast shown us the king's matter.*

God has had, and will have, a people here on earth who will know the king's matter. Why is our human race here? What is the dominion and authority that God has placed in our power? What will the consequences of all our human good intentions be?

> 24 *After this Daniel went in unto Arioch, whom the king had*

---

13   Matthew 3:13
14   See Matthew 6:22–23.

ordained to destroy the wise men of Babylon; he went and said thus unto him, Do not destroy the wise men of Babylon; bring me in before the king, and I will show unto the king the interpretation.

Notice Daniel's attitude in the midst of so much contamination and perversion. With all the terrible things these people would do, he could have said something like, "Look, king, my three friends and I are the only good ones in this place where there are magicians, astrologers, people who talk to the dead, witches, and perverts who walk in these pagan temples. So, I will tell you the interpretation if you save my three friends and me. As for these other people, kill them, but do not kill us; we are the real deal." Religion, including much of organized Christianity, has functioned like this for centuries, but not Daniel.

How many so-called prophets and people who say they have the word of God would do something like this? They would say something like this: "I have the answer, and I deserve something in exchange; we are going to do these wise men in and impose our beliefs because our group, our denomination, our ministry, our gift of prophecy is the real thing, and we are not going to allow anyone to deceive the king anymore." I fear that this is what many would say today. But this is not what Daniel did.

Daniel had already had encounters with these people. He'd had problems, and later some of these same people tried to kill him in the lions' den. They named him "Baal will preserve his life," yet Daniel was sentenced to death because of them. Their lives, however, were saved because of Daniel. So, where is Baal?

²⁵ Then Arioch brought Daniel in before the king in haste and said thus unto him, I have found a man of the captives of Judah that will make known unto the king the interpretation.

Scripture is clear in that if we try to save our life, we will lose it; but if we lose our life for the Lord and for the gospel, we will find it.[15] When we are in his life, we have the liberty to do God's will. Arioch realized that the life of God was in and with Daniel; he noticed that Daniel behaved in a different way than how all the magicians and wise men of Babylon would have if they had received this revelation.

²⁶ The king answered and said to Daniel, whose name was Belteshazzar, [the king still did not have the revelation] Art thou

---

15   Matthew 16:25 and more.

*able to make me understand the dream which I have seen and
its interpretation?*

*27 Daniel answered in the presence of the king and said, The
mystery which the king demands cannot be shown unto the
king by wise men, astrologers, magicians, nor fortune-tellers.*

*28 But there is a God in the heavens who reveals the mysteries,
and he has made known to the king Nebuchadnezzar what
shall happen at the end of days. Thy dream, and the visions of
thy head upon thy bed, is this:*

Daniel began where the other wise men ended. They had said that no
king had ever demanded such a thing from any magician, astrologer,
or Chaldean. Daniel made them look good when he affirmed the same
thing.

But they said there were angels of God in another realm whose dwelling is not with flesh, and who could reveal the dream to the king, but
they had no access to them. What were they forced to do? They were
forced to admit that they didn't have true wisdom.

However, Daniel gives the answer, lifts God up, and gives them all a
second chance.

*29 Thou, O king, in thy bed, thy thoughts rose up to know what
should come to pass in the future; and he that reveals the mysteries showed thee what shall come to pass.*

*30 And unto me this mystery has been revealed, not for any
wisdom that is in me more than in all those living but that I
notify the interpretation to the king and that thou might understand the thoughts of thy heart.*

Right now, God is raising up a ministry for the same purpose for which
he raised up Daniel: to explain to the human race what their forgotten
unfulfilled dream is. If God is allowing a clean word to flow purer and
purer, it isn't because we are something special but because he has decided that this is the time. The Lord who gave the dream is the same God
that took it away and the same God that broke the king's spirit; he is
doing this now with the entire human race.

31 Thou, O king, didst see and behold a great image. . . .

Nebuchadnezzar's Dream

We were created in the image and likeness of God, and God said that everything he had made was good. But then after a while, God himself repented (turned around) of having made man. He said that men's hearts were perverse and only evil came from them. God wanted to destroy the human race, but Scripture says Noah found grace in the eyes of the LORD (Genesis 6:5–8). Jesus Christ also found grace and favor before God and men (Luke 2:52), and this is what happened with Daniel.

> ³¹ . . . *This image, which was very large and whose glory was very sublime, stood before thee, and its form was terrible.*

His glory was sublime but very terrible, perplexing the king. The inquiry the king had is the same question the entire human race has. There is a great purpose for our existence here, but the present situation has not improved; it has only gotten worse.

> ³² *The head of this image was of fine gold, its breasts and its arms of silver, its belly and its thighs of brass,*
> ³³ *its legs of iron, its feet part of iron and part of baked clay.*

The state of the image began more or less okay, but it progressively deteriorated down to the feet made of iron and clay, which do not mix well. In other words, this image had very sublime, almost divine thoughts, and very capable arms, but it had no ability to walk or function. Gold symbolizes God's nature, and silver symbolizes redemption, but the image had the belly made of bronze, which symbolizes judgment. Humans are terrible at judging others because we all have our own excuses and blame others for the state in which we are in.

The image stood on legs of iron, which represent the law. The feet were made of iron and clay; humans who are of the dust of the earth (or clay) have never been able to fulfill the law. Because we cannot fulfill the law, judgment fails, our redemption fails, our sublime and even divine thoughts end up being hopeless because we cannot walk, and we cannot function. This is what the king saw. Sadly, he didn't fully understand the explanation even though he received it with great joy.

How do I know that he didn't understand it? Later in the third chapter, the king made a statue of himself of pure gold, sixty cubits high and six cubits wide, so that everyone would worship it. How many people who have received a revelation from God have failed because they have tried to implement it their own way?

> ³⁴ *Thou didst see until a stone was cut out, not with hands,*

which smote the image upon its feet that were of iron and baked clay and broke them to pieces.

This stone that crushed the image (representing all our seemingly good human capacities and every empire that ever was or ever will be) was cut without hands. This means we will not be able to bring down this Babylonian system (which is the head of everything man does) with our own hands, or with our own effort. To accomplish this, a stone must be cut without hands. In other words, God is the one who must do it.

> [35] *Then was the iron, the baked clay, the brass, the silver, and the gold broken to pieces together and became like the chaff of the summer threshingfloors; and the wind carried them away that no place was found for them again; and the stone that smote the image was made into a great mountain that filled the whole earth.*
>
> [36] *This is the dream, and we will tell its interpretation before the king.*
>
> [37] *Thou, O king, art king of kings, for the God of heaven has given thee the kingdom, the power, and the strength, and the majesty.*
>
> [38] *And everything that is inhabited by children of men, beasts of the field, and fowls of the heaven, he has given into thine hand, and has made thee ruler over them all. Thou art this head of gold.*

Sometimes we believe we are here in the hands of the devil or other things, and it's true that we have sold our birthright and fallen. But God has given man true authority over all of nature, over everything that can be seen. This has tremendous implications in the realm of the unseen.

> [39] *And after thee shall arise another kingdom inferior to thee, and another third kingdom of brass, which shall bear rule over all the land.*
>
> [40] *And the fourth kingdom shall be strong as iron; and as iron breaks in pieces and subdues all things, and as iron that breaks all these things, it shall break in pieces and bruise.*
>
> [41] *And whereas thou didst see the feet and toes, part of baked potters' clay and part of iron, the kingdom shall be divisive; but there shall be in it some of the strength of the iron, such as thou didst see the iron mixed with baked clay.*

> *[42] And as the toes of the feet were part of iron and part of baked clay, so the kingdom shall be partly strong, and partly fragile.*
> *[43] Concerning that which thou didst see, the iron mixed with baked clay, they shall mingle themselves with the seed of men, but they shall not cleave one to another, even as iron does not mix with clay.*

Human beings have not been able to abide by the imposed laws placed by man. Even when there is a death penalty, they still have not been able to keep them.

> *[44] And in the days of those kings [or kingdoms] the God of heaven shall raise up a kingdom which eternally shall never become corrupted, and this kingdom shall not be left to another people, but it shall break in pieces and consume all these kingdoms, and it shall stand for ever.*

Every human kingdom continues to degrade; corruption is increasing. Right now, no one suggests having one man reign over a country or over the world. Many countries have declared it necessary to have three separate powers: for example, the executive, the legislative, and the judicial. The goal with this system is to distribute the power among many people, but unfortunately, this may actually increase corruption. It does not take very long to run up huge fiscal deficits.

In the Babylonian kingdom, they believed it better for one man to run everything because it made things less complicated. What they accomplished was incredible. They had no debates or political formulas; if the king wanted something to be built, they did it, and fast, because if they didn't, their heads would be cut off. Others would replace the disobedient ones. This was the protocol for war or conquest, and it was a very efficient system.

As far as the systems of this world are concerned, God himself said that the kingdom of Babylon was the head of gold, meaning it functioned better than anything else. Where are we now? After going through Babylon, the Medes and the Persians, the Greeks, the Roman Empire, we are in the time of the democracies. These descendants of the Roman Empire do not function; they cannot walk.

Our society is corrupted more and more each day, and God says this will all end, but not because of the capitalists who exploit their workers, or because of the guerrillas who live in the jungle, or the Muslim extremists – not even because of the world powers or the third world countries. God says it will all collapse without the intervention of hands, in just one hit. There will be a different kingdom that will never become corrupted. For this to happen, there must be a change of life because our life is corrupt, but his life is incorruptible.

In order to fill the whole earth with the kingdom of God, people need to be filled with the life of God instead of their own life. This is what Scripture promises. The exact date is unknown, but we are coming to the point in history when this will happen.

People fight for oil, for money, for power, etc. They fight for things that are not important, and sooner or later, this will all cease. Even if a person gets a chance at power, how long will they be able to enjoy it? How long will it last: five, ten, twenty, years? We need God's wisdom, but even more than that, we need to be understood in heaven before the throne of God in order to understand true knowledge so that we can see where we have been and where we are going. How can we be understood in heaven if we don't speak God's language,[16] if the love and nature of God doesn't flow from our hearts? Scripture says that out of the abundance of the heart the mouth speaks (Matthew 12:34).

> [45] *In the manner which thou didst see that out of the mountain was cut one stone, not with hands, and that it broke in pieces the iron, the brass, the clay, the silver, and the gold; the great God has shown the king what shall come to pass hereafter; and the dream is true, and its interpretation sure.*
> [46] *Then the king Nebuchadnezzar fell upon his face and humbled himself before Daniel and commanded that they should sacrifice presents and sweet odours unto him.*

The kingdom of Babylon is compared to a golden head in a statue that represents all the empires of the earth until the time of the end. According to God, the kingdom of Babylon was the best. When the Medes and the Persians took over, the material degraded to silver; when the Greeks came, the material degraded to bronze; when the Romans came, the material degraded even more to iron; and when we get to our present time, the time of the democracies represented by the feet, the statue degraded to iron mixed with clay.

In the Scriptures, iron symbolizes the law; today we have the rule of law. Clay represents man in Scripture, so we have Roman or English law as a foundation, which is man's law instead of God's law. People try to unite on the basis of law, but they are unable to change human hearts.

16   Please don't misunderstand me; I am not suggesting that everyone learn Hebrew.

At the end of the king's dream, a stone cut without hands crashes into the image. Where does it crash? It crashes into the feet. It crashes into the democracies of our present time, and the statue turned into dust and was taken by the wind. Nothing remained of it. That stone grew and formed a mountain that filled and dominated the earth; this is the true kingdom of God.

⁴⁶ Then the king Nebuchadnezzar fell upon his face . . .

Notice he didn't fall on his back; he fell on his face.

⁴⁶ . . . and humbled himself before Daniel and commanded that they should sacrifice presents and sweet odours unto him.
⁴⁷ The king answered unto Daniel and said, Certainly the God that is your God is God of gods and the Lord of the kings and the revealer of the mysteries, seeing thou could reveal this mystery.
⁴⁸ Then the king magnified Daniel and gave him many and great gifts and made him governor over the whole province of Babylon and prince of the governors over all the wise men of Babylon.
⁴⁹ And Daniel requested of the king, and he set Shadrach, Meshach, and Abednego, over the affairs of the province of Babylon; but Daniel was at the gate of the king.

In Acts 14, when the people wanted to sacrifice presents to Paul, he didn't allow it. But here it's different; the king fell down and started to worship Daniel and asked for presents to sacrifice before Daniel. However, we must understand that in this example, Daniel represents the new man that has no corruption, of which our Lord Jesus is the head, and the rest of the body is of the same quality.

Daniel became second in the kingdom, and his three friends were placed in charge of the province of Babylon where the king was reconstructing pagan temples and mansions and building one of the wonders of the ancient world.

Using their pagan names, the three friends were placed over all the province of Babylon, and Daniel was at the gate of the king. What happened to Daniel was similar to what happened to Joseph in Egypt.

I have been told by some of those who have dug in Iraq that they found heaps of residues of everything that King Nebuchadnezzar did, and that most of the bricks they found (of which tremendous cities were made) bear the stamp of the king's name.

Daniel and his three friends were in charge of all this. They were the ones who directed all the construction in Babylon that, according to historians and philosophers, was one of the marvels of the ancient world. However, notice that the Bible doesn't mention this; it only says they were placed in authority. The rest of the book focuses on the revelations that God gave Daniel because Daniel was understood in heaven.

Babylon passed. Today it's completely destroyed, and what Saddam Hussein tried to rebuild was also destroyed. But the wisdom God gave Daniel remains written; God is still amplifying the revelation for those of us who are living in the time of the fulfillment.

Let us pray:

Lord, we give you thanks and we ask that we will be able to appreciate the purity that is needed to be understood in heaven. Allow this to be the case for each one of us. Amen.

Chapter Three

True Liberty

In the second chapter of Daniel, King Nebuchadnezzar wondered about the future. How was the world going to end? He knew God had revealed the answer in an extremely important dream, but it had been erased from his memory.

This is the condition of the entire human race. The moment we are old enough to reason, we are left with questions: How did we get here? Why are we here? What is the meaning of life? Every one of us suspects deep down that someone, sometime, may have known the answers. We have had dreams that we have forgotten. Some of us have had the answer in our hands and were about to understand it, like Nebuchadnezzar, but then we lost it.

The goodness of God was so great that he not only gave King Nebuchadnezzar a revelation, but he allowed the king to go through a difficult testing that would change his life. God used four kidnapped boys from Jerusalem to enlighten Nebuchadnezzar. He learned that the human race is not evolving into a type of superhero; the human race is degenerating.

The time we are living in is not the time of the head of gold representing the Babylonians. Neither is it the time of silver, bronze, or iron. We are in the time of democracies, but this man-made society cannot progress. Humanism cannot take us any further, and God is ready to crush all of this in such a way that it will not recover.

Nebuchadnezzar's Statue

After receiving the dream and its explanation, and after God showed him how things were going to end, Nebuchadnezzar had an idea. He did exactly what people do when they try to interpret God's mysteries with their own wisdom instead of asking God for wisdom. Daniel means "God is the judge," and here at the beginning of chapter 3, the king wanted to be the judge. He apparently thought that if this didn't work, if he was the head of gold, and if in the future humanity would be in such a hideous state, he was going to fix it himself. Look at what the king did:

Daniel 3

> [1] *Nebuchadnezzar the king made a statue of gold, whose height was sixty cubits and its breadth six cubits; he set it up in the plain of Dura, in the province of Babylon.*

Nebuchadnezzar apparently didn't accept God's explanation of the statue. Instead, he seems to have thought that if the problem was that things were going to get worse from there on, then he would make a statue that was gold all the way to the feet. He wasn't going to just be the head of gold; he was going to be the whole thing! So, he built a statue sixty cubits high and six cubits wide.

Can you imagine how much gold it would have taken to build a sixty-cubit high statue? One cubit is approximately fifty centimeters; so, we are talking about a statue of gold that was thirty meters high and three meters wide (approximately one hundred feet high and ten feet wide). That is tons and tons of gold.

These measurements represent man because the number six in the Scriptures is linked to man; ten is linked to the law. Therefore, sixty could refer to the law of man.

In Scripture, the number one represents light because on the first day God created light. Six times one (the width of the statue) could symbolize that the statue would also be under the enlightenment (light) and wisdom of man.

The kind also decided to implement his idea as an obligatory religion. This idea is rooted in every one of us. If someone does something that is against our will, we all tend to attempt to impose our will by force; since the king had a lot of power, he did it in the following way:

> [2] *Then Nebuchadnezzar the king sent to gather together the great ones, the assistants and captains, the judges, the treasurers, those of the council, presidents, and all the governors of the provinces, to come to the dedication of the statue which Nebuchadnezzar the king had raised up.*
> [3] *Then the great ones, the assistants and captains, the judges,*

> *the treasurers, those of the council, presidents, and all the go-*
> *vernors of the provinces, were gathered together unto the dedi-*
> *cation of the statue that Nebuchadnezzar the king had raised*
> *up; and they stood before the statue that Nebuchadnezzar the*
> *king had raised up.*

The king's name comes from the root "Nebo" which is the pagan god Mercury; this is the same god that is called Cupid in the Roman Empire. It is the same Cupid that is found in much religious art. It is seen in the arcs and paintings of Michelangelo in the Vatican and elsewhere. This god, Cupid (Nebo), is promiscuous, and this pagan cult engaged in these activities. The name also means "Nebo protects my borders." It is a territorial idea where the god (Nebo) possesses the land that he will secure and protect.

Surely all or most of the gold in the statue came from those places that the pagan god had obtained by force. This statue was made with melted gold and set up in the plain of Dura, which means "circle." This circle (or dura) represents a bridge of communication with the spirit world.

As if the symbolism of this place and their god was not enough, they summoned all the great intellectuals, all the government staff, and the governors of the provinces (there were possibly 127 provinces) to the dedication of the statue. The king decided to establish one religion for the world, united by that head of gold.

> [4] *Then a herald cried aloud, To you it is commanded, O people,*
> *nations, and languages,*
> [5] *that when ye hear the sound of the cornet, flute, harp, sac-*
> *kbut, psaltery, dulcimer, and of every musical instrument, ye*
> *are to fall down and worship the statue of gold that Nebuchad-*
> *nezzar the king has raised up:*
> [6] *and whoever does not fall down and worship shall the same*
> *hour be cast into the midst of a burning fiery furnace.*

The Fiery Furnace

Notice that pagans, like this king, were among the first to come up with this concept of "hell." One practice of their ritualistic cult, which also involved a serpent, was the adoration of fire. In this cult, they sacrificed humans to appease the god of fire.

The statue was likely made in the image of the king. Nebuchadnezzar's strategy (as well as that of all empires) was to establish, consolidate, and unify the provinces and nations that were already subjugated. He confiscated the riches of these nations, using some of it to construct the image. To establish this new religion, the king attempted to unite everything by imposing an obligatory ceremony.

Today, the natural man thinks much the same way. With a globalization philosophy, people try to unite the whole world around money and the economy. In order to participate, these people must worship money and gold.

Likewise, in the ancient times, people had to prove their loyalty with a test. At the sound of the music, everyone was required to bow down and worship the statue of gold. This was the test, uniting Babylon religiously, politically, and economically.

Many people think there is no problem with listening to all types of music. Music tends to prepare the way for spiritual things to be transferred or imparted.

Many people don't realize some of the music they listen to has a relationship to a cult. Music may prepare a person for sexual licentiousness; music may prepare you to worship the money god; music may prepare people to do things their own way instead of God's way. Music can practically guarantee to put the people in a state where God no longer has clear access to their thoughts and feelings. Music, where it is no longer important to understand lyrics, can block out all thought of God.

The king represents the human race since God gave us the responsibility of this earth. When we follow what we think is right and what we think is wrong, we open ourselves up for other spirits to come in. We end up with something diabolical, where whoever does not accept our will must be destroyed and exterminated. There is no goodness or mercy.[17]

Nebuchadnezzar said that when they heard this music and all the instruments, they had to worship the Babylonian statue. Remember, Babylon means confusion. This confusion is brought about when man decides to do what seems right to him, when he imposes his own justice.

> *7 Therefore, when all the peoples heard the sound of the cornet,*
> *flute, harp, sackbut, psaltery, and every musical instrument,*
> *all the peoples, nations, and languages, fell down and wors-*

---

17 In ancient Babylon, God influenced the king (directly and by using Daniel and his three friends) who was the absolute authority and used this situation to cleanse and purify a remnant of his people so that after seventy years he could send them back to Jerusalem. Today it would be extremely difficult, if not impossible, to find a country or empire in which the safety and well-being of all God's people could be preserved by a single individual.

*hipped the statue of gold that Nebuchadnezzar the king had
raised up.*

They obeyed the king, and the whole world went along with the new
world religion; but there was one problem:

> *⁸ Therefore at that time certain Chaldeans came near, and ac-
> cused the Jews.*
> *⁹ They spoke and said to the king Nebuchadnezzar, O king, live
> for ever.*

People want to live forever. Religion has the formula on how you can live
forever. It proclaims that saying this prayer or worshipping that symbol
will guarantee "life." Of course, this type of religion condemns those who
do not obey to hell, the furnace that burns. Religions even claim to have
a certain amount of power over this "hell." In this story, the king had the
capacity to make the hell he invented seven times hotter.

> *¹⁰ Thou, O king, hast made a law that every man upon hea-
> ring the sound of the cornet, flute, harp, sackbut, psaltery, and
> dulcimer, and every musical instrument, shall fall down and
> worship the statue of gold;*
> *¹¹ and whoever does not fall down and worship that he should
> be cast into the midst of a burning fiery furnace.*
> *¹² There are certain Jews whom thou hast set over the affairs of
> the province of Babylon, Shadrach, Meshach, and Abednego;
> these men, O king, have not regarded thee; they do not wors-
> hip thy gods, nor do they worship the statue of gold which thou
> hast raised up.*

The king imposed the law. He implemented it with the resources and
gold from the entire world. He unified it with the musicians and musical
instruments of the kingdom.

These religions assure you that those who comply with their requirements are not going to have any problems, but woe to those who do not
because they are destined to hell. In the same way, according to the need,
they can make "hell" hotter.

This is the problem: the three young men who were in charge of
Babylon had been placed in authority because they had obtained the wisdom of God. Daniel had set them over the province after saving the lives
of the magicians, astrologers, and spiritualists. But when men of God are
placed over the business of this world, they make those who seek their

own good and want things their own way feel extremely uncomfortable.

It's different when someone wants to do things God's way; God's way of doing things is that we seek the good of our neighbor and the good of the kingdom of God, not our own good. If we don't seek our own good, we are in direct opposition to the world system.

When the music rang out, someone was spying on these three Hebrew boys and saw that they did not obey the command. For them, these three, who had helped save the Chaldeans' lives, were nothing but a disgrace, and the fact that they ruled over the province was revolting. Seeking personal gain, the spies decided to eliminate them.

The serpent in the garden of Eden did a similar thing. Seeing God had given Adam authority, it demonstrated an attitude similar to this: "Now God is going to place me under Adam, but I want to reign here. And this recently created Adam is very young, and he's naming all the animals. I'm not taking this!" (In ancient times, the one who gave the name was the one with the control because the name is the essence of a being.) The serpent invented a lie to provoke mankind to disobey God and be expelled from the garden.

In Babylon, only three boys who did not want to disobey God remained. In order for the people to feel okay about doing this, they had to eliminate the three righteous Hebrews. When the Chaldeans came to the king with the story, the king did what any one of us would have done in our natural state. When someone goes against our will, instead of being grateful for previous good deeds, we retaliate. So, the king decided to teach them and the entire world a lesson.

> [13] *Then Nebuchadnezzar in his rage and fury commanded to bring Shadrach, Meshach, and Abednego. Then they brought these men before the king.*
>
> [14] *Nebuchadnezzar spoke and said unto them, Is it true, O Shadrach, Meshach, and Abednego, that ye do not honour my gods, nor worship the statue of gold which I have set up?*

In those days, they thought everyone could have their own god. Look at what Nebuchadnezzar did: the same thing that most religious people do. Many theologians in Catholic or "Protestant" seminaries (protestants in quotations because they don't protest anymore), even some evangelicals and charismatics, invert the role.

Instead of believing we were created in the image and likeness of God and have lost the breath of life that God placed in Adam and Eve, they invert things and create a god in their own image and likeness. King

Nebuchadnezzar created a god, his god, and he made it in his own image and likeness. He thought he had God's blessing doing it this way because God had shown him the future of human history. God had said the head of gold on the statue was his own.

Nebuchadnezzar's problem came when the three governors didn't want to worship the image. Even though they were good administrators in Babylon, the Bible doesn't mention details of the huge city (referring to Babylon) or of the hanging gardens or other fabulous constructions. The Bible doesn't tell us how much money that thirty-meter statue cost. What the Bible does say is that these righteous men were placed in some of the highest positions that true men of God had ever had in the history of the world.

> [15] *Now, are ye ready when ye hear the sound of the cornet, flute, harp, sackbut, psaltery, and dulcimer, and of every musical instrument to fall down and worship the statue which I made? For if ye do not worship, ye shall be cast the same hour into the midst of a burning fiery furnace; and who is that god that shall deliver you out of my hands?*

The king had said that those who did not obey this command were to be burned immediately, but he had enough respect for these three that he decided to give them one last chance. The king decided to play the music one more time: For if ye do not worship, ye shall be cast the same hour into the midst of a burning fiery furnace; and who is that god that shall deliver you out of my hands?

The king had received the revelation of God, and he knew that God was the one who had revealed it to him, so he had placed Daniel and his three friends over all the business of Babylon. But he still thought he was above God. For Nebuchadnezzar, God was his little helper who would benefit his prosperity in Babylon.

This happens in the world religions everywhere, and we will soon see another attempt to consolidate it. In this world religion, a god in the image of man will be created; the treacherous love of man will be god, operating with conditions.

God's true love is unconditional and born out of sacrifice, redemptive by nature. Man's love is conditional. It isn't born out of sacrifice; it's born out of the desire to obtain some benefit. It doesn't redeem; it destroys. The love of man caused Eve to believe the lie that she could be like God, discerning good and evil. But when this is placed in man's hands, it only produces death and misery.

> *[16] Shadrach, Meshach, and Abednego, answered and said to king Nebuchadnezzar, We are not careful to answer thee in this matter.*

They didn't even give the king a chance to let the choir sing or to make all the musicians play. Their response essentially said, "Look king, it's very simple."

> *[17] Behold, our God whom we serve is able to deliver us from the burning fiery furnace, and he will deliver us out of thine hand, O king.*
> *[18] But if not, be it known unto thee, O king, that we will not worship thy god, nor honour the statue which thou hast raised up.*

Shadrach, Meshach, and Abednego would not bow. They said their God could deliver them from the fiery furnace, and even if he didn't, they would not worship his god or honor his statue.

Observe this response very carefully. The statue is one thing; Nebuchadnezzar's god is something else, and they knew how to differentiate. They responded that God could deliver them from the fiery furnace. (Notice how it appears in the original. It appears differently in many translations.) Our God whom we serve is able to deliver us from the burning fiery furnace, and he will deliver us out of thine hand, O king.

What I understand them to be saying is, "Look, king, God can deliver us from the furnace that you put us in. That is up to him. But God will deliver us from your hand because God is first and foremost. You are not bigger than he is. God is bigger than you."

> *[19] Then Nebuchadnezzar was full of fury, and the form of his visage was changed against Shadrach, Meshach, and Abednego; therefore he spoke, and commanded that they should heat the furnace seven times more than it was customary to be heated.*

In church history, when there were theological differences, anathemas were launched. One group determined the fate of the other by saying it was going to be destroyed forever in hell. Like the king of Babylon, during the inquisition, religious leaders burned alive whoever did not recant.

Even John Calvin, the great reformer, burned Michael Servet at the stake for having differences in doctrine over the trinity. Sadly, the word "trinity" doesn't even appear in the Bible. For centuries, they condemned people to the stake to defend beliefs that did not necessarily line up with the Scriptures. Nebuchadnezzar thought he owned hell and ordered it to be heated seven times more than customary. This is where he threw the three Jewish boys.

> *20 And he commanded the most mighty men that were in his army to bind Shadrach, Meshach, and Abednego and to cast them into the burning fiery furnace.*
>
> *21 Then these men were bound in their coats, their undergarments, and their hats, and their other garments, and were cast into the midst of the burning fiery furnace.*

In ancient times, clothes were the covering and signified under what authority that person operated. Every detail was significant: the hair, the beard, and the dress.

Today, many groups and churches teach an idea that people need to be under "the covering" of a perceived spiritual authority (other than the Holy Spirit and those delegated authority by the Holy Spirit), and in order to be under someone else's authority, it is usually necessary to pay a tithe. If you pay that tithe and are under a person, you gain a false security, as if you are not going to hell. Here, the king orders the three boys into "hell" with their "covering," and look at what happened:

> *22 Therefore because the king's commandment was urgent and the furnace exceeding hot, the flame of the fire slew those men that took up Shadrach, Meshach, and Abednego.*
>
> *23 And these three men, Shadrach, Meshach, and Abednego, fell down bound into the midst of the burning fiery furnace.*
>
> *24 Then Nebuchadnezzar the king was astonished, and rose up in hast and spoke and said unto his counselors, Did we not cast three men bound into the midst of the fire? They answered and said unto the king, True, O king.*
>
> *25 He answered and said, Behold, I see four men loose, walking in the midst of the fire, and they have no hurt; and the form of the fourth is like the Son of God.*

When they were thrown into the furnace, only the cords that bound them and the men who threw them in burned. More astonishing, upon seeing a fourth man in the fiery furnace, the king declared him to be like the Son of God.

True Freedom

In the king's "hell," which is like the devil's Hades or Sheol, if those who have the true covering are thrown in, nothing happens to them. In that moment, a fourth man appeared. The symbolism of the covering became reality, and they walked with the Lord himself. This actually happened, but it was also a symbol of a future event even more important.

Ephesians 4:9–10 is often translated wrong when it says that the Lord descended into "hell." The hell that is referenced in this verse is really Hades or Sheol, which is the "first death." (This translation problem happens when multiple diverse Hebrew and Greek words are lumped together and all translated by only one English word in most of our Bibles.) This Hades is something like Nebuchadnezzar's fiery furnace in that true followers of Christ are protected from the power of death or the grave.

In the parable of the rich man and Lazarus, Hades had two compartments, and Lazarus was with Abraham on the better side, still bound by death. The rich man was in flames and torment on the far side of a great gulf. (See Luke 16:19–31.) While the grave contains both for a while, to the one with God's covering, the fire does no harm.

The king was probably not seeing clearly through the fire. The king saw the part where there is nothing but flame. In reality the three Hebrew boys and the Lord were in a situation that was beyond that flame. They were in a realm where the flame couldn't harm them. They passed through the fire, but the fire didn't harm them.

Hebrews 11 says that Enoch didn't see death, but at the end of the list (which includes Enoch) it says, "they all died." Enoch didn't see death when he died because he didn't go to Hades or Sheol (they are the Hebrew and Greek words for the same thing); he went to the presence of God instead.

The book of Revelation speaks of the "lake of fire" reserved for the devil and his fallen angels and whoever joins their rebellion. This lake of fire is referred to as the "second death" and is the real hell from which there can be no escape.

The time came when the Lord Jesus himself descended into the devil's jail (Hades), broke it, and took his own people. He passed through that fire, and nothing happened to him; death could not hold him.

These boys were bound when they went in, but when the king came to look at them, they were free. The king's fire of "hell" burned up their bonds and the king's mighty men to reveal their true covering, which was the Lord Jesus himself. This is where we find true religion.

What does the Word of God say concerning true religion? It says that true religion is to visit the orphans and widows in their affliction and to not be contaminated or corrupted by the world. What is the world? The world is a way of doing things; it is the Babylonian way of doing things.[18]

Daniel's three friends suffered because they were practicing true religion. If we are going visit the orphans and widows in their affliction, their problems will become our own. How many orphans are there? How many widows are here in Colombia where I live? There are many because of the violence. There are also many orphans and widows in the spiritual sense. We practice true religion if we accompany them and keep ourselves unspotted from the world as the Spirit of God leads us.

Many nongovernmental organizations claim to help the needy but end up living off the needs of the people instead. They ask for help for the poor, but they also take a large share of it and live like kings. There are plenty of needs every month, and we must ask God for discernment because we can't supply all the needs. But we can supply the needs that God wants us to supply. We can accompany those that God wants us to accompany. We can do things God's way instead of this corrupt world's way.

The world will condemn us when we do not dance to the rhythm of their flutes, or eat their food, or when we do not bow to this world's music, its politics, its economy, or its religion. As the world degenerates, it will create a hell seven times hotter than before. But God's true nature will be revealed when others try to harm us.

After indirect dealings of God, King Nebuchadnezzar had a revelation of the Son of God that was not a dream or a vision; it was a reality. He saw the fourth man walking in the fire! The king himself said the fourth man was like the Son of God. How did the king know that this man was like the Son of God? We don't know, but he sure did.

> [26] *Then Nebuchadnezzar came near to the mouth of the burning fiery furnace and spoke and said, Shadrach, Meshach, and Abednego, ye servants of the most high God, come forth and come here. Then Shadrach, Meshach, and Abednego, came forth of the midst of the fire.*
> [27] *And the great ones, the governors and the captains and the king's counselors gathered together to see these men upon*

---

18   The pure and undefiled religion before God and the Father is this, To visit the fatherless and widows in their tribulation and to keep thyself unspotted from this world. (James 1:27)

*whose bodies the fire had no power, nor was a hair of their
head singed, neither were their coats changed, nor the smell of
fire had passed on them.*

They came out of the fiery furnace completely intact with their glory,
which is their "hair," and their "covering," which is their clothes. They
didn't even smell like smoke. The Bible says we must be careful because
the day of the coming of the Lord is near. Malachi 4:1 says that day will
burn like an oven for all the wicked.[19]

Second Corinthians 5:3 indicates that some will be ashamed in that
day because they will end up "naked." But these three Hebrews passed
through the fire and did not come out naked or ashamed. They came
out as worthy representatives of the Lord. Notice that they say very little
in this book. Daniel is the main character, but these three basically say,
"King, don't make the orchestra play, because in any case, we will not
bow down. God can deliver us out of this furnace; but if he doesn't, he
will free us from your hand because we will not remain under your slavery; king, we are of God." This point is very important because of where
it ends:

> [28] *Then Nebuchadnezzar spoke and said, Blessed be the God
> of these . . .*

Notice that the king still had a bit of pride. He was burning his last straws.
Now he tried to get out of it because he could not deny the miracle. Everyone saw it, and the unscathed men of God confirmed it. The law and the
statue were brought to nothing, but the king wanted to save his power
and pride by blessing the God of these men. The king may have thought,
"Blessed be 'their' God. I won't submit even though I have to bless their
God."

The king was humiliated. The hell he fabricated didn't work. The hell
of many theologians is fiction before a true son of God with a pure heart.
But it was real for the king's "mighty men!"

> [28] *. . . of Shadrach, Meshach, and Abednego, who has sent his
> angel and delivered his servants that trusted in him and have
> changed the king's word and yielded their bodies that they mi-
> ght not serve nor worship any god, except their own God*
> [29] *Therefore I make a decree, That every people, nation, or lan-*

---

19   For, behold, the day comes that shall burn as an oven; and all the proud, and all that
do wickedly shall be stubble; and the day that comes shall burn them up, said the
LORD of the hosts, that it shall leave them neither root nor branch.

guage which speak blasphemy against the God of Shadrach, Meshach, and Abednego shall be cut in pieces, and their houses shall be made a dunghill because there is no other god that can deliver after this sort.

The king had a difficult time learning. After every fight, he would give God the glory and send documents out, but then he would go back to the same old thing. Scripture says a dog always returns to his vomit, and a clean pig always goes back to the mud (2 Peter 2:22); it also says a leopard cannot change his spots (Jeremiah 13:23).

What does this mean? It means that when we are born for the first time, there are things governed by genetics (such as the color of our hair and eyes) that we cannot change. What God wants to do is replace our life with his. This is what Daniel exemplified. Daniel looked for his existence in the life of God, and he received it in the midst of many problems, while receiving power and authority from a pagan king.

However, this supremacy is not the most important thing. Even though Daniel and his friends were in charge of Babylon during the construction of many wonders, Scripture only tells us they were given authority over the provinces of Babylon, and when the king had a dream that no one could interpret, Daniel was given the revelation of it from God.

King Nebuchadnezzar accepted some things, but he still had a way of imposing his will. Instead of using his conscience, he wanted to impose things by brute force. This is also a serious problem with the world's system. We often say that terrorism must be fought. Terrorists hurt and threaten anyone who does not pay them a certain fee each month.

But who is the worst terrorist? Is it the person who says, "If you don't pay us to fund our revolution, we will harm you or our family," or the person who says, "If you don't pay us your tithe, God will harm you"? I think the person who threatens by twisting something God has said is worse.

Despite everything, look at how this chapter ends:

> ³⁰ *Then the king promoted Shadrach, Meshach, and Abednego, in the province of Babylon.*

The Spanish translation of this verse says that the "king ennobled Shadrach, Meshach, and Abednego..." Two kinds of people existed in the ancient world: those who were born free and those who were born slaves. Everyone, except the ruling noble class, was a commoner or a slave.

In the English language, there is no distinction between a man who was born free and one who was not. However, in Spanish, the word for nobleman, or a man born in freedom, is varón.

Note that in the original language of the Bible, in the book of Genesis when God creates man, the Hebrew word adam is used, implying that God made man with free will. In the original, it doesn't say that God took a rib from Adam to create a woman. It says instead that he took from his side, from his heart. This is where Eve came from. They called her woman or in the original, ishshah.[20] In Spanish it is varona, which is the female version for varón

How could this be? This means that this varona would be a free woman. This was in the beginning. But as part of the curse, man had to sustain himself by the sweat of his brow. The woman lost her freedom and became subject to the man. The serpent lost its autonomy and was cursed and sentenced to slither on its belly with its insatiable corrupt appetite for the dust of the earth.

But look at how chapter 3 ends. King Nebuchadnezzar decided these three boys deserved their freedom. They had placed their own lives at stake, so the king's mandate was changed. He'd had them as slaves, and now he ennobled them.

The word "ennobled" means "to place in liberty." The king still had many lessons to learn, particularly the importance of giving the true people of God liberty. The "kings" of this world (religious or otherwise) who insist on enslaving God's people will never be free from the curse they live in.

Abraham's promise is fulfilled for those who have been born again in the Lord Jesus and are, therefore, part of his true seed. God told Abraham that he would make his seed as the sand of the sea (Genesis 32:12). He was going to have natural sons who would still be slaves even though they are like the grains of sand separating the sea from the earth (or dry land), or in other words, separating the nations without God from the church.

But the Lord also told Abraham he would bless him and multiply his seed as the stars in the heaven that shine, give light, offer an example, and are above everything on earth and residents of the heavenly realm. Some are natural sons; others are sons of the promise. Some have Adam's nature with ministries and gifts from God; others have the nature of Christ.

---

20   The Hebrew word for woman, ishshah, is derived from iysh (meaning a unique, individual man).

In any case, the three Hebrew boys had freedom to follow the Lord no matter what the circumstances were. The king's fire only served to burn their bonds, to kill the king's mighty men who threw them into the fire, and to show the world and the king their true covering. Finally, the king had to accept a completely obvious fact that these boys were not slaves in Adam; they were free in Christ!

Scripture says that true liberty is when the Son sets us free (John 8:36). This is obvious freedom. Freedom is found where the Spirit of the Lord is (2 Corinthians 3:17), and our true covering is found in the Spirit of the Lord. Being directed by the Spirit of God can cost us our position in this world; it can cost us our life in this world; but this is where we will find true freedom.

Let us pray:

Lord, we thank you for this very clear example, and we ask that we may be part of your great plan to show these truths to the entire world. Amen.

— 42 —

Chapter Four

Seven Times Over The Beast

Nebuchadnezzar Continues to Rebel

Liberty exists wherever the Spirit of the Lord is.[21] You can use it to do God's will, but it is impossible to do God's will without it. True liberty presents two options: the first one is the opportunity to do God's will, and the second one will default into a zigzag between two extremes. One of the extremes is licentiousness (or lawlessness with no moral restraint), and the other is legalism, where people try to fulfill God's law (or the law they have invented) with their own strength, and they revert to bondage.

Neither of these two extremes will work. The harder the repression is, the greater the licentiousness will be. This is the reason for man's laws and legalism becoming stricter.

For example, when a religious leader (a pastor, an elder, or a bishop) has problems in the sexual area, and this person tries to control the problem, he goes to the opposite extreme and tries to make the opposite sex wear clothes up to their neck. That kind of repression has never been able to stop corruption within the heart. History proves that the problems only get worse when religious communities become excessively strict. On the one hand, they establish norms that are impossible for the old nature to keep. On the other hand, they hide the evidence when rules are broken.

In order for true righteousness and justice of God to flow through us, we need him living in us. Religion's covering cannot save us from danger. My father used to tell me, "Our doctrines cannot save us even when they are true. Make no mistake; only the Lord Jesus Christ can save us."

John 8:36 says, If the Son therefore shall set you free, ye shall be free indeed. King Nebuchadnezzar had no capacity to set the Hebrew

---

21   2 Corinthians 3:17

boys free because they were already free. They were free from the moment they decided to follow the Lord with their whole heart, when they allowed the Lord to clean their hearts, and when they decided to reject the contamination and the corruption of the kingdom of Babylon.

It's interesting to recognize how God first dealt with the pagan king. He used these same boys that had been taken as slaves to bring truth to the king.

The king saw the wisdom of God, he saw God's power, and he saw God's signs; and then, even though he was willing to bless God, he was not willing to let go of his throne and let the Lord take control.

Daniel 4

¹ King Nebuchadnezzar, to all the peoples, nations, and languages that dwell in all the earth; Peace be multiplied unto you.

The king wrote this chapter after a terrible disgrace that God brought him through.

² The signs and wonders that the high God has wrought with me are such that I must publish them.

Nebuchadnezzar represents the entire human race. The smallest person on this planet has the God-given free will to decide for themselves whether they are going to appreciate the truth and reject the lie, whether they are going to receive God's intervention and authority, or not. It doesn't matter if you are born a slave; you could have been born into a native tribe where the name of Jesus Christ has never been mentioned; you could be a person who was raised in a guerrilla camp or someone from a military school, a Catholic seminary, or an evangelical church. Regardless of where we come from, we all have the same opportunity to receive the truth and reject the lie.

God has placed a conscience in each one of us, and it tells us what we should do, but most of us don't do it. We all choose to go against our conscience at some point. If God dealt with us as he did the king, what would we do? Would we be willing to bow our heads and recognize our mistake? The king comes to the place where he recognizes his mistake after something very terrible happened to him.

³ How great are his signs! and how mighty are his wonders! His kingdom is an everlasting kingdom, and his dominion is from generation to generation.

> *[4] I Nebuchadnezzar was quiet in my house and flourishing in my palace;*

He flourished in his natural life, with his own wisdom and strength.

Another Dream

> *[5] I saw a dream which made me afraid, and the imaginations and visions of my head troubled me in my bed.*

Unlike the first dream he had, this dream remained in his memory.

> *[6] Therefore I made a decree to bring in all the wise men of Babylon before me that they might show me the interpretation of the dream.*

Nebuchadnezzar didn't send for Daniel first. Once again, he called the other "wise men" first. Politicians, governors, and presidents of this world keep doing the same; when they are in trouble, they don't seek a true man of God to tell them the truth. They look for all the other magicians and diviners and listen to them first.

Only when it is completely clear that there is no solution do they remember there is a Daniel around, and they send for him. Why does this keep happening? Because what God is going to say is contrary to what we want to hear.

> *[7] Then the magicians, the astrologers, the Chaldeans, and the fortune-tellers came in and I told the dream before them; but they never showed me its interpretation.*
> *[8] But at the last Daniel came in before me, whose name is Belteshazzar . . .*

Daniel, whose name means "God is the judge," was renamed Belteshazzar. Bel[22] means "lord," and Belteshazzar means "Bel protects his life."

> *[8] . . . who when I name him it seems to me that I name my god, and in whom is the spirit of the holy God; . . .*

The king identified Daniel with God. Many people claim to be God's representatives, but if we analyze their attitudes and actions, we cannot relate them to God because they are not worthy representatives of him. However, politicians, religious leaders and those with economic power usually call these people first.

22　Bel, meaning "lord," is the god of Babylon. Bel is another name for Nimrod, Adonis, Baal, Tamuz, or Marduk.

The king knew from before that something terrible was going to happen. Since no one could give him an explanation, he was very disquieted, and his curiosity got the best of him. Nebuchadnezzar was trying to avoid this sentence.

> [8] . . . *and before him I told the dream, saying,*
> [9] *Belteshazzar, prince of the wise men, now that I have understood that the spirit of the holy God is in thee, and that no mystery is hidden from thee, tell me the visions of my dream that I have seen and its interpretation.*
> [10] *Thus were the visions of my head in my bed: It seemed that I saw a tree in the midst of the earth, and its height was great.*
> [11] *The tree grew and made itself strong, and its height reached unto heaven, and its sight to the end of all the earth:*
> [12] *His leaves were fair, and his fruit abundant, and in him was food for all; underneath him the beasts of the field lay down in his shadow, and in his branches dwelt the fowls of the heaven, and all flesh was fed of him.*
> [13] *I saw in the visions of my head upon my bed, and, behold, one who was a watchman and holy descended from heaven;*
> [14] *he cried aloud and said thus, Hew down the tree, and cut off his branches, shake off his leaves, and scatter his fruit; let the beasts get away from under him and the fowls from his branches:*
> [15] *nevertheless leave the stump of his roots in the earth, even with a band of iron and of brass shall he be bound in the green grass of the field; and let him be wet with the dew of heaven, and let his portion be with the beasts in the grass of the earth:*
> [16] *let his heart be changed from a man's heart, and let a beast's heart be given unto him; and let seven times pass over him.*
> [17] *By sentence of the watchmen is the matter resolved, and the case by the word of the holy ones to the intent that the living may know that the most High takes rule over the kingdom of men and gives it to whoever he will and sets up over it the man who is the lowest.*

What did our Lord say? He said that in his kingdom, the greatest would be the servant of all. What did the Lord Jesus come to do? He came to serve. He humbled himself like a slave.

Philippians 2:7–11 says this about him:

. . . but emptied himself, taking the form of a slave, made in the likeness of men, and being found in fashion as a man, he humbled himself and became obedient unto death, even the death of the cross [Gr. stauros or stake]. Therefore, God also has highly exalted him and given him a name which is above every name, that at the name of Jesus every knee should bow, of things in heaven and things in earth and things under the earth, and that every tongue should confess that the Lord Jesus Christ is Lord in the glory of God the Father.

Daniel 4

[18] I, King Nebuchadnezzar, saw this dream. Now thou, O Belteshazzar, shall declare its interpretation, for as much as all the wise men of my kingdom could never show me its interpretation; but thou art able, for the spirit of the holy God in thee.

This image carried the same message as the vision the king had in the beginning: all of our works will be destroyed. Nebuchadnezzar did not want this to happen, so he made a statue of gold. His efforts failed when God rescued the three boys from the furnace.

After all this, Nebuchadnezzar kept on with his madness. God said in effect, "If you are going to keep on like this [and it's an insanity we all have] then I am going to really make you crazy. I am going to take away your human side, and I am going to turn you into a beast for seven 'times.' You are going to eat grass like an ox, and your nails are going to grow like those of an eagle, and dew from heaven is going to bathe you. We're going to see if, at the end of this, you will discover true reason. Let's see if you're sane in the end."

Notice the seven times. God's concept of time is much different from ours. In the prophecy of Daniel, a day can represent a year of human history. And a day can also represent one thousand years. This is stated twice in the Bible – once in the Old Testament and then in the New Testament.

For a thousand years in thy sight are but as yesterday when it is past and as a watch in the night. (Psalm 90:4)

But, beloved, be not ignorant of this one thing, that one day before the Lord is as a thousand years, and a thousand years are as one day. (2 Peter 3:8)

In God's prophecy, one day can sometimes be one year. He has a different concept of time. On the equator, we think 365.4 days make a year. But it would be different if we were at the North Pole.

Someone told me that at the North Pole there will be six months of darkness and six months of light, but this isn't true. I have been in the arctic and can say there is a phenomenon that alters that balance. The atmosphere refracts the light of the sun. When the sun is on (or even below) the horizon, it looks higher than it really is.

This deviation is similar to a pole in a stream of water. The pole does not look straight; it looks crooked because of the refraction.

The atmosphere does the same thing at the North Pole. If we saw everything correctly, there would be six months of day and six months of night. In actuality, it is closer to seven months of day and five months of night. The Bible says God lives on the sides of the north, and in the true north, one of our years would be the evening and the morning of one day.

God has designed everything for light to always exceed darkness. In Colombia, we calculate that the sun comes up about 6:00 a.m. and sets at 6:00 p.m.[23] If we really do the math, there is more time of the light of day than the darkness of the night.

Make the calculations when you are out in the plains with no mountain ranges because these mountains around Bogotá hide the truth. Measure it in the plains, and if the day is clear, there will always be more light than darkness during a twenty-four-hour period. We really have twelve and a half or up to thirteen hours of light, versus eleven or so of darkness.

God declared seven times over Nebuchadnezzar. In this context, seven times were seven years, and this story is documented in pagan history. The archeologists know that Nebuchadnezzar experienced a problem in the middle of his reign that obligated him to leave his throne due to a mental disease.

But in the bigger picture, the entire human race has had to desist from the true kingdom that God wanted for us for a period of seven thousand years. Six thousand of those years have already passed. The man who was created in the image and likeness of God fell and lost his reflection of the nature of God.

What man has now is the beastly nature with all its carnal desires. Scripture says all of creation fell along with Adam, and all of creation

---

23   At the equator, the length of daylight is about the same all year long.

suffers and waits for a glorious change (see Romans 8).

God has this period of seven thousand years divided up into stages, or times, and the last time is called the day of the Lord. At that time, God will make changes in the midst of fallen nature (as the curse is lifted) and will openly reestablish his government. After the thousand years described in Revelation 20 comes another stage, which is called "the new heavens and the new earth." The plan of God is much greater than we can imagine. The Bible sums it up like this:

> *But as it is written, That which eye has not seen nor ear heard neither has entered into the heart of man is that which God has prepared for those that love him.* (1 Corinthians 2:9)

What Daniel was running in Babylon was not his true destiny; it was not his real inheritance or his true job. We will see at the end of the book that God sends Gabriel to tell him something similar to this: "Seal this Daniel, for at the appointed time, you shall be raised up and receive your true inheritance" (Daniel 12:4, 13).

> [19] *Then Daniel, whose name was Belteshazzar, was silent for almost one hour, and his thoughts troubled him. Then the king spoke and said, Belteshazzar, do not let the dream or its interpretation trouble thee. Belteshazzar answered and said, My lord, let the dream be to thine enemies, and its interpretation to those that wish thee evil.*

Daniel's Interpretation

Next, Daniel gives the interpretation the king would become insane and be thrown out of his kingdom.

> [20] *The tree that thou didst see, which grew and made himself strong, whose height reached unto the heaven and the sight thereof to all the earth;*
> [21] *whose leaves were fair and his fruit abundant and in him was food for all, under whom the beasts of the field dwelt, and in whose branches the fowls of the heaven dwelt:*
> [22] *it is thou, O king, that grew and made thyself strong; for thy greatness has grown and has reached unto heaven, and thy dominion to the end of the earth.*
> [23] *And regarding that which the king saw, one who was a watchman and holy who came down from heaven and said, Hew*

the tree down and destroy it; yet leave the stump of its roots in the earth, and with a band of iron and of brass let it remain bound in the green grass of the field, and let it be wet with the dew of heaven, and let his portion be with the beasts of the field until seven times pass over him:

[24] this is the interpretation, O king, and this is the decree of the most High, which is come upon my lord the king:

[25] that they shall drive thee from among men, and thy dwelling shall be with the beasts of the field, and they shall feed thee with grass of the field as the oxen, and with the dew of heaven shalt thou be bathed, and seven times shall pass over thee, until thou shalt understand that the most High takes rule over the kingdom of men and that he shall give it to whoever he will.

[26] And whereas they commanded to leave the stump of the tree roots in the earth; thy kingdom shall remain sure unto thee, that thou shalt understand that the rule is in the heavens.

Then, in verse 27 Daniel gives the king advice. Daniel had every reason to hate the king because Nebuchadnezzar had taken him captive and destroyed his city and his people. Daniel heard what God was going to do to the king, and it saddened him so much that he wasn't able to talk for an hour. Then he not only gave the king the interpretation, but he also gave him advice on how to avoid such a sentence.

[27] Therefore, O king, approve my counsel and redeem thy sins with righteousness and thine iniquities with mercies unto the poor: behold the medicine for thy sin.

Today's religious leaders probably would have said to Nebuchadnezzar, "Listen, you are a depraved sinner, and you are going to go to hell if you don't repent." But in this case, the one who wants to send everyone to hell is Nebuchadnezzar, and the one who is kind and tries to save a wicked despot is Daniel.

God gave Daniel a heart for a terrible dictator. The truth is that we are all terrible dictators. We see it in our children, and we think it's funny and cute when they are little, but they become brats who think they are the center of the universe. This causes many problems: marriages do not function, community farms do not work, businesses fail, governments do not succeed. They all want to run things with a heavy hand.

The king still had to go through yet another situation where God was going to teach him a lesson. It hurt Daniel to reveal this vision to the king because God's dealing this time would be extremely hard. For seven years, Nebuchadnezzar lost his human capacity and turned into a "beast."

> *28 All this came upon the king Nebuchadnezzar.*
> *29 At the end of twelve months as he was walking upon the palace of the kingdom of Babylon,*
> *30 the king spoke and said, Is this not the great Babylon that I have built for the house of the kingdom by the might of my power and for the glory of my greatness?*
> *31 The word was yet in the king's mouth when there fell a voice from heaven, saying, O King Nebuchadnezzar, to thee it is spoken; The kingdom is departed from thee;*
> *32 and they drive thee from among men, and thy dwelling shall be with the beasts of the field; and they shall feed thee as the oxen, and seven times shall pass over thee until thou know that the most High takes rule in the kingdom of men and gives it to whomever he will.*
> *33 The same hour the word was fulfilled upon Nebuchadnezzar: and he was driven from among men and ate grass as the oxen, and his body was bathed with the dew of heaven until his hair grew like eagles' feathers and his nails like birds' claws.*

This continues today: people who don't want to submit themselves to the God of heaven who created them are becoming more and more like beasts. They aren't getting better.

Nebuchadnezzar's Restoration

God wants something different. Without God, humans are crazy. Sometimes God allows a person who thinks they are so smart to experience real insanity. In the end, the king did give God the glory and he made this proclamation:

> *34 But at the end of the time I Nebuchadnezzar lifted up my eyes unto heaven, and my understanding was returned unto me, . . .*

He looked toward the right place after all the time had passed. The human race has not looked up yet. But this prophecy implies that they will do so in the end.

34 . . . and I blessed the most High, and I praised and glorified him that lives for ever, whose dominion is an everlasting dominion, and his kingdom is through all ages:

35 and all the inhabitants of the earth are counted as nothing; and in the army of heaven and in the inhabitants of the earth, he does according to his will; nor is there anyone who can interfere with his hand and say unto him, What doest thou?

36 In the same time my reason was returned unto me, and I turned to the majesty of my kingdom; my dignity and greatness returned unto me; and my governors and my great ones sought me; and I was restored in my kingdom, and more excellent greatness was added unto me.

37 Now I, Nebuchadnezzar, praise and build up and glorify the King of heaven because all his works are truth, and his ways judgment: and he is able to humble those that walk with arrogance.

We are coming to the last of the times, and this will end with "Nebuchadnezzar" (who represents the human race and the free will God has given each one of us) completely sane and whole again before God.

This is the first time King Nebuchadnezzar talked about the King of heaven. Before this, he referred to himself as the king. In biblical history, Nebuchadnezzar's story ends here. It ends with this phrase: Now I, Nebuchadnezzar, praise and build up and glorify the King of heaven because all his works are truth, and his ways judgment: and he is able to humble those that walk with arrogance.

Notice that even in this, Nebuchadnezzar respected God's will. He didn't say, "And God is going to humble those who walk with arrogance." He left it in God's hands instead, saying . . . and he is able to humble those that walk with arrogance. The king was practically saying, "I know this is true because I was the most arrogant, and now I know that God can humble anyone."

God was patient with the king, but Nebuchadnezzar was anxious and wanted to know the truth. God showed it to him. Submitting to the truth was hard for the king. He continued to fight and play his cards to keep his own kingdom. He began to allow God to work when he placed Daniel as head of all his business.

In the end, however, God had to knock him out of his kingdom by turning him into a beast that ate grass. Only then did he find true reason.

The Bible says that the kingdom of God is as if a man should cast seed into the ground and should sleep and rise night and day, and the seed should spring forth and grow up, he knows not how. But Scripture affirms that the blade (of grass) comes first, then the flower, and finally the seed (Mark 4:26–28). The king thought he was on top of everything. God turned him back to the stage of eating grass and receiving dew from heaven.

This is God's remedy for humanity. The only way out of the insanity is by eating and digesting the true Word of God and letting the dew from heaven wash and clean us. And if, in due time, this makes us lift our eyes to heaven, he can give us back our sanity and our reason. He can humble us too; he doesn't have to do it, but he can.

Let us pray:

Lord, please send us your word and your rain from heaven. If on our own we are not able to take the medicine for our own sins, we ask that you, Lord, would submit us to your dealings, to your remedy, until we focus our eyes on you. We ask this for all nations and for all of humanity. Amen.

CHAPTER FIVE

The Writing on the Wall

Belshazzar's Feast

God had used Daniel to humble Nebuchadnezzar. However, the king's son Belshazzar never learned his father's lessons, and when he eventually took the throne, his conduct was wicked. Belshazzar means "Bel preserves the king." (We will discuss the similarity between the names Belshazzar and Belteshazzar a little further on in this chapter.) Bel was the main god out of the many pagan gods of Babylon. Chapter 5 begins many years later, when Belshazzar made a banquet and drank "against" his lords; Belshazzar competed to see who could drink the most alcohol and remain standing.

Daniel 5

> [1] *Belshazzar the king made a great banquet to a thousand of his lords, and against the thousand he drank wine.*

He not only drank against his lords, but look what he did next:

> [2] *Belshazzar, under the influence of the wine, commanded that they bring the vessels of gold and of silver which Nebuchadnezzar his father had brought from the temple of Jerusalem; that the king and his princes, his wives and his concubines, might drink with them.*

In his drunken state, Nebuchadnezzar's son decided to bring the vessels that were from the house of the Lord and fill them with Babylonian wine. He included his wives and concubines to create a greater party. This happened in Babylon more than 2,500 years ago, but it is a picture of how the present church age will end.

Right now, we have man's way of doing things, the "Babylonian" system. In the original, "Babylon" means "confusion" and comes from the Tower of Babel where the Lord confused the languages. Babylon is the land, or system, or city of confusion.

From where did this confusion come? When man decided to make a name for himself and, in effect, said, "We're not going to accept the judgment of God anymore. God destroyed the earth with a flood, but we're going to build a tower as high as heaven. We're going to give it a name and unite the whole world under our tower and our name" (see Genesis 11:1–9).

A tower symbolizes a force or power. The people rejected the word of God and refused to scatter throughout the earth and multiply. Instead, they wanted everyone to reside in Babylon under their control.

Man continues this by elevating his own name and strength, attempting to control the world. Belshazzar's pride causes him to call for the vessels from the temple of the Lord. In the Bible, a vessel means a "servant" or a "person." If we are serving the Lord, symbolically we could be called vessels in his service. The vessels were made out of gold, silver, bronze, clay, or wood; each material had its significance. But here, even the vessels of gold and silver were in the power of the king of Babylon.

The Lord had told Jeremiah that the people of God had to go through captivity. Those who submitted might survive that judgment; but the ones who remained in the land the Lord was judging would not survive. And these did not survive.

> *And unto this people thou shalt say, Thus hath the LORD said: Behold, I set before you the way of life, and the way of death. He that abides in this city shall die by the sword or by the famine or by the pestilence, but he that goes out and falls to the Chaldeans that besiege you, he shall live, and his soul shall be unto him for a spoil. For I have set my face against this city for evil, and not for good, saith the LORD; it shall be given into the hand of the king of Babylon, and he shall burn it with fire.* (Jeremiah 21:8–10)

King Belshazzar made a tremendous feast. In Scripture, our stages of maturity in the life of God are symbolized by the word "feast." The Jews had to celebrate three feasts a year: the Feast of Passover, the Feast of Pentecost (also called Feast of Weeks or Feast of Firstfruits), and the Feast of Tabernacles (or Booths) at the time of the fall harvest (also called Feast of Ingathering). (See Leviticus 23.) Each of these feasts can also be a picture for us of an age, or an era, as well.

What happened in Babylon with the vessels of the temple symbolized the end of the age of Pentecost (the age of the church). This is a picture of how this age will end. People in churches are running around trying to gather great multitudes and handing out supposed blessings from God. Many behave as if they are drunk; some fall over backward; others come into hysterical laughter; and others exhibit various manifestations, even of animals.

Wine is a symbol of life. The Lord used the cup and the wine for a purpose as well in the last supper with his disciples. There are two possibilities as far as the kind of life we choose: we can live Adam's life, a life that is already corrupted by sin; or we can allow Jesus Christ to live his life in and through us. The person who drinks the new wine of the kingdom of God is not going to get "drunk" in the sense that they go out of control; but the person that harbors Adam's life will easily become intoxicated.

Today's Feast

When the true Holy Spirit arrives and God's gifts are used God's way, there is not only a manifestation of the gifts of the Spirit, but there is also the fruit of the Spirit. One of the characteristics of the fruit of the Spirit is that everything is under the control of the Holy Spirit.

The Holy Spirit does things with order and purity. It is a holy and clean Spirit with the purpose of leading us toward cleanness, not toward ambiguous things where we lose control. This is not to judge the thousands of well-intentioned brethren who have been misled following unclean spirits and thinking it was God's will. Here, the judgment is not against the thousand lords; it's against the king who misdirected the people.

Right now, it is as if there is some kind of a contest in the charismatic realm, which corresponds to the "holy place" (not the holy of holies). They fill the stadiums up to see who has the most power to knock people down, who has the strongest gift of healing, who prophesies better, etc. When the Lord Jesus did miracles, he didn't do them to fill stadiums. And he would leave and go to the desert when people looked for the miracle instead of the Lord. He would not walk with them anymore if that were the case.

True prophets don't say nice things to the carnal man; true prophets are rejected because they prophesy against carnal living. They prophesy that the only way to thrive in this world is by living the life of the Lord Jesus by the power of the Holy Spirit instead of living our own life. His life puts us under the control of the Holy Spirit. It does not take us out of control or leave us without reason.

> *3 Then they brought the vessels of gold that they had brought from the temple of the House of God which was in Jerusalem; and the king and his princes, his wives, and his concubines, drank with them.*
> *4 They drank wine and praised the gods of gold and silver, of brass, of iron, of wood, and of stone.*

What many are doing now is giving prophecies and other manifestations that they say are "God's new wine." All this is to tell the people that if you don't have money, all you have to do is go to Christ and "them." "They" assure you that you will receive "gold and silver" (the things of this world) if you give them your offerings and tithes. In the end, these misguided people worship the god of gold and silver, of brass, of iron, of wood, and of stone.

They may not make figures of gold and silver (although they still do in some places), but they give people the formula to get gold and silver. People who seek these things fall into the deception and give their tithes and their offerings.

The leaders ask, "Who will give a thousand dollars?" So, the people who rise up and give receive the so-called "Abraham's blessing." Then they offer a cheaper blessing that costs five hundred dollars for those who don't have a thousand dollars. They offer all the different prices and all the different styles. They will give you a special blessing if you give them your gold chain, your watch, or your ring. Some will lay a guilt trip on you to get your television or your sound system.

Many people have things they have not earned honestly, but they cannot expect God's blessing while holding these. But something is terribly wrong in many of the big churches around the world. The message given today is not, "Come and give your life to the Lord, and let him discipline you and separate you from the love of the things of this world and from the love of your own life so you can live Christ's life by the power of the Holy Spirit." Their message is, "Come and we will make sure it all goes well with your own life."

I see a similarity between these charismatic centers and churches and a terrorist who gets bewitched to prevent bullets from penetrating him.

Many ministers and ministries today who should know better are in the middle of this feast, giving out Babylonian wine that makes everyone drunk while everyone is drinking against each other to see who can stand the longest and benefit the most from the things of this world. It was possibly one of the most tremendous feasts in the history of Babylon.

Now, however, we are seeing one of the greatest feasts in the history of the church. When have we seen the multitudes that we are seeing? When have we heard all the promises that are being made? When has so much money been brought in? When have we seen all the TV and radio stations that now broadcast this perversion?

But look at what happened in the middle of that party:

> *5 In that same hour some fingers of a man's hand came forth and wrote in front of the candlestick upon the plaster of the wall of the king's palace: and the king saw the palm of the hand that wrote.*

Handwriting on the Wall

Fingers of a man's hand appeared in front of the candlestick. The Israelites kept the candlestick in the holy place, so this helps us identify this spiritually as the realm of the holy place: the realm of gifts, the realm of the showbread, the realm of the lampstand that the priests filled with olive oil, the realm of the altar of incense, the realm of the "priesthood" of all believers. But this is not the realm of the presence of God (the holy of holies); this is the realm of ministry, and the hand is a symbol of ministry, which means "service."

In that same hour, the fingers of a hand appeared in front of the light of their candlestick. It was their own light because they didn't seek God's light, represented by Daniel and his three friends. The previous king had entered into what God wanted, but his son did not.

God has sons, but a common expression says, "God does not have grandsons." This problem has existed in the church for a long time. Many descendants of great men of God have departed from him. Christian churches often create a title and job when they recognize a true man of God, but after that person dies, the church replaces him with someone not necessarily sent by God.

In some past generations of the church – Catholic, Orthodox, or Protestant/evangelical – an authentic fear of God and the life of God sometimes appeared in spite of limitations by the traditions of men. But now, we are at the last party, when the king of Babylon is unleashed.

His lords are competing to see who can drink the most Babylonian wine from the vessels of the temple of the Lord.

The priests were prohibited from drinking wine in the holy place. They had to drink the wine outside if they were to minister unto the Lord. Wine is not prohibited in Scripture; the Lord Jesus drank it, but he didn't get drunk. On the other hand, God had made it clear to people such as John the Baptist not to drink wine. If someone has that commitment with God, we must honor it. The wine in and of itself isn't the problem; the use and purpose of the wine creates the problem. If the purpose is to feed our own life, the "wine" will lead us astray.

Because of this, we see drunken people in the bars. Many die in knife or gun fights; some end up doing things under the influence of alcohol that they would not have done otherwise. On the other hand, a good glass of wine in fellowship with family around a table or with friends at a wedding opens another kind of communion (or temperance), a fruit of the Spirit.

The person who is under the control of the Spirit of God will not get drunk or lose control. The Spirit of God wants control in all areas of our life, bringing us liberty and controlling our appetites (in temperance). Without the Spirit, we have no liberty to do God's will. We either serve the flesh, the world and the devil, or the Lord. No one can serve two masters. If the Lord doesn't enter and replace the other one, we will never have the freedom to accomplish his will.

During this out-of-control Babylonian party, the Lord sent a ministry represented by the fingers of a man writing. Some say that the hand and the five fingers represent the five ministries mentioned in the letter to the Ephesians. Many false ministries have arisen that are not from the Lord, spurred by some element of symbolism. But here, only the hand was seen, and it was writing.[24]

These words were not spoken; they were written and remained visible on the wall. The people knew this was from God, but they could not understand it.

> [6] *Then the king became pale, and his thoughts troubled him, and the girdings of his loins were unloosed, and his knees smote one against another.*

When the king saw the hand, the color in his face faded, his clothes fell, and he remained naked and trembling. He didn't even understand the

---

24　Isaiah 8:18 says, . . . I and the children whom the LORD has given me are for signs and for wonders . . .

message. When the writing appeared, it interrupted their party; the music stopped, the drinking stopped, the vessels remained, and everyone watched in panic and terror.

> *7 The king cried in a loud voice that they bring in the magicians, the Chaldeans, and the fortune-tellers. The king spoke and said to the wise men of Babylon, Whoever shall read this writing and show me its interpretation, shall be clothed with purple and have a chain of gold about his neck and shall be the third ruler in the kingdom.*

The second ruler could have been the queen (who enters in verse 10).

> *8 Then all the king's wise men came in, but they could not read the writing, nor make known to the king its interpretation.*
> *9 Then king Belshazzar was greatly troubled, and his colour was changed, and his princes were upset.*

In the middle of the drinking competition, the writing was sculpted, and the king wanted someone to interpret for him. He was in trouble, and his princes started to murmur.

World-pleasing feasts and parties never end well. There is always somebody that does a terrible disgrace and ruins it. The princes who needed a strong leader in Babylon instead got a pale, naked king who trembled with fear.

The king realized that something was terribly wrong, but he couldn't interpret the writing.

Why do many church leaders have the same problem today? Because none of their "wise" men, none of their "magicians," none of those who say they know how to use the "vessels" truly know God's language.

We have a desperately sad situation in much of the church today. People say they are of God and have God's ministry and God's gifts. These people might have gifts from God, but they use them for their own life and their own good instead of seeking God's true kingdom that is not of this world. God says that if we are not faithful with the little, then the little that we have will be taken away from us (see Luke 16:10–13).

The enemy was at the door, and when God showed them the truth in the midst of confusion, they sought answers. A good part of the church is in this condition of advanced drunkenness while they nourish their own life. When God's true message comes, no one understands. God has true ministry, and Scripture is true, but no one can understand it.

Some princes were probably mad at the king for ending the party.

> *¹⁰ Now the queen, by reason of the words of the king and of his princes, came into the banquet room. The queen spoke and said, O king, live for ever: let not thy thoughts trouble thee, nor let thy countenance be pale.*
> *¹¹ There is a man in thy kingdom . . .*

In the original, the word "man" used here is the Chaldean, gebar, meaning a nobleman, a freeman (very similar in meaning to the Spanish word varón). The true body of Christ is free, no matter what the circumstances, because their freedom is inside, in their very nature. Where a free person walks, what the laws are, or what the government is makes no difference. No one can hinder their freedom because it is freedom to be in a direct relationship with God, to have a clean heart and be pleasing to God. No one can stop that kind of freedom.

> *¹¹ There is a [free or noble] man in thy kingdom, in whom lives the spirit of the holy God; . . .*

There is a man (that is outside of this feast) in whom the Spirit of the Holy God dwells. What does this mean? In the wild party, even with the vessels of the temple of God and the light that they invented, God's Holy Spirit was not there. They did have gifts that came from God, vessels that came from the temple of God, gold and silver that came from God, but God's Holy Spirit was not there. If the wine they drank was not the life of God's Holy Spirit, then what spirit was it? It was a false spirit.

> *¹¹ There is a man in thy kingdom, in whom lives the spirit of the holy God; and in the days of thy father light and intelligence and wisdom, like the knowledge of God, was found in him; whom the king Nebuchadnezzar, thy father, made prince over all the magicians, astrologers, Chaldeans, and fortune-tellers; thus did thy father, the king,*

Belshazzar had not continued on the path his father had learned. Nebuchadnezzar may have placed Daniel in charge of something, but now he no longer had authority over those people. Daniel means "God is the judge" or "the Lord judges," and this is what the Lord is about to do now.

> *¹² because Daniel, whom the king named Belteshazzar, was found to have a more excellent spirit and greater knowledge and understanding interpreting dreams, unraveling questions, and dissolving doubts. Now let Daniel be called, and he will show thee the interpretation.*

The previous king had named Daniel "Belteshazzar," whereas the present king, son of Nebuchadnezzar, was named Belshazzar, which means "Bel preserves your life." But Belteshazzar has a double meaning; it can mean "Bel preserves your life" or "leader of the Lord."

Belshazzar was not the Lord's leader and was completely off track. Now here comes Belteshazzar, or Daniel. God filled the king with terror; he was scared, pale, naked, and trembling. Then Daniel came to interpret what God was already doing before the king. Some of the best ministry opportunities happen when the person knows he is in trouble and asks for advice; then another person can come to reveal what the Lord desires.

> [13] *Then Daniel was brought in before the king. And the king spoke and said unto Daniel, Art thou that Daniel, who art of the sons of the captivity of Judah, whom my father brought out of Judea?*

Notice this: the king was not ignorant; he knew his history; he knew what had happened with his father; and above all that, he had chosen to go his own way. Those who do this today in the church are not ignorant either. They know their history and their state because they look for things of this world for their own benefit. They don't seek the good of the true people of God. Neither do they want to do the will of God because they want a God who is created in their image and who blesses whatever they want. They have turned their backs on God's true will.

> *. . Art thou that Daniel, who art of the sons of the captivity of Judah, whom my father brought out of Judea?*

Why hadn't he called on him before? He sent for him as a last resort at the last minute.

> [14] *I have heard of thee, that the spirit of the holy God is in thee and that light and understanding and greater wisdom was found in thee.*

Many "kings" along with their "prophets" pertaining to this realm do things backward. They do things thinking that light is darkness, and that darkness is light. And according to Scripture, the light inside of them is darkness, but they think it is light. The Lord Jesus said: If, therefore, the light that is in thee is darkness, how great is that darkness! (Matthew 6:23). This occurs when they do not believe or receive the truth.

The truth is not a concept; the truth is a person. It is the Lord Jesus himself (John 14:6). They give themselves over to a great delusion – a deception – represented here as great drunkenness. The king said he knew the history; he knew that Daniel existed; he knew where Daniel came from and everything that happened with his father. But up until this time, he had not wanted to accept it. He said, I have heard of thee . . .

> *15 And now the wise men, the astrologers, have been brought in before me that they should read this writing and make known unto me its interpretation, but they could not show the interpretation of the thing:*

They claimed to be spiritual guides and did miracles and prophesy, but they didn't speak God's language. They could not understand or declare it. For them, it was an enigma.

> *16 And I have heard of thee, that thou canst declare that which is in doubt and unravel difficulties: . . .*

How sad that it took an impossible situation for the king to recognize his need and feel this doubt! However, the Lord has a true people, a true body on the earth that can unravel doubts and difficulties. But people who are content with their own lives do not desire for someone to resolve their doubts or difficulties.

> *16 . . . now if thou canst read this writing and show me its interpretation, thou shalt be clothed with purple and have a chain of gold about thy neck and shalt be the third ruler in the kingdom.*
> *17 Then Daniel answered and said before the king, Let thy gifts be for thyself and give thy rewards to another; yet I will read the writing unto the king and show him the interpretation.*

Daniel answered the king, in essence, "I don't desire those things that are important to you and your princes. I don't care about the position you offered. I don't care about your gifts. I don't care about the offering you promised. Give it to someone else. It doesn't matter because your kingdom has come to an end. However, I will declare what God has written."

I have heard of ministries that go to places and rent stadiums or hold meetings in churches with large auditoriums. They send their own people to collect the offering because they don't trust the pastor of that area. Others believe the other ministry robbed part of the offering. Or they make a campaign all over the city and invite people to receive the Lord. They write down the names and phone numbers of the people, but the pastors fight because they were not given enough names (of those who went forward and signed decision cards).

They pursue these people and lay guilt trips on them to make them go to their church to get their tithes and offerings. Sadly, after someone realizes they have been deceived, they may never come back to church, or it takes years for them to give another tithe or offering.

True tithing should go to the widow, the orphan, the hungry, the needy, and also the "priest," the "Levite," and the prophet (Deuteronomy 26:12–15). But relatively few have been able to understand that an implemented rule or law is not necessary if you are truly led by the Spirit of God.

When God leads us, we will share a lot more than a tenth of our time, our resources, our things, and our money. Even more, the Lord will show us the true man or woman of God or needy person that is worthy to receive this gift. The true things of God flow naturally and not by fear. The people who are controlled by the life of fallen Adam must be motivated by fear, but those who have Christ's life are motivated by God's love.

The king called Daniel because he was trembling with fear. He had ruled for years and had never even thought of calling Daniel. Now things had changed, and this is what Daniel declared:

> [18] *O thou king, the most high God gave Nebuchadnezzar thy father the kingdom and the greatness and the glory and the magnificence:*

God did this with Adam, our ancestor: he placed everything under his authority.

> [19] *and by the greatness that he gave him, all the peoples, nations, and languages, trembled and feared before him; whom he would he slew; and whom he would he kept alive; and whom he would he set up; and whom he would he humbled.*

The Lord has given man the authority here on earth.

> [20] *But when his heart made itself arrogant, and his spirit hardened itself in pride, he was deposed from the throne of his kingdom, and they took his glory from him:*

This also happened to Adam, and for thousands of years, Adam's descendants have lost their sanity; the only way to regain it is by doing what Nebuchadnezzar did. Scripture says that he recovered his sanity when he lifted his eyes to the heavens and recognized God's authority and greatness. The human race will not return to its sanity until it does likewise.

²¹ and he was driven from among the sons of men; and his heart was put with the beasts, and his dwelling was with the wild asses: they made him eat grass like an ox, and his body was bathed with the dew of heaven until he understood that the most high God takes rule of the kingdom of men and that he appoints over it whomever he will.

God is preparing another government. He is preparing a varón or, a free man, represented by Daniel, who is not going to depend on the whims of men. Daniel did well during Nebuchadnezzar's time, but not during Belshazzar's kingdom.

From time to time in the past, it has gone well for the true sons of God, but lately, it has gone extremely badly for them; in most cases, they have been outside of the ecclesiastical governments, and they have struggled. But they don't need to be placed in high authority by the kings of this world because God himself is about to remove all of it.

God will not place people in authority in his kingdom who have not been tested and proven faithful with little. God will choose people who have been tested with receiving a surplus. He will choose people like Paul who knew how to be content in abundance and in need. He will send people who have been able to give him their best, being sick or well, with money or without. He will choose people who have been faithful to him.

²² And thou his son, O Belshazzar, hast not humbled thine heart, though thou knewest all this;

Many people, like Belshazzar, know history; they have the Scriptures; they know about millions of martyrs who gave their lives for the Lord. But they desire the things of this world and don't understand God's true language. They don't understand what true treasures of heaven are or where true investment should be, and God says your heart will be where your treasure is (Luke 12:34).

²³ but hast lifted up thyself against the Lord of heaven; and they have brought the vessels of his house before thee, and thou and thy princes, thy wives and thy concubines, have drunk wine in them; furthermore, thou hast praised gods of silver and of gold, of brass, of iron, of wood, and of stone, which do not see, nor hear, nor know; and the God in whose hand is thy soul and whose are all thy ways, thou hast never honoured.

This happens in many places that claim to be the house of God; the music is frightening and doesn't give honor to the Lord. The messages are an abomination because they tell people they can save their own lives and prosper, praising the gods represented by gold, silver, brass, iron, wood, and stone.

> [24] *Then from his presence was sent the palm of the hand that sculpted this writing.*

The hand was sent from the very presence of God, from the true holy of holies.

> [25] *And the writing that he sculpted is, MENE, MENE, TEKEL, UPHARSIN.*

They saw letters written with the palm of a hand, but Daniel said it was sculpted (not done with a pen or a pencil). The letters were engraved in high relief on the stone wall of the palace of the king of Babylon.

The king was understandably freaked out when the hand came into his palace in front of everyone and sculpted the message on what could have been a marble wall. Did the palace shake and crack during this? Did the foundations of Babylon begin to shake so much it made the king's clothes fall off, leaving him naked, pale, and trembling, and he had to stop the party and send for Daniel?

God is about to send a message through his true servants who are represented by his hand. This is going to make today's "Babylon" shake. The message is that this world is coming to an end, and whoever wants safety must flee – from the false security of religion, politics, or economics dominated by the world – to the presence of God outside the camp. The city of Babylon is about to be taken.

> [25] *And the writing that he sculpted is, MENE, MENE, TEKEL, UPHARSIN.*
> [26] *This is the interpretation of the thing: MENE; God has audited thy kingdom and finished it.*
> [27] *TEKEL; Thou art weighed in the balances and art found wanting.*
> [28] *PERES; Thy kingdom has been broken and is given to the Medes and Persians.*

Babylon Falls

The true danger was outside, and since they were inside and drunk, they didn't realize what was coming: an army that was surrounding the city. They thought that Babylon was invincible because they had conquered the whole world.

The Medes and the Persians who were outside used a similar tactic to what David had used many years before to conquer Jerusalem by going up the waterspout (2 Samuel 5:8). They threw stones into the river that flowed into the city under the great wall. That night, they deviated the river of Babylon, and the enemy army entered through the empty water way.

These kings and princes were drinking against each other in their confused state, with the vessels of the house of the Lord, and they were minutes away from losing everything.

Many people know that there will be judgment from God in the end. They think they will be fine in that day because they prayed the prayer, or they said a certain thing, or they gave their tithe, or went to confession, or church, or whatever. But they don't know the elements of judgment are now taking place, and the Lord will say in that day:

> *For I was hungry, and ye gave me no food; I was thirsty, and ye gave me no drink; I was a stranger, and ye took me not in; naked, and ye clothed me not; sick and in prison, and ye visited me not. Then they shall also answer him, saying, Lord, when did we see thee hungry or thirsty or a stranger or naked or sick or in prison and did not minister unto thee? Then he shall answer them, saying, Verily I say unto you, Inasmuch as ye did it not to one of the least of my brothers, ye did it not to me. And they shall go away into eternal punishment, but the righteous into eternal life. (Matthew 25:42–46)*

The Lord will not ask how many meetings they attended, or how many offerings they gave, or how many prayers they made. He will not ask how many night vigils they kept; he will not even ask if they read the Bible every day. He will only ask about the answer that came from their heart when someone from the Lord came with a need. He will ask how they responded. The spontaneous reaction of the heart will define the future. This king had ignored Daniel for years, even knowing his story and the information given to him, probably by his mother and his own queen.

> [29] *Then Belshazzar commanded, and they clothed Daniel with purple and put a chain of gold about his neck and made a proclamation concerning him, that he should be the third ruler in the kingdom.*

Not understanding politics, many Christians in the United States of

America fight in that realm to elect a president who will stop abortions, allow the Bible to be read in schools, and repress homosexuals, etc. First, it may be too late for that. And second, it is not possible to convert a nation by force. Even though I believe that we have a clear responsibility to vote (unless God specifically shows us otherwise), remember that our battle is not against flesh and blood but against principalities, against powers, against the lords of this age, rulers of this darkness, against spiritual wickedness in the heavens (Ephesians 6:12).

Therefore a "political" conversion of the USA is not possible because spiritual abortions have escalated so much that God is very unhappy. People come to a church and say the prayer, and then they tell the pastor, "But I still don't feel saved. I still feel condemned."

And the pastor may say, "Of course you're okay; you're in the church with me. Here, read this verse . . ." And they never ask people to repent of their own life and never lead them toward a true and new birth.

These pastors are spiritual abortion doctors. Spiritual homosexuality remains in many institutes of theology, seminaries, and Bible schools where man teaches man. Many spiritual directives do not come from God. And then these so-called Christians want to judge the transvestites and the homosexuals that walk around skid row.

The time is quickly approaching when God will dictate a final sentence over this great humanistic Babylon that dabbles in the occult. Those who stayed in Babylon waiting for the sentence waited too long. When it comes, God will execute it instantly. (See Revelation 18.)

> [30] *That same night Belshazzar the king of the Chaldeans was slain.*

As I said before, "Chaldean" means "spiritualist." He was king of the spiritualists. Belshazzar, the king of the Chaldeans, was killed.

Sadly, the spirit in some people today who say they are of God is not the Spirit of God. Some of these mega pastors who claim to represent God are not more than a band of spiritualists.

The bigger some churches get, the worse their problems get. Those who reject the truth follow a great spirit of deception[25] where their worship soon turns into a show, a spectacle in the name of the Lord. They make a great performance with the vessels of God, but they give out the wine, the life of Babylon. They teach the people that they can acquire the best things of this world without repenting of their own way.

When people decide to truly follow the Lord and turn their backs on

25   2 Thessalonians 2:10

their own life, they take up their crosses and follow Christ. They live his life by the power of the Holy Spirit.

God wants us to prosper, but his prosperity is different from the world's prosperity. If the root of corruption isn't cut, we will never be able to obtain true prosperity in the life of Christ. God isn't going to allow people with divided hearts to remain in his kingdom. He already experienced that with Lucifer and Adam, and he doesn't want any more of it. God gave us free will, but he also gave us a chance to seek the true light in this fallen world. Everyone who wants to can seek the true light, and he is that true light.

The Lord Jesus came so no one would perish. If someone does perish, it's because they turned their backs on the Light, the Truth, and the True Way.

> [30] *That same night Belshazzar the king of the Chaldeans was slain.*
> [31] *And Darius the Median took the kingdom, being sixty-two years old.*

Daniel 6

> [1] *It pleased Darius to set over the kingdom one hundred and twenty governors who should be in all the kingdom;*

Pentecost began with 120 people. Twelve is linked to divine order, and ten symbolizes the law (or Word) of God.

> [2] *and over these three presidents, of whom Daniel was first, that the governors might give accounts unto them, and the king should not be bothered.*

When Babylon fell, Daniel did not. He continued with the next king. What am I trying to say? God can give us experience in the kingdoms of this world, but his plan will not be manifested that way. The kingdoms of this world will be reduced to ruins, but the true kingdom of our Lord will come forth another way.

When the new thing came, Daniel was not placed third; he was first.

In an instant, Babylon ended. Everything came down, and God did something different. This great "Babylon" that exists today, where men think they know more than God, and they proudly say they have established their course with their own philosophy and ideas, will soon come down.

Let us pray:

Lord, we thank you because there are people that have learned your language that is only understood with a true change of heart. They have understood your message that can only be beneficial when we come into the realm of your life. Let us be your faithful representatives, Lord, not only in word but also in deed, so that in the moment that a message must be sculpted on a wall, we can be in your image and likeness and part of your true body. We ask this, Lord, and give you authority to purify our hearts and lives as you see fit. Amen.

Chapter Six

Perfection Is a State of the Heart

The fall of Babylon, as narrated in the last chapter, is also a representation of the system of this world. Babylon was a real empire, but God describes the fall of the future Babylon (representing the present world system) in Revelation 18.

The Tower of Babel began this kingdom. Mankind wanted to make a name for themselves, so they built a tower to reach the sky to avoid another destruction like the flood. The construction of the tower was an effort to avoid God's judgment without having to change their behavior. Instead of doing what God wanted, which was to go and multiply and have dominion over all the earth, they chose to stay in one place and be controlled by the same thing. So, God confused their language. Now the ancient kingdom had crumbled.

Daniel 5

30 That same night Belshazzar the king of the Chaldeans was slain.

31 And Darius the Median took the kingdom, being sixty-two years old.

Sixty-two is an interesting number,[26] but even more interesting is that Darius was possibly the same King Ahasuerus[27] who was Queen Esther's husband.

---

26   See The Tabernacle of David: A Study of How the Psalms Reveal Prophetic Numerology, Russell Stendal, Ransom Press International, Hollywood, Florida (2020).

27   Ahasuerus is a title not a name (such as Pharaoh in Egypt).

Daniel 6

¹ It pleased Darius to set over the kingdom one hundred and twenty governors who should be in all the kingdom;
² and over these three presidents, of whom Daniel was first, that the governors might give accounts unto them, and the king should not be bothered.

Daniel Obeys God

Darius put the kingdom in Daniel's hands. Daniel was no longer third; he was first. The Bible promises a day when there will be a first resurrection, and those worthy of the first resurrection will reign with Christ for a thousand years. But, if they are to reign with Christ, who are they going to reign over? (See Revelation 20.)

³ Then this Daniel was preferred above these governors and presidents because an overabundance of the Spirit was in him; and the king thought to set him over the whole kingdom.
⁴ Then the presidents and governors looked for occasions against Daniel on behalf of the kingdom, but they could find no occasion or fault because he was faithful, and no vice nor fault was found in him.

Ever since the New Testament days, there have been many theologians who say that perfection is impossible. But here, in the Old Testament, the Scripture says the pagan governors could find no fault with Daniel in spite of the terrible situation. Sometimes our concept of perfection is not the same as what the Lord shows in Scripture.

We may feel that we can never achieve perfection because our minds are forgetful or our adding skills are inaccurate. But in God's vocabulary, perfection is a state of heart, motivation, attitude, and direction. Daniel shows us it is possible to find perfection in this context.

Many people in Scripture were without fault before the Lord. To name a few, the Bible speaks thus of Job, Joshua, and Joseph (in Egypt). There are many examples of people whose goal was only to do the Lord's will and nothing more. Throughout the course of their lives, they never deviated from that purpose. This doesn't mean they never had a mishap in language; it doesn't mean they always got their multiplication tables right. It means their mistakes were of a different kind.

The Bible says Jesus Christ was a man without sin, and he was perfect to God. One day, in the midst of a multitude, the Lord Jesus asked, "Who touched me?" (Luke 8:45).

Peter replied, "Master, the multitude throng thee and press thee, and sayest thou, Who touched me?"

But the Lord wanted to highlight the woman who had intentionally touched him. As far as his humanity, Jesus had the same limitations we have; if we're looking forward, we cannot look backward. The direction the Lord had from the Spirit of his Father was his true inheritance, and it is available to us too. He came not only to show us the way but also to be that way.

Daniel is a type of Jesus, and in the book of Daniel, we don't find any errors or faults in Daniel. While he was born into the enslaved human race and raised in the midst of contaminated apostate religion, with God's power and presence, he obtained victory over the flesh and over sin, even while hostage in Babylon. Later, we find Daniel kneeling and repenting for the sins of his people, asking God to restore them. This is similar to what the Lord Jesus came to do. Because Jesus was sinless, he also carried our sins and bore the penalty for them.

Darius's kingdom was somewhat better in a certain sense, but from God's point of view, the empires of the world have gone in decline. Remember the image Nebuchadnezzar saw of the kingdom of Babylon: a statue's head of gold. In this image, the silver arms and shoulders represented the Medes and the Persians that came after Babylon. They may have conquered more, but their quality was inferior.

Greece came later, under bronze, which is a symbol of judgment. Then came the iron, and after that the iron mixed with baked clay. Every kingdom has added something that seemed like progress, but God says the human race and its governments are in a process of degradation.

In the beginning, Nebuchadnezzar could make life or death decisions over his subjects. When it came to the Medes and the Persians, they placed the law above the king. They feared that the king could become rash in a fit of rage (remember that Nebuchadnezzar was insane for seven years), so they thought it was necessary to tie him to a law that could not be changed, not even by the king himself. The Greeks and the Romans added other elements to the government. Today, in the days of democracy, we have the most degraded and corrupt form of government there has ever been or ever will be (because man without God is corrupt and in a democracy the power is spread out over many people).[28]

---

28 The United States is a modified democracy called a republic that has extensive checks and balances to provide at least some safeguards for those in minority, such as Jews and Christians. But even so, unless there is a strong percentage of godly,

> *⁵ Then these men said, We shall never find any occasion against this Daniel except we find it against him in the law of his God.*

Observe the following: the Lord has something that is parallel to what the kingdoms of men have implemented after the course of many years. The Lord has a law that almost no one has wanted to consider. These presidents and princes apparently thought, "If we are going to find a fault in Daniel, we have to find it in the law of his God because Daniel will always put the law of his God above our law."

> *⁶ Then these governors and presidents assembled together before the king and said thus unto him, King Darius, live for ever.*

They came to sweeten the king's ear with praise, and he fell into the trap.

> *⁷ All the presidents of the kingdom, magistrates, governors, great ones, and captains have agreed in common accord to promote a royal decree and to confirm it that whoever shall ask a petition of any God or man for thirty days, except of thee, O king, he shall be cast into the den of lions.*

In the prophetic books, the "king" often represents the authority God has given the human race. Today, many people believe humanism is the greatest thing ever. They say, "We're going to glorify and deify the human being above everything."

In King Darius's case, they used caution because they didn't know if he would fall for their scheme or not, so they suggested it be for thirty days. They knew thirty days was enough time to catch Daniel disobeying the law.

Lately, democracies have changed constitutions of entire countries to state that power is of the people. This sounds excellent to most voters because things change according to their taste. From God's point of view, however, humanistic democracy is the most corrupt form of government. Why? Because failures, cracks, and corruption are produced in this political system, and the interests of a few move masses by controlling information and certain stimulus.

Remember that the great statue of King Nebuchadnezzar's dream (representing a succession of world empires all the way to the end of the world system) degenerated in quality from the gold head of one-man rule all the way down to feet and toes of iron (representing law) mixed

---

moral people, the system will implode. Our republic is presently being put to the test and desperately needs a massive spiritual awakening along with divine intervention if our freedom is to survive.

with clay (representing voters) that could not adhere to one another.

The natural man is prone to falling into deception. The problem with Adam and Eve was that they wanted to have the knowledge of good and evil to be like God. In most democracies, the people are believed to be wise enough to choose their governors, but they go from problem to problem, from one extreme to the other.

The governors and presidents came to the king, and in a very sneaky manner, they presented the deal and concluded saying:

> ⁸ *Now, O king, confirm the decree and sign the writing that it not be moved, according to the law of Media and of Persia, which does not change.*
> ⁹ *Therefore king Darius signed the writing and the decree.*

There was a writing and a decree that affected Adam and Eve when they lost the sovereignty over the earth that God had given them to administer. When one person loses something, another gains it. In the laws of physics, energy cannot be wasted, neither can it be destroyed; it can only change its form. While some people lost everything in the great depressions, others gained.

The religious and political realms are like this also. King Darius signed the decree, and later it could not be changed.

> ¹⁰ *Now when Daniel knew that the writing was signed, he entered into his house; and with the windows open toward Jerusalem in his dining chamber, he knelt three times a day and prayed and gave thanks before his God as he was used to doing before.*

Daniel didn't even close the windows; he didn't modify his behavior out of fear. Making decisions based on fear and terror from people who aren't clean before God is dangerous. King Darius fell into the trap because they praised him and exalted him far above what God wanted. Daniel wasn't fooled, however. He knew that God's power was infinitely greater than the power of any law or any human government.

In reconciling this with Paul's teaching in the New Testament where he says that we should obey the governors of this earth, we recognize that we must be exemplary citizens in everything that is for good. But the governors of this earth are not above the Lord, and if they insist we praise ourselves, or the king, or the governor, or the god of money above the God of heaven, then we cannot obey them.

Daniel didn't try to hide. Daniel didn't go tell the king, "Look, king, you're falling into a big trap. Please don't sign this because they have bad intentions against me; I have to serve my God, and they're taking away my religious freedom . . ."

Many churches and pastors object and challenge the government when they notice it does something that hinders them. Even as the first president, Daniel didn't do this. These Medes went to score their touchdown, declaring Daniel's refusal to obey. But Daniel's decision to put God first allowed the king's heart to become apparent.

The Lions' Den, Then and Now

What was Daniel going to do now? Was he going to worship the king – worship humanism that idolizes man? Or was he going to worship the God of heaven? Daniel didn't change his course, because he looked toward Jerusalem, which is the city of peace. Scripture says that if we are born again, we are part of the heavenly Jerusalem that is the mother of us all (see Galatians 4:26). The pressure and the test were huge, but Daniel remained focused.

There was no mention of a lions' den regarding the former Babylon (of course there was a furnace that they could make seven times hotter). But here it existed, and these lions continued in history up until the Roman Empire. A few centuries later, the more "advanced" governments turned the lions' den into a coliseum. This, the origin of our organized sports.

We could ask what's wrong with a soccer game. Maybe nothing. But accidents happen, and fans literally kill each other. Violence and blood escalate because the foundation is wrong; it's based on the idolization of man.

We must be careful about our purpose for attending a football game or sports event. The Lord might send us there for some reason or give us the freedom and the liberty to go. However, if we go to worship man and to idolize him over God, then not only is it wrong, but these problems that have been going on for centuries will never cease.

So, they had the lions' den, which in its primitive state was the beginning of what we now call a "stadium." The most terrible thing is that some now use those stadiums for religious shows, idolizing men who might have gifts of God. Some likely do have gifts of God, but those gifts are often used contrary to the way the Lord Jesus wants them to be used.

Why does God allow all this to happen? Because he wants to reveal what is in the hearts of all these leaders who allow their followers to lift them up and idolize them. In the same manner, he proves the hearts of the people who want a man to reign over them instead of God.

Even though the nations decline in democracy, we still have a responsibility to vote on some occasions. Only God can show us. In some elections, I have not been able to decide which of the two candidates is worse, and one falls into the trap of voting for the least evil. But other times we have voted because we believed it was from the Lord.

I am not trying to make political statements. If the Spirit is in us, we are free to serve God and do everything that the Lord allows us to do. We can go anywhere the Lord gives us freedom to go.

Just because God might not allow me to do a certain thing doesn't mean he will not allow someone else to do it. I shouldn't make everyone turn off their televisions just because the Lord told me to turn mine off.

To hear directly from God is our personal responsibility. This requires maturity. Daniel didn't change his behavior; he continued praying three times a day (in a visible manner) and focused on Jerusalem without deviating from his course.

> [11] *Then these men assembled and found Daniel praying and making supplication before his God.*
> [12] *Then they went and spoke before the king concerning the royal decree; Hast thou not confirmed a decree that whoever shall ask a petition of any God or man within thirty days save of thee, O king, shall be cast into the den of lions? The king answered and said, The thing is true, according to the law of the Media and Persia, which does not change.*
> [13] *Then they answered and said before the king, . . .*

I imagine that it was quickly and with joy.

> [13] *. . . That Daniel, which is of the sons of the captivity of the Jews, has not regarded thee, O king, nor the decree that thou hast confirmed, but makes his petition three times a day.*
> [14] *When the king, heard the matter, it weighed very heavy upon him, and he set his heart on Daniel to deliver him: and he laboured until the going down of the sun to deliver him.*

Observe the difference in the situation with the three Hebrew boys who were thrown into King Nebuchadnezzar's furnace. Nebuchadnezzar had personally received the revelation from God, but he tried to prevent the world's demise by uniting the kingdom, making everyone honor a gold statue in his image. This king was the one who got mad and had these boys thrown into the furnace when they chose not to worship his statue. In much prophetic symbolism, the king represents our will (notice the king is getting better).

A time will come when many people realize what they and the entire human race have done against God, their Creator. Darius fell into the trap of these powerful people linked to the system of this world. He was seduced by the rhythm and the force that this great political movement had. They put him on a pedestal, and he wanted to be there.

Too late, he realized they were conspiring against Daniel, representative of the manifestation of God in his people on earth. They were plotting against the people of God. He knew how these things worked, and it weighed on him so terribly he desperately tried all day to free Daniel.

Revelation 20:7–9 is similar to what happened to Daniel: even when unregenerate humanity is under a good government, their hearts may not change. People say, "The problem would be solved if we had justice, if there were no corruption, and if we had a government with clean leaders."

The first resurrection involves those who have been "beheaded" for the witness of Jesus and the Word of God. They came out from under their own headship and are under his. They are the ones who are resurrected and reign a thousand years with Christ.

> *And I saw thrones, and those who sat upon them, and judgment was given unto them; and I saw the souls of those that were beheaded for the witness of Jesus and for the word of God and who had not worshipped the beast neither its image neither had received its mark upon their foreheads or in their hands; and they shall live and reign with Christ the thousand years. But the rest of the dead did not live again until the thousand years were finished. This is the first resurrection. Blessed and holy is he that has part in the first resurrection; on such the second death has no authority, but they shall be priests of God and of the Christ and shall reign with him a thousand years. (Revelation 20:4–6)*

At the end of these thousand years, Satan is unleashed for a time to deceive and unite all the kingdoms in the world to fight against the people of God. They will try to destroy the people of God. They had righteous, trustworthy Daniel over the presidents and governors and wise men of this kingdom, but the problem within their hearts continued.

Likewise, the desire for power in these presidents, governors, and magi didn't disappear. They continued to feel they should be in power, even with their corruption. Their hearts hadn't changed.

> *15 Then those men assembled near the king, and said unto the king, Know, O king, that this is the law of Media and of Persia: No decree nor statute which the king has confirmed may be moved.*
>
> *16 Then the king commanded, and they brought Daniel, and cast him into the den of lions. Now the king, speaking unto Daniel, said, Thy God whom thou servest continually, may he deliver thee.*

The difference between King Nebuchadnezzar and King Darius is obvious. Nebuchadnezzar got angry and sentenced the three Hebrew boys to the fiery furnace, while Darius recognized that Daniel served the one true God. Darius was ashamed, and with his head down, he had to say to Daniel, essentially, "Look, this is out of my control, and I must leave it in the hands of your God. I am a witness of the complete faithfulness you have toward your God."

Scripture says there will be people in whom the true love and charity of God flows so that the world can see it. Everyone will know who the Lord is. This happened when Darius saw what Daniel was like. Daniel didn't have to speak on behalf of himself because he was what he was, and this defined the case, creating a problem for the king.[29]

> *17 And a stone was brought and laid upon the mouth of the den; and the king sealed it with his own signet ring and with the signet ring of his princes that the agreement concerning Daniel might not be changed.*

It was sealed. Where else in Scripture do we see a stone used to seal something? After the death of Jesus, a stone was placed to seal his tomb. The power of death could not defeat the Lord Jesus. The Lord descended to this den administered by the devil, where the devil had imprisoned the souls of the dead (Hebrews 2:14). He not only broke the seal and rolled away the stone, but he also took captivity captive. He broke the jail and took his own. (Daniel is a symbol of this.)

> *18 Then the king went to his palace and lay down without ea-*

---

29 Something similar to this will eventually happen to the human race. Destroying Babylon is only the beginning. The other problem begins after the true and pure government of God replaces the authority of "Babylon."

ting; neither were instruments of music brought before him, and his sleep fled from him.

Daniel probably slept with ease in the lions' den. The Lord not only closed the lions' mouths, but perhaps Daniel didn't even feel cold that night. I have a friend who thinks he could have covered himself with two or three of those nice big fluffy lions because the true authority was in the hands of Daniel. The one who didn't sleep well, despite his castle and all his comforts, was the king.[30]

King Darius couldn't sleep, and he spent the whole night repenting. Most of the twenty-five verses that mention King Darius refer to the decision he made in the second year of his reign to restore God's house in Jerusalem and return God's vessels to the temple. He'd made a decision that he would not be like Belshazzar the partier. He'd decided to stop the insanity and restore the true foundations of the house of God. He had to restore each vessel one by one and place one stone on top of the other in order to accomplish this. But now he wrestled with the consequences of a poor decision.

According to the Lord, the human race in its fallen state is nothing. If we are to return to what God wants, we must do it step by step, always directed by God. The prophets Zechariah and Haggai began to prophesy in the second year of King Darius's reign to wake up the spirit of a remnant that returned to Jerusalem with precise instructions about how to lay the foundation and restore the house of the Lord.[31] Darius had begun that restoration, but now his own decision had caused the Lord's agent, Daniel, to face harm.

> [19] *Therefore, the king arose very early in the morning at dawn and went in haste unto the den of lions.*
> [20] *And when he came to the den, he cried loudly with a sad voice unto Daniel; and the king, in speaking to Daniel said, Daniel, servant of the living God, has thy God, whom thou servest continually, been able to deliver thee from the lions?*

The king had some faith mixed with doubt. He showed he had faith because he was talking, but he still asked the question. The king didn't

---

30   Much of the human race is spiritually asleep. They have illusions of their own grandeur, and their thoughts are deluded. They believe themselves to be wise, when in reality God sees them as insane. They may think that they are very awake, but to God they are deluded and dreaming. Like King Darius, they are in serious need of a wakeup call.

31   This is expounded in chapters 14 and 15.

know what he was going to find. Who knows what would have happened to that poor king had he found Daniel dead? He may have been close to taking his own life; he was terribly upset.

> [21] *Then Daniel said unto the king, O king, live for ever.*
> [22] *My God has sent his angel, who shut the lions' mouths, that they do me no evil because before him righteousness was found in me; and even before thee, O king, I have done no corruption.*

Scripture says that if the Spirit of God is leading us, we are not under the law because the law of God's Spirit is superior.[32] The law of the Spirit is a law of life and not death.[33] Here Daniel, in representation of God, says that God desires for the king to live forever. This is God's desire for each one of us – for the entire human race. How are we going to live forever? Death must be overcome in order to live forever, and the only one who has been able to defeat death is the Lord Jesus. If we hope to take part in that victory, we must be willing to do what Daniel did.

Daniel was not looking for power as the first president of the Medes and the Persians. He hadn't sought power in Babylon either. He didn't seek his own good, and he didn't try to defend his own life. He sought only what God wanted of him, and he would not modify what he had covenanted with God out of fear of man or of the lions' den.

God is looking for this same attribute now. He looks for a people who are willing to follow him. We continue to hear preachers say, "Come to Christ, and he will give you a house, a car. All you have to do is be faithful here with your offerings, your tithes, and your presence, and you will not lack anything; you will have perfect health and everything you need for your kids; if you ever have a need, all you have to do is come and give more money. God will multiply what you give many times more . . ."

These preachers and their followers really worship the god of money. They would be happy with Nebuchadnezzar's statue of gold and all the music. However, the true message is different. It consists of deciding to not contaminate yourself even before being placed in a position of power like Daniel's. Daniel had to decide whether he would obey the people and the king, or if he would obey the commitment he had made with God. He didn't deviate. He didn't move the curtain of the window, and the lions couldn't handle him.

---

32   See Galatians 5:18.
33   See Romans 8:2.

> *23 Then the king was exceeding glad because of him and commanded that they should take Daniel up out of the den. So Daniel was taken up out of the den, and no injury was found upon him because he believed in his God.*

This is a complete dependence on God, not just a mental statement.

> *24 And the king commanded, and they brought those men who had accused Daniel, and they cast them into the den of lions, them, their children, and their wives; and even before they reached the bottom of the den, the lions had the mastery of them, and broke all their bones in pieces.*
> *25 Then king Darius wrote unto all the peoples, nations, and tongues, that dwell in all the earth: Peace be multiplied unto you.*

God's Protection and Our Future

After Daniel escaped unscathed, they took the ones who had condemned Daniel and threw them into the same den. It didn't go well for them. Likewise, in Revelation it says that the Lord makes war in righteousness.[34]

Revelation 11 confirms that when the two witnesses come with the testimony of the life of the Lord, whoever wants to hurt them will have that same harm fall upon them.

> *And I will give my two witnesses, and they shall prophesy a thousand two hundred and sixty days, clothed in sackcloth. These are the two olive trees and the two candlesticks standing before the God of the earth. And if anyone desires to hurt them, fire proceeds out of their mouth and devours their enemies; and if anyone desires to hurt them, he must in this manner be killed.* (Revelation 11:3–5)

God allows this to prove the hearts of the people. If we are clean and we represent the Lord, and someone does us good or receives us, they do it to the Lord himself. If someone hurts us, they hurt the Lord. The Lord Jesus said, Father, forgive them; for they know not what they do (Luke 23:34). But he also said the consequences were going to come upon that generation,[35] and they did.

---

34 And I saw the heaven open, and behold a white horse; and he that was seated upon him was called Faithful and True, and in righteousness he judges and makes war. (Revelation 19:11)

35 The generation that crucified the Lord came to an end with the destruction of Jeru-

The two generations that still exist are Christ's and Adam's. What we have received from Adam doesn't have a good future. The future is in Christ, in his life. Adam, the first man, was made a living soul by the breath of God, but Jesus Christ is the Lord of heaven and was made a life-giving Spirit.

> *And so it is written, The first man Adam was make a living soul; the last Adam was made a life-giving Spirit.* (1 Corinthians 15:45)

> *He that has the Son has life; and he that does not have the Son of God does not have life.* (1 John 5:12)

Scripture says that God the Father has life in and of himself, and he has given Jesus life in and of himself, but our life is found in Jesus Christ. If we have found eternal life, it's because we have found him. If we don't have him, we don't have life. If he isn't in us, then we don't have life. Religious leaders have deceived many by telling them they have to do religious rituals. Many people do religious things, but it's a waste of time if they don't have him.

God's Math

We like to add, but God likes to multiply. Good things for God can be multiplied. Bad things can be multiplied as well. People who are heading toward destruction multiply their sentence; the people who are heading toward eternity multiply their blessings. They are both like a geometric progression.

The good gets better, and the bad gets worse. Everything gives its fruit at the end: wheat provides bread and good seed, and the tares give out poison. A huge difference isn't seen in the beginning, but in the end, it's very evident.

Daniel's story ends in a great blessing, but these others didn't even reach the bottom of the den before they were completely broken. Daniel said he had been found righteous before God. If we are righteous before God, it's God's righteousness in us because our own righteousness is like filthy rags (Isaiah 64:6). But it will not go well for us in the "lions' den" if true righteousness isn't found in us.

Daniel told the king that he had done no corruption and had not

---

salem by Roman armies circa AD 70. This is also prophetic of what will happen at the final judgment to anyone who has done damage to the body of Christ and remains unrepentant.

broken the king's commandment either. Why? Because the king's commandment was insane. Many things that the world requires are insane, even though there are times when we look like the crazy ones.

Good works are not something we invent; the Bible says good works are the works God has prepared for us to walk in beforehand.

> *For we are his workmanship, created in Christ Jesus for good works, which God has prepared that we should walk in them.* (Ephesians 2:10)

We won't make it through the final judgment if we aren't found walking in these good works. Our own works cannot save us; but at the same time, if his works aren't found in us, it's an indication we aren't saved. The lions ate these people with everything they had. Some people will be very surprised when they face death. Scripture speaks of two deaths: the first death and then after the judgment comes, the second death. The ultimate hell is the lake of fire, which is the second death.

> *And fear not those who kill the body but are not able to kill the soul, but rather fear him who is able to destroy both soul and body in hell.* (Matthew 10:28)

God isn't interested in never-ending torture of his enemies. He's interested in resolving issues in his government to eliminate corruption. He wants us to come to a future where there is no more corruption on earth or in heaven. And Scripture says even the heavens are contaminated by all the problems there have been.[36]

The prophecy in the last chapters of Isaiah, where righteousness dwells in the new heavens and the new earth, comes to pass at the end of the book of Revelation. Corruption doesn't exist where righteousness dwells. Daniel proved that he had no corruption before the king, or in his house, or before the lions when they threw him in the den.

If we come into a total dependence on the Lord like Daniel did, if by the Spirit we live the Lord's life and not our own, no one will be able to terrorize us because we will not be making decisions based on the fear of man.

When we represent the Lord, our life is in his hands. The Lord's words to his disciples in Matthew 10:23 are true: But when they persecute you in this city, flee ye into another, for verily I say unto you, Ye shall not have gone over the cities of Israel until the Son of man be come.

Israel is "the people" of God. The Lord tells us to flee when supposed

---

36   See Job 15:15.

Christians don't want to receive us but want to harm us. Under other conditions, the true men and women of God may remain. Daniel didn't flee. The trouble they planned for Daniel fell upon his enemies instead.

King Darius may have had a heart for God from an early age. His mother may have taught him well. He had seen the things of God, but he was still susceptible to the adoration and idolization of men. However, he did have a functioning conscience.

> 25 *Then king Darius wrote unto all the peoples, nations, and tongues, that dwell in all the earth: Peace be multiplied unto you.*
>
> 26 *On my behalf a statute is put into effect, That in all the dominion of my kingdom everyone tremble at the presence of the God of Daniel for he is the living God and endures for all ages, and his kingdom is such that it shall never come apart, and his dominion shall be even unto the end:*

Darius recognized that God was above him. Darius understood that the kingdoms of men will end, but God's kingdom will endure.

> 27 *that saves and frees, and makes signs and wonders in heaven and in earth, who delivered Daniel from the power of the lions.*
>
> 28 *So this Daniel was prospered during the reign of Darius and during the reign of Cyrus, the Persian.*

After all these tests, God revealed more truths to Daniel that have to do more with our time. He told Daniel to seal the book until the time of the end. He said that when the prophecy is fulfilled (after the end of the years prophesied), Thou shall go to the end and shalt rest, and thou shalt raise up in thy lot [or in thine inheritance] at the end of the days (Daniel 12:13).

After managing so many kingdoms, being the first president, gaining the trust of Darius and the trust of those who ruled in the ancient world – including King Cyrus (Daniel's prayers and intercession even contributed to Jerusalem being restored and the vessels of the Lord being returned) – the Bible says that this was still not Daniel's true inheritance. He would receive his true inheritance at the end of the "days."

Being like Daniel is attainable. We must simply recognize God's authority instead of our own, allowing the Lord to clean us. From the beginning, Daniel purposed in his heart to not contaminate himself; the Lord honored that and blessed him. He didn't allow Daniel to be contaminated at any time. He allowed Daniel to work his whole life in delicate positions, in some of history's most difficult kingdoms, without corruption. If God could do that with Daniel, he can keep us clean in any circumstance, in any group, and in any rank. But none of these positions are our true inheritance. We are only taking a course, receiving training to be able to handle the true riches that are coming.

Let us pray:

Heavenly Father, we thank you, and we ask that what happened with the kings in Daniel's time could happen to us, that God, you would awaken the Spirit in these kings and rulers in order to fulfill your will on earth. We ask that we could come to a time when you will awaken your Spirit in our governors, in our president, the Congress, the Senate, the courts, and all the public offices so that there will be men and women like Daniel who are willing to give up their lives before compromising in corruption. We ask this in the name of our Lord Jesus. Amen.

CHAPTER SEVEN

The Sum of the Matters

Daniel 7

¹ In the first year of Belshazzar king of Babylon, Daniel saw a dream and visions of his head upon his bed: then he wrote the dream and penned the sum of the matters.

Up until now, the king was the one who had the dreams, and Daniel was the one who interpreted them. After he did this for the king, Daniel began to have visions.

In a dream, the person is sleeping, while in a vision, the person is awake. Daniel, being awake, was able to foresee things to come. He was able to see the end result of the empires that existed and the ones that were to come until the time of the end (our time).

The first part of the book of Daniel represents the revelation God gives to unbelievers in their fallen state. Scripture declares that no one has an excuse because even nature demonstrates the glory of God. They might not see this if they do not have the wisdom to interpret the things that surround them.[37] But now, God begins to give Daniel direct revelation that represents what God is doing in the new man in Christ.

Jesus Christ is the beginning of the new creation, and Daniel is a representation of the Lord Jesus. When the king saw Daniel, he thought he was seeing "God" because Daniel represented God. The Lord Jesus told his disciples that if they had seen him, they had seen his Father.[38]

---

37 For the wrath of God is revealed from heaven against all ungodliness and injustice of men, who hold back the truth with injustice; because that which is known of God is manifest to them; for God has showed it unto them. For the invisible things of him, his eternal power and divinity, are clearly understood by the creation of the world and by the things that are made so that there is no excuse. (Romans 1:18–20)

38 Jesus said unto him, Have I been such a long time with you, and yet thou hast not

What does this mean? The Lord Jesus left his heavenly glory and came here as a man (John 1:14). Scripture says he was the temple of God (John 2:19–22). Since he was God become man, he was like us in every way except that he was born alive spiritually. His Father dwelled in him through the Spirit because he was clean.

The Lord Jesus didn't come to do his own will but his Father's will. He didn't come to speak his own words or to do his own works; he came to speak what his Father was speaking and to do what his Father wanted him to do.

We have a part in his ministry, too. According to the Bible, the "body" of Christ is a body of many members of which Jesus is the head. Everyone who is redeemed and cleansed by his blood is part of this body. (According to Leviticus 17:11, the life is in the blood, so we could also say that we are cleansed by his life. See Romans 5:10.) Ephesians states that if we belong to the body of Christ (the true church), everyone will have a different function, just like different organs in the human body have different functions. We all have need of each other, and the Lord Jesus is the head who is over all of us.

> *From whom the whole body fitly joined together and well tied together among itself by the nourishment that every connecting bond supplies, by the operation of each member according to the measure they have received, making increase of the body unto the edifying of itself in charity.* (Ephesians 4:16)

God says that when he has a clean people, when he has a people he is pleased with, he is going to have them reign and even judge nations together with the Lord Jesus.[39] In this sense, Daniel is a representation of what God wants to do with his people. While he was on the earth, Jesus said he was not here to judge anyone, but if he did, his judgment would be true because he did not come to do his own will but his Father's (John 12:47–50).

Horses of Zechariah and Beast of Revelation 17

Now, Daniel's revelation had details that require more wisdom to interpret them. Daniel saw a dream and visions of his head during Belshazzar's first year, and Belshazzar ended up being the last king of Babylon. The Bible says that this happened while Daniel was awake in his bed (at

known me, Philip? He that has seen me has seen the Father; and how sayest thou then, Show us the Father? (John 14:9)

39   1 Corinthians 6:2; 2 Timothy 2:10–12; Revelation 20:4–6

night). He was in a kingdom and a situation that had no spiritual light, only darkness, but God gave him a revelation that was above this.

Daniel 7

¹ . . . then he wrote the dream and penned the sum of the matters.

To understand, we must take everything into account – to get the sum of it all. The next verses of this chapter describe the four beasts Daniel saw in his vision. In Revelation 17, John says he only saw one beast that had "seven" heads: the sum of the matters. In Daniel 7, the first beast had one head, the second beast had one head, the third beast had four heads, and the fourth beast had one head. If we add this up, there is a total of seven heads, just like Revelation 17.

John saw the same vision, but instead of seeing four beasts, he only saw one that represents the sum of all the world's empires. It's ultimately the same story of the statue that the king saw and Daniel interpreted.

But Daniel's vision is more of a complete revelation given directly for the sons of God.

² Daniel spoke and said, I saw in my vision by night, and, behold, the four winds of the heaven fought the great sea.

Men believe their great civilizations and corresponding religions are light, but God says all that is night and darkness. The Lord Jesus taught in the Sermon on the Mount that if the light that is in us is darkness, how great is that darkness!

But if thine eye is evil, thy whole body shall be full of darkness. If, therefore, the light that is in thee is darkness, how great is that darkness! (Matthew 6:23)

Daniel saw his vision during the prime time of the kingdoms of men, and God said it was night. In King Nebuchadnezzar's dream, only a stone cut without hands destroyed the image, but in this chapter, Daniel's vision is a greater example of the coming kingdom of God.

² . . . the four winds of the heaven fought the great sea.

Zechariah 6 speaks of four chariots pulled by four kinds of horses. Zechariah says these are the four spirits of the heavens that are sent throughout the four cardinal points of the earth with the judgments of God. "Four" symbolizes God's divine dealings and his divine love.[40]

---

40   See Genesis 1:14–19.

> *And I turned and lifted up my eyes and looked, and, behold,*
> *there came four chariots out from between two mountains,*
> *and those mountains were of brass. In the first chariot were*
> *red horses and in the second chariot black horses; in the third*
> *chariot white horses and in the fourth chariot grisled and bay*
> *horses. Then I answered and said unto the angel that talked*
> *with me, What is this, my lord? And the angel answered and*
> *said unto me, These are the four spirits [or winds] of the hea-*
> *vens, which go forth from standing before the Lord of all the*
> *earth.* (Zechariah 6:1–5)

God wants to change us. He wants to plant his Word and his life so that his life replaces ours. He wants to take us out of the old creation and bring us into the new creation, of which the Lord Jesus is the first of the firstfruits according to the Scriptures;[41] he is the first in the resurrection and represents the whole harvest.

These horses of many colors symbolize what God wants to do with us. Compare these horses in Zechariah 6 to the ones in Revelation 6: the order in which they appear changes, and one of the horses is a different color. It was impossible to begin with holiness (to begin with being separated exclusively for the work of God) in the old covenant. The blood and the law had to be applied first. Sadly, the law cannot be fulfilled in our own strength. The new covenant begins with a white horse because the Lord is not trying to sanctify us in our fallen state; he desires to bring us into his body, which is already holy. It's a change of government. Instead of us being the head, he wants to be the head. When this happens, he applies the blood (the red horse) and begins to cleanse us.

The third horse in Revelation 6 is black because, for us, God's ways seem very black. God wants to put an end to what we think is good. What may seem right to us may not be right to God, and this is a terrible situation. This black horse is linked with the three feasts of God (Revelation 6:5–6).[42] It represents walking with the Lord and being faithful until the end. He who is faithful with a little will receive more.[43]

The fourth horse is the one that changes. Zechariah 6:3 says that in the fourth chariot, the horses were grizzled and bay. This symbolizes death; therefore, the horses are an ugly color and full of spots. (Up until

---

41   Romans 8:29; 1 Corinthians 15:20–23

42   See Revelation Unveiled, Russell Stendal, Ransom Press International, Hollywood, Florida (2019).

43   Luke 19:17

Jesus's work of redemption, the devil had the empire of death and the title to the earth.) The way God, by his Spirit, fights the "sea" of unconverted humanity is not by being lenient; God's solution for the old man is to kill it. Therefore, we must identify ourselves with the death of the Lord Jesus on the cross. The actual death to our life under the whims of the flesh is a slow one, little by little and drop by drop.

The Lord Jesus can place us on this path, even in this lifetime, and root out the bad desires so that they never come back again. But the way was extremely hard before the work of redemption of Jesus Christ; so much that it was almost impossible for anyone to walk it. Death had a lot of power, and those who died were held prisoner by its power in Hades (or Sheol) while they waited for the coming of the Lord.

Remember that according to the parable of Lazarus and the rich man, Hades (or Sheol) had two compartments, one for those who belonged to God and the other for those that did not. The Lord Jesus broke that jail of death and took his own to be with him (see Ephesians 4). Now the apostle Paul says he is willing to be absent from the body and to be present with the Lord (2 Corinthians 5:8).

Revelation 6:9 is also referring to the souls of those who lost their own lives in order to be under the Lord's authority and live his life. They are not in Sheol: they are under the altar of heaven, under the provision that Jesus Christ gave them through his life, which is the same as through his blood because Scripture says the life is in the blood.[44]

In Revelation 6:7–8, the fourth horse is not grizzled and bay, as it is described in Zechariah. In the original text it is green. Most Bibles have not translated it this way because green colored horses do not exist in the natural realm. But God is going to take us out of this creation and introduce us into something new, something that does not exist yet. The Greek word used here is the one from which we derive our word "chlorophyll" to describe the life of the plants. It is the color in Scripture that illustrates resurrection because God's plan is to end our life and give us new life after being born again into the life of Jesus Christ. This is the plan of redemption.

God is showing all this to Daniel – the four winds of heaven fought the great sea (Daniel 7:2) – because the four winds of heaven can also be translated as the four "spirits" of heaven ("spirit" and "wind" are the same word in Hebrew). The Holy Spirit works to transform us from the old man into the new man. This is the fight God has against the great sea

---

44   Genesis 9:4; Leviticus 17: 11, 14; Deuteronomy 12:23; John 6:53–54

of unconverted humanity.

Flesh and blood cannot inherit the kingdom of God (1 Corinthians 15:50). God has to take us out of one in order to place us into the other. This is summarized here in one line, but it's important in order to understand this vision. The four winds of heaven are fighting against the great sea; God offers his plan of redemption to a world of fallen humanity and has all the power of his Spirit to implement it.

The way of salvation in the Old Testament is exactly the same as in the New Testament: no one will ever be saved by anyone but the Lord Jesus Christ, and it's because of his life.

> *For if, when we were enemies, we were reconciled with God by the death of his Son, much more, now reconciled, we shall be saved by his life.* (Romans 5:10)

Scripture is clear in saying we are reconciled by his death. The death of the Lord gave us the possibility of entering into communion with God, but the verse ends by saying we shall be saved by his life. There is no salvation unless his life is in us.

> *He that has the Son has life; and he that does not have the Son of God does not have life.* (1 John 5:12)

He is coming again as the head, as the authority, as Lord.

Daniel's Vision

After seeing this, the vision continues in Daniel 7.

> *³ And four great beasts came up from the sea, different one from another.*

In Scripture, the "beast" symbolizes the natural man with his carnal appetites. In order for King Nebuchadnezzar to learn the lesson, God had to dethrone him and take away his sanity. In his sentence, he had to eat grass like an ox and endure the heart of a beast instead of a man's heart.

This is happening now. Mankind is not evolving into some sort of super race; it's degenerating at every level. Even in genetics, we're losing what we once had. Humanity is turning more and more into an animal and a beast. Read the headlines of the newspapers everywhere to discover the inhumane, beastly things people do.

Our world is getting worse, and a beast represents each of the four kingdoms of the world. The words "king" and "kingdom" were virtually the same in the original languages. The context determines the meaning. Everything that belongs to the king, including people and land, makes up the kingdom.

> [4] *The first was like a lion, and had eagle's wings; I beheld until its wings were plucked off, and it was removed from the earth, and it stood up on its feet as a man, and a man's heart was given to it.*

A beast in this prophetic sense depicts fallen men with the appearance of nobility. The lion and the eagle are two of the more noble animals. This beast could fly and had access to the heavenly realm, but what happened? Babylonians wanted to have access to the heavenly realm, so they built the Tower of Babel.

Fallen man is a beast that wants to stand on its two feet and pretend to be a man asserting the importance of his own wisdom. People think they can avoid another judgment like the flood by making their own great name and uniting everyone under that name. But King Nebuchadnezzar recovered his sanity after he learned his lesson and cried out to God and turned his gaze toward heaven. He was given a man's heart again, and he understood the reason why he was here. Nebuchadnezzar faced a hard trial, but he came out with an understanding of what his position was in relation to the God of heaven.

In the same way Belshazzar lost the kingdom and didn't learn from his father's mistakes, every generation has the opportunity to learn the same lessons, and the consequences are usually worse because humanity is getting worse. Man, in his fallen state, has lost his "wings" (his ability to interact in the heavenly realm). This beast is a symbol of the kingdom of Babylon that God said was the head of gold in the image; it was the best that man had been able to come up with.

> [5] *And behold the second beast, like unto a bear, which went off to one side, and it had three ribs between its teeth; and thus was said unto it, Arise, devour much flesh.*

Man's philosophy was considered good, and it was admirable for a man to be like God. But this second kingdom is linked to the earth (no wings) and symbolized with a bear. A bear can eat grass and herbs, but it can also eat meat. Once a bear becomes carnivorous, there is no turning back.

This particular bear had three ribs in its mouth, an insatiable appetite. The number three in Scripture relates to producing fruit and multiplying things. It can be linked with green things, such as hope and resurrection, but also the color green pertains to envy, greed, and the god of money. This happened to the second beast.

The kingdom began to disintegrate. In Scripture, silver symbolizes redemption. God speaks of a judgment day when all things that are corruptible are not going to survive. Only those things that cannot be burned in fire, the incorruptible things, survive.

> *For no one can lay another foundation than that laid, which is Jesus the Christ. Now if anyone builds upon this foundation gold, silver, precious stones, wood, hay, stubble, the work of each one shall be made manifest, for the day shall declare it because it shall be revealed by fire; the work of each one, whatever sort it is, the fire shall put it to test. If the work of anyone abides which he has built thereupon, he shall receive a reward. If anyone's work shall be burned, he shall suffer loss, but he himself shall be saved, yet so as by fire.* (1 Corinthians 3:11–15)

Shadrach, Meshach, and Abednego did not burn when they were thrown into the fire, but their captors and bonds did burn. The fourth man like the Son of God appeared in that instant, just like Daniel did before the king.

Notice the difference between the two kingdoms. In the first, the king gave the orders, and God said this was cleaner than the second kingdom where they placed the law above the king. During the second kingdom, not even the king, who loved Daniel, could change that law, and Daniel was sentenced to the lions' den. By saving Daniel from the lions, God showed that he was above the law, above the king, even above death, symbolized in the lions' den.

The Medes and the Persians knew that humans could not be trusted, so they elevated the law that they thought provided more security. So, what happened? The law caused more killings, more devouring of flesh, because no one can fulfill the law. The only thing the law accomplished was to bring everyone under the death penalty.[45] This second beast keeps on devouring flesh. Hope and resurrection are replaced by greed. No one can serve two masters: one cannot serve the God of heaven and the god of money.[46]

> [6] *After this I beheld, and behold another, like a tiger, which had*

---

45   Romans 7:7–13
46   Matthew 6:24; Luke 16:13

> *upon the back of it four wings of a fowl; this beast also had*
> *four heads; and power was given to it.*

The next beast was even more savage. This third kingdom, or king, started with Alexander the Great and the Grecians. The Medes and the Persians had added the legal and judicial aspect, but this new kingdom consolidated the legislative branch. The Greeks came, and they opened the legislature and started listening to the people who were "free" in the city.

The beast became more vicious and could not remain united. Alexander the Great's kingdom was divided into four parts; thus, this beast had four heads. When we approach democracy, we accumulate many heads, and this produces more confusion.

On the other hand, this beast received "wings," signifying that the fate of humans is to get out of this earthly realm and return to their previous liberty. The four-headed tiger tries its best to escape, but it's too heavy and doesn't fly well. Unfortunately, the Greeks tapped into dark spiritual forces, and their mythology depicts gods that have superpowers combined with all of the failings of fallen humanity. They created gods in their own image and fell prey to demons.

> [7] *After this I saw in the night visions, and behold the four-*
> *th beast, dreadful and terrible, and exceedingly strong; and*
> *it had great iron teeth; it devoured and broke in pieces and*
> *trod down that which was left with its feet; and it was very*
> *different from all the beasts that had been before her; and it*
> *had ten horns.*

In Scripture, iron symbolizes the law and absolute power; this beast describes the Roman Empire. The Romans applied their power and defined the powers of the tribune (legal court) enforced by their armies. They held the powers of the senate and considered Caesar to be deity. Roman citizens had rights, but the rest of the people were like slaves.

This beast was not compared to an earthly beast. Daniel was terrified by this horrible monster. When John saw the sum of the matters in Revelation, he saw a woman riding on the beast, drunk with the blood that had been spilled, a woman who thought she reigned, but at the end, the beast leaves her naked and with no power. In time, the great dragon that is behind all this comes and loses its wings. A clean woman (the church) is given the wings of an eagle.[47]

This part (especially the four-winged tiger) has its counterpart. In

---

47   See Revelation 12.

Greek mythology, Greeks believed there were many gods, and mortal beings could marry these gods and have children with them. They conceived the idea of creating gods in the image of men. Men's attempts to reunite with God through carnal means is characteristic throughout Greek mythology.

This effort to gain access to the spiritual realm is naturally impossible. However, spiritual union with demons is quite another possibility because God is not the only one in the heavenly realm; other spirits dwell there that are not clean. Gaining access to the spiritual realm is possible by creating an unholy link with these unclean spirits.

Man has done this throughout his existence. This access to a supernatural spiritual realm (full of miracles) when there is no holiness or purity leads to another series of problems and comes to fruition in the fourth beast, dreadful and terrible, and exceedingly strong; and it had great iron teeth; it devoured and broke in pieces and trod down that which was left with its feet.

The fourth beast does not leave leftovers; it consumes everything. We are experiencing this with our present governmental systems. Man thinks he has perfected his system with all these ingredients and he can place judgment and justice on the earth. But in reality, he has created an even stronger monster: uglier, dreadful, and more terrible than has ever existed.

Roman law dictates that a person is guilty until proven innocent. Defending yourself under this premise is hard to do. It's the Holy Inquisition all over again.

Try proving your innocence after the IRS has filed a lawsuit against you, and you are automatically considered guilty.

> [8] *As I was considering the horns, [in Scripture, horns are a symbol of power, and this beast has ten horns; his power was the law] behold, there came up among them another little horn, before whom three of the first horns were plucked up by the roots; and, behold, in this horn were eyes like the eyes of man, and a mouth speaking grand things.*

This horn is man who thinks he is above the law and tries to pass himself off as God. Ten factions or kingdoms comprised the Roman Empire. However, historically, when the papacy began, it plucked out three of these kingdoms and replaced them. Take note of what happened: in this horn were eyes like the eyes of man. The eyes of man do not see things like God sees them.

Documents such as the writings from Vatican II, which are not based on Scripture, opened new horizons for the church. These are based on human philosophy, the eyes of man, and a mouth speaking grand things because they believed that whatever came out of the mouth of the pope was infallible. Now they say it's infallible when it comes from their whole counsel (which has splintered into opposing factions).

The Throne of God

[9] I beheld until thrones [for judgment] were placed, and an Elder of great age did sit, whose garment was white as snow,[48] and the hair of his head like pure wool: his throne a flame of fire, his wheels burning fire.

In the book of Ezekiel, one of the things that can be found in the vision of the throne of God are the "wheels that turn." It is hard to describe because some wheels turn one way, and others turn the other way, while all this was moving up and down and to the sides. Everything that is associated with the throne of God was there – wheels, fire, and a rainbow – making this is almost impossible to put into words.

[10] A river of fire issued and came forth from before him; thousands of thousands served him, and ten thousands of ten thousands stood before him; the Judge sat down, and the books were opened.

The kingdoms of men are the sum of the four empires previously described. Today, man has decided, through democracy and the deification of man, that absolute power comes from the people and not from God. Scripture says this will continue until the judge sits on the throne of judgment. God is the true Judge, and his description here is as an Elder: of great age, of absolute purity, and of absolute power.

Fire in Scripture can be a symbol of destruction, or it can be a symbol of love. Depending on whose life you live, it can be a fire that destroys or a fire that restores. It depends on whether we live in corruption or not. If we live under the government and head of the Lord Jesus Christ in incorruption, we cannot be under the authority of these beasts (not even under the little horn that elevates itself and sees with the eyes of man and speaks grand things). In the true kingdom of God, the smallest person, the servant, is the greatest.

[11] I beheld then because of the voice of the great words which

---

48   See also Matthew 28:3; Mark 9:3.

> *the horn spoke; I beheld even until the beast was slain and its*
> *body was undone and given over to be burned in the fire.*

God will bring this system down.

> [12] *They had also taken from the other beasts their rule because*
> *their lives had been prolonged until a certain time.*

Revelation says this beast is thrown into the lake of fire, which is the second death. This is complete and eternal death.

> *And the beast was taken and with it the false prophet that*
> *wrought miracles in its presence, with which he had deceived*
> *those that had taken the mark of the beast and had worshi-*
> *pped its image. These two were cast alive into the lake of fire*
> *burning with brimstone. (Revelation 19:20)*

Daniel 7:12, if read in Spanish, says, "their lives had been prolonged a time and time." The lives of these other beasts had been prolonged for a "time and time" because they all unite in the end (but with "seven" heads), which describes our present-day world situation. "Time" in its simplest sense means one day in Scripture.

Scripture says one day is as a thousand years and a thousand years as a day. So, time and time are two thousand years of prolongation. The first coming of the Lord Jesus is somewhat parallel to the rise of the Roman Empire. This is known as the church age that is now coming to the end of its two thousand years prior to the second coming of the Lord Jesus.

> [13] *I saw in the vision of the night . . .*

This night covers six thousand years of human history where people proclaimed the great day of man, but God says it's dark like the night. The true light has not yet been perfectly revealed. Scripture says the day of the Lord is coming where the light will shine everywhere, and righteousness will reign.

> [13] *. . . and, behold, in the clouds of heaven like a Son of man*[49]
> *that came and drew near unto the Elder of great age, and they*
> *brought him near before him.*

One of the titles that the Lord Jesus has is "the Son of Man."[50] The same title seems to be referred to in Revelation 12:5 (in old English it is trans-

---

49   Here the Chaldean word, enash, is used in the original (this is comparable to the Hebrew, iysh).

50   In Spanish, the word used here is again varón, which means "born free of noble blood."

lated as "manchild").

When Adam lost the life of liberty that God gave him, Jesus, the last Adam (1 Corinthians 15:45), came after him and was born free, giving us the opportunity to be born free in him by the Holy Spirit. Many members form this manchild; many are still being born. In Revelation 6:10 the souls under the altar ask the Lord how long it will be until he intervenes and avenges the earth.

> *. . . and it was said unto them, that they should rest yet for a little while until their fellow servants and their brethren, that should be killed as they were, should be fulfilled* (Revelation 6:11)

Essentially, he says he will wait until the number is complete. When this many-membered body of Christ, this manchild, is complete, he will intervene.

At the time of judgment, the "Son of Man" will be presented. Jesus Christ and his many brothers come before the throne and begin the judgment. God the Father is the Judge, but he delegates the judgment. This judgment has different connotations than Roman or even English law (which accepts a person's innocence until proven guilty). However, both of these human laws are unjust and imperfect.

Revelation 11 says that whoever mistreats or wishes to kill or harm a representative of God will have the same thing happen to them. Everyone dictates their own sentence according to how they have treated God's representatives.

Scripture also says that whoever helps one of God's little ones, even with a simple glass of water, will not be left without reward.[51] Some will be removed from the presence of God because they refused to help those sent by God.

In Matthew 25:35 the Lord says, for I was hungry, and ye gave me food; I was thirsty, and ye gave me drink; I was a stranger, and ye took me in. And they will say, Lord, when did we see thee hungry? (v. 37). And He will reply, Inasmuch as ye have done it unto one of the least of these my brothers, ye have done it unto me (v. 40). This judgment is based on a person's words, deeds, and the fruit they produced.

It says that if you receive someone because they are sent from God (because they are a prophet) you will receive a prophet's reward.[52] It also

---

51 Matthew 10:42
52 He that receives a prophet in the name of a prophet shall receive a prophet's reward, and he that receives a righteous man in the name of a righteous man shall receive a

says that if we are among his saints, we will be able to participate in the judgment of the world.[53] Imagine standing in the judgment, and someone is about to be condemned for a list of terrible things they did, and someone else stands up and says, "Wait a second, when I went to his area in the name of God, this person received me well." What will happen with the judgment? I don't know; he might be saved. Many people want to say "so and so is lost" or "this person is saved." Most of us are in no condition to say anything. Only God sees the hearts, and the judgment that is coming is going to be just.

> [13] *I saw in the vision of the night, and, behold, in the clouds of heaven like a Son of man that came and drew near unto the Elder of great age, and they brought him near before him.*
> [14] *And he gave him dominion and glory and kingdom; and all the peoples, nations, and tongues served him: his dominion is an eternal dominion, which shall not pass away, and his kingdom such that it shall never be corrupted.*

This corporate man, with Jesus Christ as the head was brought before God. Jesus gives glory and dominion to his Father because he lives to do the will of his Father. The Lord Jesus not only wants us to know him as our King, Lord, and only Master, he wants us to know and have a direct relationship with his Father as he does (John 17:21).

"Eternal dominion" does not only mean that it lasts forever but that it is of a different essence. The Lord Jesus said that his kingdom was not like the kingdoms of this world with everyone trampling on one another for power. It is not like the beast that devours with iron teeth and tramples on everything with its feet like the corruption in the democracies today. They don't leave any leftovers for those who are truly in need. Even if they cannot devour them, they will trample them with their feet.

> [15] *My spirit was troubled, I Daniel, in the midst of my body, and the visions of my head astonished me.*

Daniel saw all of man's corruption and its progression. He saw how it will end and how God's incorruptible kingdom will come. He was astonished because this will not happen the way our human mind imagines, not like the little horn with the eyes of man. God showed him this through his own eyes, and God's eyes are full of love but also justice.

> [16] *I came near unto one of those that stood by and asked him*

---

righteous man's reward. (Matthew 10:41)
53   1 Corinthians 6:2–3; Jude 1:14–15

the truth of all this. So he told me and made me know the interpretation of the things.

This vision has many facets. When is this going to end?

[17] These great beasts, which are four, are four kings [or kingdoms], which shall arise in the earth.

[18] And they shall take the kingdom of the Holy One who is most High and possess the kingdom until the age and until the age of the ages.

What is going on with these man-made governments? What did man do? He took the knowledge of good and evil and elevated himself above where God had ordained. He made decisions that belonged only to God, deciding what was good and what was evil on his own. Even in the highest interpretation of human religion, or of human justice and government, man only lets God decide what is wrong, but he keeps on deciding what he thinks is right, and that's why he can never get rid of corruption. Many times, what seems good to us is evil in God's eyes, and what God says is good may seem evil to us.

[19] Then I had the desire to know the truth regarding the fourth beast, which was so different from all the others, exceeding dreadful, whose teeth were of iron, and its nails of brass; which devoured and broke in pieces and trod down that which was left with its feet;

This beast leaves nothing remaining. Nothing is left over; there is always a deficiency.

[20] also regarding the ten horns that were in its head, . . .

Man places the law, their source of power, above everything. Observe the democracies of today; they have nothing left over; they always operate in deficit.

[20] . . . and of the other which came up, and before whom three fell; . . .

These systems remove the possibility of producing fruit.

[20] . . . and that same horn had eyes and a mouth that spoke very grand things, whose appearance was greater that his fellows.

In these democracies, the powerful speak of all the great things that they cannot even accomplish. They see everything from their own points of view, and they make promises regarding the religious as well as the economic and political aspects of life. It's the same beast that had its beginning in Babylon before the Tower of Babel.

> *21 I saw that this horn made war against the saints and overcame them;*

The ones who have power in the things of this world don't allow anyone that is clean before Lord to come in. God's people aren't compatible with the economic, political, and religious components of this realm.

> *22 until such time as the Elder of great age came, and the judgment was given unto the saints of the most High; and the time came, and the saints possessed the kingdom.*

When this body of Christ comes before the Elder of great age, they give up everything, but they will also receive everything. God doesn't give the saints everything in the beginning. This grave mistake has been made in many places by those who try to obtain the things of this world in the name of God. They try to mix the religious and political together, and the economic aspects that get mixed into it all lead to great corruption. They have never been able to overcome this corruption because they seek corruptible things. God allows his own sons to receive all things in the time of the end and not in the beginning.

> *23 Thus he said, The fourth beast shall be a fourth king in earth, [a fourth kingdom in the earth] which shall be greater than all the other kingdoms and shall devour the whole earth and shall tread it down, and break it in pieces.*
> *24 And the ten horns signify that of this kingdom ten kings shall arise; and another shall rise after them; and he shall be greater than the first kings, and he shall bring down three kings.*

In addition to history, God has opened many possibilities here, but the world is already in the hands of those who seek to foment, sustain, and increase the system of this world (as well as their own good). Man strives to do things for his own benefit instead of seeking God's will.

The beast that John saw in Revelation had "seven" heads (the complete number of heads), which sums up our present world situation quite well and coincides with the typology of the feet of the image that Nebuchadnezzar saw (ten toes on feet made of iron mixed with baked clay). Neither example portrays a homogenous one-world dictatorship at the time of the end (the appointed time) when the saints are given the kingdom. Although it is clear all along that all the kingdoms of this world are under the prince of this world, the devil.[54]

> *[25] And he shall speak great words against the most High and shall break down the saints of the most High and think to move the times and the law; and they shall be given into his hand until a time and times and the half or dividing of a time.*

Times and the Law

It says . . . and they shall be given into his hand until a time and times and the half or dividing of a time. Literally, this would say, "time, times, and the division of time." There were a thousand years from King David to Christ, and Daniel was about halfway between, finishing the Jewish time of the law. Then came the times (plural) of the Gentiles because God knew they would last two thousand years. The day of the Lord comes after these two thousand years as the "division of time."

Man decided to divide time (using the birth of the Lord Jesus) into before Christ (BC) and after Christ (Anno Domini – AD). However, God didn't declare it this way, even though there was a big difference from the old covenant to the new covenant, which greatly affected the world. Nevertheless, the people of God have been given into the hand of the beast until a time and times and the half or dividing of a time.

It has almost been universally accepted that God created a man and a woman to live as a couple, one man to one woman (and this has become painfully clear under the new covenant). The natural man, however, cannot keep this, so divorces and perversions increase.

Many things have cleared up little by little after the first coming of Jesus, but it is nothing compared with the change that will take place when the day of the Lord dawns. When this corporate "new man" receives the kingdom, and when God, in a first resurrection with Jesus Christ as the head, brings all the men and women in history that have overcome (from righteous Abel on, including Daniel himself) to receive the kingdom, then a true kingdom of righteousness and justice, where God is represented the way he really is, will be revealed.

God will be represented throughout the entire earth in his true character. This will be the true division of time and the demise of those who think to move the times and the law; we already know that man has moved the law of God, and he has also moved the times because man

---

54 Matthew 4:8–9; John 14:30; Revelation 11:15

doesn't know what's coming or how the future is going to be. Many are declaring the beginning of the new age of men, or the rise of a one-world government ruled by the Antichrist, when in reality, God's new day is what is coming.

Scripture says God's law is eternal,[55] and it's impossible to keep by our own merit while we seek our own good.[56] Jesus said, The heaven and the earth shall pass away, but my words shall not pass away.[57] If we're going to fulfill our duty of keeping God's law, it must be in the life of Jesus Christ (Romans 8:3). He fulfilled the law for us, and he can cover and protect everyone who places him first.

The Lord Jesus summarized the spirit of the law like this: that we would love God with all our mind, all our strength, and all our heart; and that we would love our neighbor as ourselves.[58] It's impossible to love in this manner if we don't have God's love and light.

Fulfilling the Law

Around 1988, I was on a committee working on a project for national reconciliation (of Colombia) with a charismatic Roman Catholic priest named Rafael García-Herreros. One day we discussed the publication of a booklet of key Scripture portions. The little book was to cover the Ten Commandments, the Sermon on the Mount, and 1 Corinthians 13. In the middle of our meeting, García-Herreros requested that I bring the human rights manifesto from the French Revolution. He took me to his prayer garden to ask God for wisdom concerning in which part of the booklet it should be included (at the beginning, in the middle, or at the end).

As we were praying, with the human rights papers in his lap, a dove flew over and bombarded us with dung that landed right in the middle of those papers. It splattered all over the priest: his glasses, his shirt, everything. I tried to clean it up with a handkerchief. He looked at me; I looked at him. We didn't say a word, but he took the human rights papers and threw them in the garbage. He told me to print the little book without them.

We had one other problem with this project because we needed the approval of the priest's superiors. This involved having the ecclesiastical authorities of the state church stamp the Imprimatur and the Nihil

---

55   Psalm 119:160
56   See Matthew 19:20–22 for an example.
57   Matthew 24:35
58   Matthew 22:37–39; Mark 12:30–31; Luke 10:27

Obstat onto this publication. Even though we had taken all the references from the Catholic Bible, translated by Chekel (which could possibly be one of the more accurate Spanish Catholic Bibles), our request was not approved.

The priest in charge of revising our document of Scripture portions told me, "This can't be published. It will only create great confusion because the Ten Commandments are different in the catechism.[59] And people are going to look at the Ten Commandments that you took from Father Chekel's Bible, and they are going to think the church has changed the law of God. They will think the church has made a big mistake, and this cannot be."

I had to bring this verdict to Garcia-Herreros. But his decision was that we publish the little book without the official approval of the Catholic Church (which eventually caused no small commotion). He also wrote a dedication saying that whoever fulfilled the Ten Commandments in the Spirit of the Sermon on the Mount would be fulfilling their duty with their neighbor. He spoke of duties instead of rights.

Man may change the laws. He may attempt to change the times. But God's law is eternal.

> [26] *And the Judge shall sit, and they shall take away his dominion to destroy and to cast out unto the end;*

Then this beast of the system of man will not be capable of doing any more harm.

> [27] *and that the kingdom and the dominion, and the majesty of the kingdoms under the whole heaven, be given to the holy people of the most High, His kingdom shall be an eternal kingdom, and all the dominions shall serve him and hear him.*

This kingdom will be given to the holy people of God. "Holy people of God" means that they are clean and separated for the exclusive service and use of the Lord. That is what the word "holy" means.

> [28] *Up unto here was the end of the word. I, Daniel, was very troubled in my thoughts, and my countenance changed in me: but I kept the word in my heart.*

At least 2500 years or more would pass before this word could be fulfi-

---

59   In the catechism to which he referred, the commandment about not worshipping any graven images had been deleted and the last commandment about not coveting your neighbors' goods or your neighbor's wife had been split into two so that they would still have ten commandments instead of nine.

lled (it is, in fact, still pending). It was a word that left Daniel weak and trembling, but he received it and kept it in his heart. And this is what God wants from each one of us – that we keep what the Lord is saying in our hearts.

Let us pray:

Lord, we ask for wisdom and understanding to comprehend that the systems of this world are getting worse. Let us be separated for your use only and not for the system of this world. Allow us to be under your power and authority so that a cleansing of our hearts and thoughts can take place. Amen.

CHAPTER EIGHT

Walking in the Light

Understanding the first part of the book of Daniel is crucial to understanding the last part of the book. Daniel's theme is basically the same one repeated from different angles: truth and revelation flow from God. The breath that God breathed into Adam (making him a living soul) did not get transferred to future generation, because of disobedience and rebellion. The only one born after Adam with God's light and life was the Lord Jesus.[60]

> *And so it is written, The first man Adam was made a living soul; the last Adam was made a life giving spirit.* (1 Corinthians 15:45)

The Lord Jesus can restore in us everything that was lost in the garden of Eden (and more). Not only can we be restored into the breath of life that Adam had, but we can be restored into the Lord Jesus, who is the Lord of the heavens – entering into him, being part of him, submitting to his headship and his authority. Even though the natural man had a good start, he is in decline. The natural man is not evolving into a superman or a super race because corruption works in every level.

The book of Daniel continues to show pictures of the judgment that is coming. As stated earlier, "Daniel" means "God is (the) judge." As man strives to recreate God in his own image, the sentence is dictated by the Supreme Judge.

The fact that Daniel was able to interpret the revelations given to pagan kings shows that God is willing to reveal the truth to whomever has the desire to find it. He can reveal through nature itself because everything bears witness to what the Creator has done. Lessons exist everywhere for all of us. Paul says in the letter to the Romans that

---

60 Colossians 2:9

everyone is without excuse because of creation (Romans 1:20).

Let's review. Daniel's first vision consisted of four beasts. The first, like a lion with wings, represented Babylon. In this kingdom, the second generation failed to learn the lessons of the first. Belshazzar failed to learn from his father Nebuchadnezzar. This is the sad reality in America today, where past generations have known God and placed him first, but the next generations haven't learned the same lessons or come to know God.

The second beast is like a bear, and the vision continues with a sequence of beasts, each one more terrible and beastly than the one before. The third beast, the tiger with four heads and four wings, represented the Greek empire of Alexander the Great. During this time, man headed toward democracy, toward considering the opinion of everyone, until the time of the fourth beast that began with the Romans. This beast symbolizes the moment we are in now because our present democracies come from a compilation of all these systems.

They are the fourth empire, the beast that is destroying everything, and Daniel is astonished and gets sick from watching it until thrones are placed, and the "Elder of great age" begins to open the books and dictate judgment. In this vision, someone who is like the Son of Man comes and is given the kingdom, and it is a kingdom that can never be corrupted.

Daniel passed through the stage of knowing the dreams and interpreting them for others to having his own dreams; then his visions began.

Daniel 8

> *¹ In the third year of the reign of King Belshazzar a vision appeared unto me, Daniel, after that vision which had appeared unto me before.*
> *² And I saw in the vision; (and it came to pass, when I saw it, that I was at Shushan, which is the head of the kingdom in the province of Persia); so that I saw in that vision, being by the river of Ulai,*

Babylon was going to fall, and its authority was going to be handed over to the Medes and the Persians. Before this happened, Daniel was in Shushan (the head of the province of Persia) to receive the vision. I have checked many different sources, and it is very difficult to find a satisfactory translation of the word "Ulai." It is possible that it could mean, "pure water."

The first vision came while Daniel was on his bed at night; this vision was in the place of the actual happenings next to a river. Some rivers come from God, and others are man-made. In prophecy, many things happen next to a river.

Rivers are made of sweet water (as opposed to salt water). Rivers may symbolize "the Word"; they may symbolize the provision God has for the earth. These were dry lands, and the rivers were the salvation to the dryness because irrigation canals could flow from them. Rivers may also symbolize humanism, (particularly man-made rivers).

God used pagan kingdoms to fulfill his purpose. Even though God is the one who places kings and replaces them, we are still responsible for our actions in the midst of everything that happens. God describes these kingdoms before they appear, and he knows the consequences of man's ways will get progressively worse until they become unbearable. He's waiting for this to ripen and reach its ultimate consequences, so the repercussions of man's rebellions are clear throughout eternity to everyone.

In our democracies, man's laws and judgments are unjust. When have we seen any money left over from a government budget? Almost never. The ones who control budgets are experts in spending more than they have and trying to create money out of nothing. They manipulate paper money, but there are secondary effects: inflation, deflation, etc.

It is sad that most of man's laws, and especially in the system that comes from Rome, have a foundation where the person is guilty until proven innocent. This is truly monstrous. Even English law has its problems if you consider the courts and the philosophy that reaches such an arrogant extreme because people think that the world's problems can be solved by the countries that are economically and militarily more capable. In the same way, extradition cannot completely solve Colombia's problems, and neither can the International Criminal Court. Everything that man develops brings apparent solutions, but this always causes secondary effects. The result of all this is that it creates a lot of resentment and feelings of injustice. What has not been understood is that God is the true judge, and he sees things differently.

Daniel's Second Vision

> [3] *and I lifted up my eyes and saw, and, behold, a ram was standing before the river, which had two horns; and even though they were high, the one was higher than the other, and the higher one came up last.*

This ram was a government with two arms and possibly two

situations happening at the same time. Cyrus the Persian and Darius the Mede both began by fulfilling some of God's purposes, such as the release of God's people and vessels from Babylon and the restoration of God's house in Jerusalem. At that moment, the Lord began to send his word through the prophets Zechariah and Haggai for the rebuilding of Jerusalem and its wall. It didn't seem to be a big deal in the beginning, but they pressed on with a trumpet in one hand and a sword in the other as their enemies became more and more paranoid. In a similar way, the Lord is now restoring the truth as the enemy gets increasingly desperate.

All this happens alongside a river. The rivers of God's blessings can have different purposes. When Gideon's army quenched their thirst at the river, 9,700 men didn't know how to drink the water. They focused on drinking the river's water and forgot about everything else; they were sent back home. It's possible to make mistakes, even in the midst of God's provision and blessing; most of God's people have erred this way, concentrating on the provision (seeking our own blessing) instead of fixing our eyes on God and seeking him only.

If we find the Lord, he will give us what we need. If we seek the kingdom of God and his righteousness, he will add everything else (Matthew 6:33). If we seek provision and blessing, it's possible we will find it in a temporal sense, but it's also probable that we may be disqualified from God's army of overcomers.

So, in the same way that this ram had two horns (one appeared first and then the other one came up), Cyrus the Persian came first and then Darius the Mede. The kings that came after them had the same problem that God's people have always had, where corruption catches up to us a lot faster in prosperity than in adversity. Many people seek God in the midst of their problems, but as soon as he takes them out of those problems, they turn their back on him and make even greater mistakes than before. What happened? The third kingdom was sent, and in the vision, Daniel saw it like this:

> ⁴ *I saw that the ram smote with the horns to the west, to the north, and to the south and that no beast could stand before him, nor could anyone escape from his hand; but he did according to his will and made himself great.*

The second kingdom ended similarly to the first. They were not able to pass on the lessons they had learned from God to their sons and successors. Even the fact that they elevated the law did not help them.

⁵ And as I was considering, behold, a he goat came from the west upon the face of the whole earth and did not touch the earth: and the goat had a notable horn between his eyes.

This begins as a picture of Alexander the Great, but it changes in the middle. What began as a picture of the natural empires became a spiritual statement two or three verses later.

⁶ And he came to the ram that had the two horns, which I had seen standing before the river and ran against him in the fury of his power.

An interesting truth is expressed here and highlighted in other Scriptures. James 1:20 summarizes it like this: for the wrath of man does not work the righteousness of God.

Those who believe they can solve injustices with wrath are wrong. Injustice cannot be solved with more injustice, and the wrath of man always produces more injustice. Alexander the Great was a reaction against the injustice and arrogance of the eastern kings. He came from the west with all his fury and broke them. But look at what happened:

⁷ And I saw him come close unto the ram, and he rose up against him and smote him, and broke his two horns: because the ram did not have the strength to stand before him; therefore he cast him down to the ground and trod him under; and there was no one to deliver the ram out of his hand.
⁸ And the he goat made himself very great, and when he was at his greatest strength, that great horn was broken; and in its place came up another four marvelous ones toward the four winds of heaven.

The Generals of Alexander the Great

Each of his four generals seemed to feel that they were more dignified than Alexander the Great. This is where the vision of the tiger with four heads and four wings is fulfilled. Instead of uniting, the situation deteriorated. They sought the people's will, not only idolizing the king, but also the entire race.

⁹ And out of the first of them came forth a little horn, which grew much toward the south and toward the east and toward the desirable land.

This little horn later gave way to the Roman Empire. Everything was destroyed when one of Alexander the Great's generals entered Jerusalem: the reconstruction of the temple, the kings' orders to return God's vessels to their proper place, the payment for the reconstruction with the royal treasury, the work of Nehemiah and Ezra, and all that was accomplished by Queen Esther. (Darius was possibly the same person as Ahasuerus. Cyrus may also have been related.) All of this ended after not very many generations.

The situation with Alexander the Great caused this carnage. They began worshipping man. They aimed their destruction directly at the representation of the God of heaven on the earth, quenching the fire upon the altar in the temple to end all the sacrifices.

> [10] *And it magnified itself unto the host of heaven, and it cast down part of the host and of the stars to the ground and trod them under.*

We know that Lucifer cast down a third part of the heavenly host (or stars). But we also know we were created to represent God's image. We didn't fall from heaven like Lucifer and his angels did. Adam was never in heaven; God's presence was with Adam on the earth, and Adam lost it. He was kicked out of God's paradise. Like Adam, we are also from the dust of the earth.

God still wants to plant something good in us, and the remnant that returned to Jerusalem understood this. They made a fatal mistake, however, when they made an oath with a curse, a covenant that made them slaves to the law.[61] God's true glory never filled the rebuilt temple like when his glory filled Solomon's Temple.

They made an oath with those who were going to fulfill God's law, but natural man cannot fulfill God's law. The consequences of the law fall upon man when he tries to fulfill the law in his own strength because the law states that whoever fails in just one point is guilty of the entire law.

The problem is that even though whoever fulfills it receives the blessing, whoever doesn't fulfill it receives the curse. Man has never been able to get back out from under the curse. So, the curse returned to Jerusalem once again,[62] not only because of its inhabitants but also because of Alexander the Great, whose people wanted to idolize the human

---

61 See Nehemiah 10:29.

62 Strengthened with their brethren, their nobles, they came forward in an oath with a curse that they would walk in God's law, which was given by the hand of Moses, the slave of God, and observe and do all the commandments of the LORD our Lord, and his judgments and his statutes. (Nehemiah 10:29)

race instead of God.

On one hand, some humans wanted to commit to fulfilling something they could not fulfill, but others wanted to abolish all that and said something to the effect of, "What God? We are god! We will recreate god in our image. That's how we will fix the problem of all these terrible demands of the law. If even the Jews cannot fulfill them, we're going to make gods that will be like us who get angry, commit adultery, and do all these beastly things. This is how we're going to regain access to the heavenly realms."

The heavenly realms are also contaminated; Scripture says there is a need for new heavens and a new earth.[63] Many spiritual forces are not clean. Many people who believe in miracles don't care what the power source is. They become deceived.

Scripture says a great delusion comes over those who reject the truth (see 2 Thessalonians 2:10). So, God allows the person who doesn't really want to know the truth to be deceived. For God, it is preferable that the person is deceived and not that they rebel against him with their eyes wide open.

Some rebel even when they know who God is. This is why the devil cannot be restored by the gospel. Nothing more can be said to him; no way exists to evangelize him with more good news because he already knows it. He already experienced all of it, and knowingly, he turned his back on God and tried to set himself above God. This is the position from which he fell.

But the devil is not our main problem. Our main problem is ourselves because we have the capacity for choosing between our own will (that will lead us to deception and worse: to be under the devil's dominion), or we can choose to place our life under God's authority and let him clean us. Only as we have a clean heart can we understand why we're here, what is happening, and where we're heading as individuals and as a human race.

> [11] *Even against the prince of the host did he magnify himself,*
>
> . . .

Human beings have once again formed a rebellion against God with a government they believe is the most modern and progressive of all time. The Greeks were convinced they had perfected what had begun in Babylon and what the Medes and the Persians had refined by elevating

---

63 Nevertheless we, according to his promises, wait for new heavens and a new earth, in which dwells righteousness. (2 Peter 3:13)

the law. The Greeks included a new ingredient: they began their philosophy based on man. Look at Aristotle, the Greek thinkers, the debates. They put man's intellectual capacity into practice; not only did they give the king power, but many people had power. For God, the bronze belly symbolizes this kingdom.

Bronze is the symbol of judgment, and man's justice doesn't work righteousness. This is the reason Greek myths almost always end in tragedy. They don't end well; they end like Mexican movies where everyone gets killed, including the heroes.

> [11] *. . . and by him the daily sacrifice was taken away, and the place of his sanctuary was cast to the earth.*

The Greek generals went to Jerusalem and removed the daily sacrifice. They did this literally, but the symbol is that the natural man wants to remain on the path of corruption, in insanity, on the path of being a beast instead of being man (in order to truly be human, one must follow God, who created us in his image and likeness). They broke the commandment and the conditions of God represented by the altar over which the daily sacrifice was offered.

Adam and Eve were created free, but it appears they only lasted a few years in the garden before they lost their freedom and were expelled. After this, they were slaves of their own will (according to the desires of their flesh) when they decided to become judges of what was good and evil.

The book of Daniel is the way to return to where "God is (the) judge," the way that leads to true freedom, freedom to do God's will. A slave to anyone or anything other than God is not able to consistently do God's will.

> [12] *And the host was given over by the reason of the prevarication upon the daily sacrifice; and he cast the truth to the ground; and he did whatever he would and prospered.*

The Sacrifices

God's people turned themselves over to humanism and man's governments. No more prophets emerged for almost four hundred years until John the Baptist and Zacharias, his father, appeared. Even though the mistakes have produced sad consequences, God has not abandoned us. We live in a time when God is willing to intervene directly.

Some translations refer to "the abomination" upon the daily sacrifice.

"Prevarication" is a contaminating offense that is premeditated and planned. When man degrades what should be God's house, God respects our will and leaves. We were created to represent God, and this is deteriorating. When we are right with God, we represent him, but this was disgraceful. God wanted his people in Jerusalem to represent him as he is.

In King David's time and in part of Solomon's reign, people came from everywhere to hear and observe the wisdom, beauty, and purity these kings exhibited. In Solomon's time, even the utensils in the palace were made of gold.

Scripture says, in those days, silver was not a big deal. Never in the ancient world was there a place displaying cleanness in such magnitude. That was a shadow of what God wanted to do with us. But everything collapsed.

The church should have been a display of God's incorruptible life for the entire world. Sadly, only a handful of individuals throughout history have accomplished this. What has the organized church done? The church decided this handful of individuals were saints and placed them at the center of adoration. Now, many worship them instead of God!

The daily sacrifice is also called, "the sacrifice of praise."[64] Many people erroneously believe this is something that is done with instruments and good voices, so they hire "good" musicians and begin their ritual.

What we can do with musicians and voices must be the consequence of a life that is clean twenty-four hours a day, seven days a week. If we meet with clean hands, clean hearts, and clean minds, God is happy even if our voice is off tune.

If true cleanness is reestablished in God's people, we will hear incredible musicians and music with choruses as angelic as heavenly choirs because God's will is to bless the earth with clean music again. He did this before the first coming of his Son. The shepherds were awake, praying and watching through the night, and they saw a multitude of heavenly hosts worshipping with the angel. Wouldn't he do this again before the second coming?

The daily sacrifice is where we place our own life as a continual sacrifice for the Lord. What were these sacrifices like? The first one was the sacrifice of sin. It was not for the sin or instead of the sin; it was the sin itself that God wanted to kill. A bullock or another animal with no defect was brought before the Lord to the door of the tabernacle of the testimony. Depending on who had committed the sin, they placed it on

---

64   Psalm 107:22; 116:17; Hebrews 13:15

the altar, and this became the sin that had to be sacrificed. The sin was slaughtered; the life-blood bled out (for the life of the flesh is in the blood); and the person identified with this by placing their hands on the sin so that God could do the same in their life (Leviticus 4:33; 17:11). Then the fire of God was applied to the whole ugly mess.

Next, the sacrifice of a male goat took place. This represented the guilt. After killing the sin in us, God wants to kill the guilt as well, so the enemy cannot haunt us with our past sins. The guilt would bleed to death upon the altar of God, and the blood would be applied to the horns of the altar that symbolize the power of God to kill sin and guilt.

Finally, the sacrifice of peace could take place, a symbol of us before God – clean, without sin and without guilt. It is the offering of our free will, our own life to God; this is a daily sacrifice and it is voluntary.[65]

The fire had to burn continually because it was God's fire on the altar, the lamp, and in the altar of incense. When through carelessness the fire went out, God, in his sovereignty, had to light it again. If he didn't, they would have strange or false fire that was not God's true fire. False fire, false miracles (miracles done by other spirits, not the Spirit of God), and unclean supernatural events are abundant everywhere. These may move multitudes, but they are not clean. They serve to inspire great offerings and idolize man once again.

Helen of Troy is considered by some to be a role model for the church even though she was an adulteress who caused the Greek Empire terrible death and pain. She was a beautiful woman, but very treacherous. Hellenistic art and culture continue along the same lines. Today, immense congregations look beautiful with much supernatural movement, but they are deceiving if it turns out that it is not God's fire.

The daily sacrifice that Nehemiah, Ezra, and others had restored was taken away. This was a sacrifice where they didn't live their own lives, but the Lord's life. Sodom could have been saved if it would have contained ten righteous men; Jerusalem could have been spared for the sake of only one just man that would execute judgment and seek the truth (Jeremiah 5:1). If the Lord has even the smallest remnant that is the light and the salt, he can multiply it and thereby create hope where there is none.

The two raptures in Scripture are part of this hope. First, the wicked are taken from among the righteous, and a pure representation of God remains (Matthew 13:41). The second rapture is when the true church is gathered up to meet Jesus in the air and accompany him as he returns,

---

65   See Leviticus 7.

and this entire world's systems fall (1 Thessalonians 4:17).

In the previous picture, the systems of the world will continue their course until the judge of righteousness sits; we are close to this point. Romans 5:10 says we were reconciled with God by the Lord's death, but we shall be saved by his life. His death can reconcile us, but his life is required if we want to be saved. This restoration is not in Adam's life but in the Lord Jesus's life. God plans something for us that is much better than what Adam and Eve lost. The rebellion of Satan and Adam frustrated things temporarily and caused a ruckus, but God will use this for something much better.

> [13] *Then I heard one saint speaking, and another saint said unto the one which spoke, How long shall the vision of the daily sacrifice last and the prevarication of desolation that places both the sanctuary and the host to be trodden under foot?*
> [14] *And he said unto me, Unto two thousand and three hundred days of evening and morning; then shall the sanctuary be justified.*

Two Thousand Three Hundred Days

Two thousand and three hundred days of evening and morning; when I was kidnapped in the jungle for five months, I contemplated this with a subpar Bible translation, but in any case, God used it, and he opened it up to me. Some Bibles are imperfect, but this doesn't limit God. God is above everything. Even with the best Bible possible, if the Spirit of God is not there to open up and reveal these truths, the message will remain closed.

Alexander the Great conquered Jerusalem in the year 333 BC. In the year 1967, exactly 2300 years after it lost its sovereignty, Jerusalem returned to the sovereignty of the natural Jew.

Other prophecies confirm the same date, one of which is an indirect revelation of the sabbatical year of judgment prophesied in Deuteronomy. Leviticus 26 says four different times (verses 18, 21, 24, and 28) that the Lord would punish Israel seven times for the disobedience to the decrees, the rights, and the laws that the Lord had established between himself and the sons of Israel on Mount Sinai through Moses.

This means seven times (or seven years)[66] of judgment, a day for a

---

66   Then I will walk contrary unto you also in fury, and I, even I, will chastise you seven times for your sins. (Leviticus 26:28)

year.[67] If you multiply 365.2422 (days in a year) by seven (the seven times judgment dictated in Leviticus 26) you get 2556.6954.

If we apply this number to June 6–7 of 1967, the day when the Jews recovered Jerusalem from the Arabs during the Six-Day War, the date that we come to is March 7 of 588 BC. This was the date of the beginning of the siege of Jerusalem by Nebuchadnezzar in Babylon.

$$2556.6954$$
$$-\ AD\ \ 1966.4333$$
$$590.2621\ BC$$

Once the error in the Christian calendar is corrected by compensating the "0" BC – AD (because this is fictitious according to the Jewish calendar), the result would be March 7 of 588 BC. In this way, the same date for the fulfillment of the prophecy is confirmed.[68]

The third line that gives us the same date is the prophecy in Daniel 12:11–12 that speaks of 1290 days and of 1335 days. (This will be explained later.) For example, if the age of the law began in the Exodus in the year 1488 BC with the receiving of the law in Sinai, and it ended when the Lord Jesus presented himself at the temple at the age of twelve, then our present age (of grace) may have begun when the Lord Jesus was twelve years old. This is when his life representing the law ended, and he entered into an eighteen-year period of time representing grace until his true ministry began at age thirty.

If this is true, then 1500 years with the Jews under law passed before this present age began. So, the age of the law would have lasted 1500 years.[69]

In the year AD 678 in the present age, we get to Pope Agatho[70] who may have been the first pope to declare himself infallible, proclaiming he

---

67   After the number of the days in which ye spied out the land, even forty days, each day for a year, ye shall bear your iniquities forty years, and ye shall know my reason for annulling my promise. (Numbers 14:34)

68   The confirmation of the date (1967) as the fulfillment of the judgment dictated by the Lord against Israel (the judgment of seven times explained in Leviticus 26 and other references in Scripture) can be observed in more detail in the reference used in this explanation: Carl F. H. Henry (edited by Harold John Ockenga), Prophecy In The Making (Creation House: Carol Stream, Illinois, 1971) 309.

69   Note that there are other explanations regarding how the dates may have worked out. The Yom Kippur war of October, 1973, is also a key date. See Appendix.

70   Or it could have been the next pope. Looking back on history, it seems to me that Gregory the Great, as Bishop of Rome, was not the one who initiated the abomination of desolation. This came after and led into what are known even by secular historians as the Dark Ages that did not begin to let up until the Renaissance and the Reformation.

was the Vicar of Christ on earth, displacing the Holy Spirit. This could have been the spiritual fulfillment of what Alexander the Great did in the natural. In Daniel 12, it says that 1290 days must be counted from that point. The book of Daniel is based on the fact that one prophetic day equals a year. If we count 1290 years from Pope Agatho, we come to AD 1967, to the Six-Day War, confirming that this is a key date in the work of God.

> [15] *And it came to pass, as I, Daniel, was considering the vision and seeking to understand it, behold, there stood before me the likeness of a man.*
> [16] *And I heard a man's voice between the banks of the Ulai, which called and said, Gabriel, teach this man the vision.*

Beginning with a night vision and continuing into the day, everything is clearing up for Daniel. And God wants these things to be clarified for people like Daniel. Daniel symbolizes Christ, and Christ is a body of many members where the Lord Jesus is the head, and we can be members in particular.

What happened since the Six-Day War? A new and clean word began to flow. An understanding of what had been lost regarding justification began. We cannot be justified or made righteous before God in our "old man," in our natural state.

The only way to be justified is if the old natural man dies; this is the only way to completely erase sin. It is impossible to condemn a dead person, and if we are dead with Christ, every charge against us is erased. A door of new life in him is opened.[71]

God began to restore a new word. Not a Passover word or a Pentecost kind of word, but an end-time Tabernacles word. The picture of the feasts began to unite as something that goes far beyond the literal feasts observed by Jewish people. You are reading this book because you hunger and thirst for this word.

After justification comes sanctification, being separated exclusively for the Lord's use. After the death of sin, after the death of our guilt, we can decide if we are going to be a voluntary sacrifice of peace (see Romans 12:1).

Are we going to offer ourselves once again for the Lord's exclusive use like the slave that was set free in the seventh year? After six years of service, having the opportunity to leave, the slave said, "I love my master. I wish to stay here." They would have taken him to the doorpost

---

71   See Romans 7 and 8.

and pierced his ear as a symbol that he would serve his lord forever (Deuteronomy 15:16–17). This is the option that the Lord is offering us.

The Feast of Tabernacles for Israel was a feast to celebrate ingathering and God's protection. For us, the "feast" is symbolic of spiritual development and not merely an event. When thinking of this in terms of serving God as our Master, "tabernacles" type of servitude is not by force; it is not through fear. God is looking for friends who will love him freely. We can choose to take advantage of the liberty God gives us to live our life.

If we want our inheritance to be on this side of the "Jordan" with the things of this world, God will not deny us this, just as he didn't deny it to the two and a half tribes that chose that. But if we want our inheritance to be where thieves cannot break in and where neither moth nor rust corrupt,[72] we will only find it in the Lord's life.

Daniel was one who managed Babylon's resources and those of subsequent empires; but none of that is mentioned in the Scriptures. What is mentioned is that Daniel was worthy of receiving the true revelation, and at the end of the book it says, Go thy way, Daniel, for these words are closed up and sealed until the time of the fulfillment . . . for thou shalt raise up in thy lot [or in thine inheritance] at the end of the days (12:9). This will include us because we cannot receive the inheritance without them (Hebrews 11:40). This is God's plan.

We're counting the days; we're counting the years that are left. Whenever the justification began (1967, 1972, or ??) the Lord says that those who wait and come to the 1335 days are blessed (Daniel 12:12). The carnal or natural man has never had the full blessing after Adam and Eve's defeat, and God is promising that a remnant will come out from under the curse and enter into his blessing once again.

I'm not trying to decipher the second coming or many other things that many people want to know. The only thing I'm saying is that God has a blessing, a true blessing for all those who have chosen to live his life instead of their own. This blessing has been found by individuals, not only throughout the "age of grace" but also throughout the "age of the law." After Daniel was thrust into the midst of a pagan situation by a kidnapping, after they destroyed his city and the surrounding areas, God put him into blessing as an individual, at the upper limit of what was possible for a human being to manage in those times. But this was not his true inheritance. Something is coming that is more important, and now God is promising a blessing for all his people who have Jesus Christ

---

72 Matthew 6:20

as their head.

I don't know when the Lord is coming. In one of the Gospels he arrives during the middle of the feast. I don't know. He will return whenever God the Father decides. Will his people come into the fullness of his blessing (by the Spirit) and break the curse? Yes. I also firmly believe that he will return in person according to Luke 24 and other Scriptures. The most interesting thing is that the Lord Jesus himself said that he didn't know, that only the Father knows when. There are indications that he will return when he finds the fruit he is looking for on earth. This is what the Song of Solomon says. When his clean people bring forth the fruit that he desires, it says that he will come back (Song of Solomon 6:11–13).

> [16] *. . . Gabriel, teach this man the vision.*

When have we heard something like this? Many people say they have seen angels and have had supernatural experiences. But, for the heavens to open and God himself to give the order and have it fulfilled! Notice that when Gabriel arrives, he looks like a man, and Scripture implies we all have our spiritual counterpart.[73]

Right now, there is a separation between God and us, which makes it hard for us to see clearly. It's similar to the veil in the temple, but God is about to remove it, and whatever is not clean, whatever is not pure, and whatever has corruption will not last in the presence of God. All those who say they are God's representatives and have God's Spirit but are mixed up in other things could soon be eliminated from among the representatives of God.

> [17] *So he came near where I stood, and with his coming, I was afraid and fell upon my face; and he said unto me, Understand, O son of man: for at the time appointed by God the vision shall be fulfilled.*

Notice that faithful people who experience the presence of God in the Bible fall on their faces. Now, however, some fall over backward; they fall like Judas did when he came with his mob to take the Lord.[74] But what happened here is different.

---

73 See Acts 12:15.

74 Judas then, taking a company of soldiers and ministers of the high priests and of the Pharisees, came there with lanterns and torches and weapons. Jesus therefore, knowing all the things that should come upon him, went forth, and said unto them, Whom seek ye? They answered him, Jesus of Nazareth. Jesus said unto them, I AM. And Judas also, who betrayed him, stood with them. And when he said unto them, I AM, they went backward and fell to the ground. (John 18:3–6)

When Daniel saw a clear representation of the presence of God, his glory, and his messenger, Daniel fell on his face, on his knees, and he fell bowing. This is what happens with true encounters with God, with true men of God.

On the other hand, when the Lord gives the order, it's because it can be understood. This vision was not for Daniel's time. This vision was for 2500 years or more into the future. This vision is for us.

The Lord's Cleansing Touch

> [18] *Now as he was speaking with me, I fell into a deep sleep on the ground upon my face; and he touched me and changed my state.*

We need a touch from the Lord in order to awaken from this dream that we are in. Without a true encounter with the presence of the Lord, we will never come out from under corruption. The Lord's presence is what cleans us. It is the touch of his hand that heals us (and changes our state).

He is the High Priest, and there is no justification if he doesn't apply the blood. Only he can erase our past and forget it; kill our sin, burn our sin; kill our guilt, burn our guilt; take the ashes and the residue of all this and throw it into a place where it will be forgotten forever. That is justification; then comes restoration.

But this cleansing also depends on us, on our decision; it depends on restoring the daily sacrifice (the continual sacrifice) that is true worship, living a clean life before the Lord. True worship is a willing heart to do what God wants, giving our life to him as a daily and continuous sacrifice.

The Lord Jesus was the morning sacrifice, but the evening sacrifice can represent us, where he is the head, and we are members of his body.

> [19] *And he said, Behold, I will show thee that which is to come in the last end of the wrath; for at the time appointed this shall be fulfilled.*

Another View from Zechariah and Revelation

Many details of these prophecies still remain. There are the four winds with everything that is related to them; four horns come out of the four winds, but God also comes out of the four winds. God is waging war against man's beastly and carnal nature. This picture is in Revelation 6, represented by four horses.

The order is different in Zechariah, but after the redemptive work effected by the Lord Jesus, in a new beginning, he wants us to enter into his holiness (the white horse). He wants to apply the blood, which is the red horse, and cut out everything that is not good in us with the sword of his Word.

Then comes the black horse of the ways of God, where he begins to tell us what we do not want to hear, and begins to end some things we do not want to leave behind. God's ways look black, but this is the way of blessing; it's about being faithful with the little. At the end it says, and see thou hurt not the oil and the wine (Revelation 6:6). This is the Feast of Tabernacles where we dwell with the Lord and he with us.

The last horse in Zechariah that changes color is a horrible death that used to trap virtually everyone in Hades, but after Christ's redemption, death has no power over those who are in him. Death becomes resurrection, which is represented by the green horse. (See Revelation 6 and Zechariah 6.) It isn't a resurrection of the natural man; it's a resurrection where we see Christ, and we will be like him (1 John 3:2).

The resurrection will place us bodily into the new creation. Many people believe a great tribulation will come for three and a half or seven years. This could happen, but we have been in conflict for a long time, and everyone who has consistently put the Lord first throughout human history has experienced severe tribulation.

The Lord has had great wrath against the carnal man who persists in doing horrible things. God's will and his wrath do work the righteousness of God. Our wrath does not work the righteousness of God because the Lord is the one who fights the war in righteousness, not us.

The war between Saul and David was long and hard. Even after David received the kingdom of Judah, the house of David clashed long and hard for another seven years with the house of Saul. The natural man does not desist easily, and God wants us to learn how to fight his way when he works through us.

Salvation in the Lord's Life

The most powerful weapon available to us is the truth, and the truth is a person. It is Jesus himself. He wants to come into our hearts and work. He doesn't prefer to do things by remote control, like when he gives us some gifts and we decide how to use them. This is what many like Saul have desired, and it leads to a lot of problems. He wants to truly come in and work in us.

In Gideon's story, the Hebrew words were inverted. Instead of saying Gideon clothed himself with the Spirit of Lord, it says the Spirit of the LORD clothed himself in Gideon (Judges 6:34). Man clothing himself with the Spirit of the Lord is the feast we're in now, where many people walk around clothed with God's gifts, but many of them continue to be the same unclean people inside.

The Word says the Spirit of the LORD clothed himself in Gideon. It was God inside, pure and clean, and it only looked like Gideon on the outside.[75]

Daniel is the same; the king would see God when he saw Daniel. He was there, but inside Daniel was filled with God. Jesus told Philip, He that has seen me has seen the Father (John 14:9).

Daniel had the heavens opened. Because of problems and obstacles, it was necessary for Daniel to pray and intercede for his people, and Daniel had direct contact in a time when it was supposedly not the season. Many people say we have to wait in order to see certain promises fulfilled. Until when? It's true that many good things await God's people in the future, but if we want direct contact with God the Father, the Lord Jesus can do it with us now if we are willing to receive his dealings and have him clean our hearts. This requires our will as well as his.

> [20] *The ram which thou didst see having two horns are the kings of Media and Persia.*
> [21] *And the he goat is the king of Grecia, and the great horn that he had between his eyes is the first king.*
> [22] *Now that being broken, whereas four stood up in its place, means that four kingdoms shall stand up out of the nation, but not in his strength.*
> [23] *And at the end of their empire [of their heavy hand], when the prevaricators are come to the full, a king of arrogant countenance and expert in enigmas shall raise himself up.*

When do you think we are going to see these prevaricators (deceivers) in their fullness? It's one thing to watch the news and see what happens in the world around us, but it's another thing to hear of the abominations that happen in those who are supposedly the people of God. And every time I think it has reached the "fullness," the horrors keep on growing. If we haven't reached the top, we must be very close.

---

75   And the Spirit of the LORD clothed himself in Gideon, who when he had blown the shofar, Abiezer joined with him. (Judges 6:34)

> [23] *. . . a king of arrogant countenance and expert in enigmas shall raise himself up.*

This seems to indicate a personal representation of how these abominations will be manifested in somebody, but this isn't the most important thing. More important is that we need to be in that sanctuary that will be justified. We are the true temple – the true sanctuary.

Until this point, justification has been for individuals, but God will do something new, and he will be represented collectively. Many people have maintained a vision for living in community, and some have established communities, but these fellowships can rupture and have problems.

Nevertheless, there is a true community that is not even global, much less local; God's true community is universal. Those who are justified and have clean hearts enter into this new sanctuary, which is his body. This includes Daniel and all those who came before.

Men have had problems for many centuries. There have been many martyrs, but we need not fear those who can only kill the body; however, we should fear him who can destroy both the soul and the body in the second death (Matthew 10:28). If we have God's seal on our forehead, we need not fear any enemy, judgment, or problems that may come, because to be absent from the body is to be present with the Lord (2 Corinthians 5:1–11).

Whoever is from God has received tribulation from men, from the government, and from humanized religion during this whole time.

> [24] *And his power shall be strengthened, but not by his own power; and he shall destroy marvelously and shall prosper and do according to his will and shall destroy the mighty and the people of the saints.*

This "king" (or kingdom) has always wanted to destroy everything that auto proclaims itself as the people of God. The only solution is to be found in incorruption instead of in corruption because those who name God and have gifts from God but continue in corruption will come to an end. But if the Lord's incorruptible life dominates our being, it doesn't matter what they do to us. The same thing that happened to the three Hebrew boys when they were thrown in the fire will continue to happen to people like us. It's impossible to destroy something that is incorruptible.

Those who are sealed by the Lord cannot be burned with fire; nothing in this world can harm us. What saves us is the Lord's life; our life has to be forsaken. If the seed doesn't die and fall to the ground, it cannot be multiplied (John 12:24). We cannot come into what God has for us if we don't leave our own life. God isn't asking us for a suicide. He's asking that we follow where Jesus walked: toward a cross, toward a slow death, but this way leads to resurrection. It isn't the resurrection of our life; it's the resurrection of his life in us. It's where people see us, but inside we have him. Inside is clean; inside is incorruptible. Instead of the Feast of Pentecost (where we have leaven inside and outside while we may be clothed with gifts and ministries that God has given us), the Lord wants to introduce us to the spiritual maturity of "Tabernacles," which is clean through and through.

In the state of "Pentecost," we're only dressed this way in order to give us time so that he can deal with our inner parts. And if we don't let him deal with us inside, the time of grace will expire, and the time of judgment will come. If we're found naked without his covering, we'll be like the king of Babylon when the sculpture on the wall appeared: drunk with the gifts of God, drinking from the vessels of God's Temple, but this is as far as he got. He had this feast to perfection with a thousand princes all competing with the wine. This is what we have with God's gifts nowadays, as previously mentioned, where some move the cape, and others fall backward; one says that he does miracles in all the services and on and on and on; and some say that if you pay them your tithe, who knows how much money you are going to get back; and if you listen to them you will never get sick . . . and so forth.

They're having a party that has never before been seen in the history of the church. The thousand princes are all using God's sacred vessels; they are betting on who can give more and who can do more, telling their tales while all this dishonest prevarication is reaching its fullness.

God is preparing to shake anything that can be shaken and once again will write on the wall with something to this effect: "This entire realm has been weighed in the balance, and even though there are many gifts, where is the fruit? What you have been doing doesn't qualify; therefore, you are cut off."

It all happened in just one night when the enemy deflected the river that flowed through the city and came in, entering where the word was supposedly flowing. The fall of Babylon came in through their provision.

Look at how this king who is coming (later identified as the king of the north) will be:

²⁵ *And with his understanding he shall cause the deceit in his*

hand to prosper, and he shall magnify himself in his heart, and
by peace he shall destroy many; . . .

Leaders speak of peace and of peace processes, but if they don't submit
to the Prince of Peace, they will deceive and destroy many with peace. In
the final time they will say, "Peace, peace," but there will be no peace.[76]
Or, as they say in the jungle, "peacepeacepeace" (the sound of a weapon).
This is what happens if you leave the Prince of Peace out.

25 . . . he shall also stand up against the Prince of princes, and
without hand he shall be broken.

This is the same picture of the statue that receives a devastating impact in
its feet, the feet that cannot walk. God will fatally impact the present-day
democracies, all without hands.

26 And the vision of the evening and the morning which was
told is true; therefore shut thou up the vision; for it shall be for
many days.

Something different has happened ever since 1967, and God is preparing
a special people. It would be sad, after all this revelation, if we were to
end up like those with no oil in their lamps in such a critical moment
(Matthew 25:1–13). The vision of the evening and morning of the 2300
years is true and real.

27 And I Daniel was broken and was sick certain days; and
after I rose up, I did the king's business; but I was astonished
at the vision, and there was no one who could understand it.

If this happened with Daniel so long ago, how will we react? Are we
going to encourage our own life, or are we going to allow the Lord to
break us? It's necessary for God to deal deeply with us in order to rid us
from our sickness: this sickness of pride, of arrogance, of corruption in
the natural man. God's prophetic time clock is ticking. I don't know how
much more time we have, but Scripture says if God had not cut the days
short, no flesh would be saved.[77] Are we going to let him circumcise our
hearts and cut the control and power of the flesh in us? Corruption has
to do with the flesh when the flesh imposes itself on the soul. Or are we
going to allow the Spirit of God to impose his will – to impose his true
presence that only comes in his life?

The abomination in the holy place and the prevarication that Daniel

---

76   Jeremiah 6:14; 8:11
77   Matthew 24:15–25

is speaking of is not just something that happened out there in the re-constructed temple. And it isn't just something that happens out there in corrupt churches along with the entire apostate world. This is something that can happen in this temple, which is us, if we consent to a spirit that isn't God's Spirit. The two can remain in close proximity for a while, but no one can serve two masters.[78] We will either end up with the mark of the beast, thoughts of the beast, and works of the beast, or we will end up with the mind of Christ, with our hearts and hands being used exclusively for the work of Christ.

Let us pray:

Heavenly Father, we thank you for clarifying the vision. Help us understand that with this clarification comes the responsibility to walk in your light until we find your presence, until we find your purity, until we leave this horrible realm of corruption. We ask this in the name of our Lord Jesus. Amen.

---

78   See Ezekiel 8–11.

CHAPTER NINE

Confirming the Covenant

Daniel 9

¹ In the first year of Darius the son of Ahasuerus, of the seed of the Medes, who was made king over the realm of the Chaldeans;

Darius, the son of Ahasuerus, could also have been called Ahasuerus upon his father's death (because this is a title and not a personal name). Therefore, Darius could have been the Ahasuerus of Queen Esther.[79] Darius means "preserver," and he was obviously involved in allowing the return of the Jews who were in captivity by carrying out the decree of his mentor, Cyrus.[80] The vessels of the temple of the Lord that were in Babylon were returned, but the rebuilding of the temple had deeper implications.

² in the first year of his reign, I Daniel saw diligently in the books the number of the years, of which the LORD spoke unto Jeremiah the prophet, which would conclude the desolation of Jerusalem in seventy years.
³ And I turned my face unto the Lord God, seeking him in prayer and supplication, in fasting and sackcloth, and ashes:

Prayer and Fasting

We find Daniel praying, confessing the sins of his people, counting the days until the seventy years prophesied by Jeremiah would come to pass,

---

79   Darius (if the same person as Ahasuerus) would have been the one who also commanded (at a later date) the walls of Jerusalem to be rebuilt so that the Jews who returned out of captivity could have a greater measure of security.
80   Ezra 6:14

until the day when there would be the possibility of a restoration. Daniel was involved with this problem because of the collective sin of the people of God. (We are in a similar situation today and still have a collective problem.)

God is looking for people with hearts like Daniel's to lift up those who have erred and to bring about true and authentic repentance in the hearts of the people of God. The world will not notice anything if there is no repentance within God's people. The Lord said he wanted everyone to see our good works so they would praise our Father in heaven, but we cannot do good works if God doesn't do them in and through us (see Matthew 5:16).

The natural works that Daniel and his friends directed do not appear in Gods' history. What is recorded is when they saved their enemies' lives, when they clarified what God was saying to the king, when they interceded for the people of God, and when they received a vision of what would happen to all the human empires until the present time of the end.

What they called fasting was not what we know as fasting. Back then, when people fasted they wore rough, black clothes that showed they were repenting. They also applied ashes and sat on them as a symbol that they did not want to promote their own lives, but instead, they were seeking the Lord's life to sustain them.

In our present age, we still fast, but I don't know of anyone who fasts in sackcloth and ashes. The true meaning of fasting is found in Isaiah 58, and it isn't what most people do today.

True fasting comes when people deny themselves in order to follow the Lord, which produces true freedom for those who were slaves to the flesh, the world, and the devil. Anyone who tries to free others with the things of God but keeps on seeking their own benefit will never free anyone, not even themselves. True freedom comes from the Spirit of God, and this goes the opposite direction from those who live for personal gain at the expense of holiness. Our own life is full of corruption and will never produce holiness, but the Spirit of God is holy. Holiness is only found in God's life. This doesn't come little by little; it's either there or it isn't; we're either led by God's Spirit or we aren't.

Many Christians remember a time when the Spirit of God led them. If they didn't persevere in it, however, they went back to their own ways. God's plan is to destroy the nature that goes against the Lord. Whoever is worthy of being his disciple must be willing to take up his cross and follow him.

What is the cross for? It's meant to crucify the flesh with all its desires. This isn't an instantaneous death, and it isn't suicidal either. It's a long path and a slow death that may possibly even be caused by people who ought to be our friends.

Daniel is one of the few people of whom no wrongdoing is recorded in Scripture. Daniel represents the body of Christ in this last time. This is a corporate man with the Lord Jesus as the head. And like Daniel, the body (also referred to as the bride) of Christ must be clean, without spot or wrinkle or any such thing (Ephesians 5:27). The Spirit of the Lord not only brings freedom, but it also brings purity. Daniel didn't receive this prophecy by saying, "It's been prophesied that this captivity is going to end in seventy years, so let's go back to Jerusalem." He took it as an initiative to pray and intercede to see how the Lord would fulfill the prophecy because the Lord can fulfill prophecy any way he wants.

> *⁴ and I prayed unto the LORD my God and made my confession and said, Now O Lord, thou great God who is worthy to be feared, who keeps the covenant and the mercy with those that love thee and keep thy commandments;*
> *⁵ we have sinned, we have committed iniquity, we have done wickedly, and we have been rebels, and we have departed from thy commandments and from thy judgments.*

To sin is to transgress the law. But to blatantly take the opposite direction from the truth is to deny God with full knowledge. This is rebellion. This is what the people of Israel did, and it's what many continue doing in much of the Christian church.

We should react to prophecy as Daniel did. In that day, Babylon had come to its end, and this motivated him to pray and intercede until Jeremiah's prophecy was fulfilled as a result of the decree of King Cyrus that allowed the Israelites to return (Ezra 1:1–4).

We are also in the time when the prophecy of Daniel 12 is about to be fulfilled. This isn't likely to be an automatic fulfillment; instead, it may require a people who are willing to humble themselves like Daniel.

> *⁶ We have not hearkened unto thy slaves the prophets, who spoke in thy name to our kings and to our princes, to our fathers, and to all the people of the land.*
> *⁷ O Lord, the righteousness belongs unto thee, but unto us the confusion of face, as at this day; to the men of Judah and to the inhabitants of Jerusalem, and unto all Israel, that are near*

and that are far off through all the lands where thou hast driven them because of their rebellion with which they have rebelled against thee.

The sins were grave, and the consequences were drastic. The consequences in our days have been drastic as well. The true people of God are scattered everywhere (in numerous sects and denominations), and others are using his name in vain. God's true nature hasn't been shown and communicated to many who walk in darkness. More responsibility rests on those who have received more light, and the present Christian church has had more light than the present-day Jews or the Jews from before Daniel's age.

> ⁸ *O Lord, to us belongs confusion of face, to our kings, to our princes, and to our fathers, because we have sinned against thee.*
> ⁹ *Of the Lord our God is the ability to have mercy and to forgive, even though we have rebelled against him*

Daniel knows that forgiveness and restoration will not depend on the merits of God's people but on God's mercy toward those who ask him. We cannot work righteousness in our own natural state. We can try, but our intents for righteousness will result in even more injustice because the only one who can work righteousness is the Lord. (The word for "righteousness" in Spanish and in Hebrew is the same word as for "justice.") We can either be in our own life that is corrupt and full of unrighteousness, or we can be in his life that is incorruptible and full of justice and righteousness. There is no middle ground; either God is moving us, or we are being moved by ourselves, another person, this world's system, or by some demon. Corruption is the same as anything that goes against God.

Sadly, many Christians operate in God-given gifts and abilities, but they don't seem to value his life. We can talk about the resurrection, or as Paul said, the full restoration (life from among the dead), but if we want to see the transformation, we must personally hear God's voice until we have a direct encounter with his presence. It's possible to have access to God's voice and not have an encounter with his presence because in order to receive gifts from him, all we have to do is agree with his plan. But if we want a direct encounter with his presence, everything must be placed on the altar: all our plans, all our purposes, our money, our belongings, and our future; it will cost us our own life.

Moses Sees God

The problems with the people in Daniel's time went all the way back to Moses and beyond. The people of Israel wanted to preserve their own life, so they didn't want to continue hearing God's voice. God's voice calls us, it cleans us, and his voice will lead us to the presence of God that will consume us. In essence, the people said, "We cannot stand the sound of this trumpet anymore and this mountain where the presence of God is burning and shaking; if we continue to hear the voice of God, we're going to die." (See Exodus 19 and 20.)

Moses only saw God's back when he went up Mount Sinai, and even so, God had to place his hand on Moses's face to cover him. But the Bible says later that never in history was there a man like Moses who spoke face to face with God. That face-to-face encounter with God may have cost Moses his life.

Moses was 120 years old, and he was still in good physical shape. God said, Climb up into this mountain Abarim, unto Mount Nebo . . . and die in the mountain (Deuteronomy 32:49–50). God brought him up the mountain and showed him the promised land. Not just what is now known as the Holy Land, which is only an example, a shadow, an imitation, or a reflection of the true inheritance that is the Lord Jesus (because he is the true "promised land").[81] From the mountain, Moses saw a landscape in the distance, but that was not what killed Moses. It's very likely that Moses died due to a direct encounter with the presence of God.

Due to an incident at Meribah, where Moses disobeyed and struck the rock twice because of the bad attitude of the people, God had said that Moses could not enter the promised land (see Numbers 20:7–12), and he didn't enter in his own life. Yet after Moses was dead, the devil could not hold him (Jude 9), and in the Gospels, Moses appears in the promised land on the Mount of Transfiguration, glorified in the life of Jesus!

And there never arose a prophet since in Israel like Moses, who had known the LORD face to face. (Deuteronomy 34:10)

That encounter Moses had with the Lord had the same effect as the burning furnace with the three Hebrew boys. The fire and dying in obedience to the Word of God only destroys the bonds and reveals the true presence of God in the person who gives themselves to do his will.

---

81   Hebrews 11:39

On the other hand, the Bible says the prince of this world, who had the empire of death back then, couldn't hold Moses. When he went to pick up Moses's body, he couldn't take it, even when almost all of those who had come before him were captives to death.

In the Mount of Transfiguration in the Gospels, Moses appeared in the glory of Jesus instead of being held captive in Sheol. He appeared with Elijah, and the glorified Lord Jesus was in the midst of them. This is the picture of the transfiguration. God gave Israel an opportunity to hear his voice and come into his presence, and it was rejected. God gave the Christian church this same opportunity, and it has also rejected it, with the exception of certain individuals and a few relatively small groups.

> [11] *And all Israel transposed thy law, departing by not hearing thy voice; by which the curse has fallen upon us and the oath that is written in the law of Moses, the slave of God, because we have sinned against him.*

Old Law or New Nature

This curse is clear throughout the law, and it is even more so in the last chapters of Deuteronomy where a blessing or a curse is offered. The blessing is for those who keep God's law, and the curse is for those who do not. Even so, with the exception of the Lord Jesus, no one has been able to fulfill God's law because whoever fails on just one point is guilty of all the other points as well. However, the Lord not only desires for us to be with him but to be in him, under his covering, under his head and authority, to be led by his Spirit, and to have his life.

Three words are translated "sin" in the New Testament. In the Old Testament there is only one. True, we have all sinned and are imperfect, but God is the one who defines, who gives the final word.

The Greek word hamartia shows a unique definition in the New Testament. John said that whoever was born of God cannot sin. It doesn't say, "does not sin" as many people have misunderstood it. The word hamartia doesn't mean "to transgress the law," which is a definition of sin in the Old Testament.

Hamartia has to do with your intentions, your direction, and your purpose in life. It's derived from a word that signifies to shoot your arrow at the bull's-eye, but it isn't about missing the mark, as some clergy have tried to translate it. This sin is when you intentionally aim for the wrong target when you have the right target in sight. It has nothing to do with scoring a perfect bull's-eye every shot.

In the Christian sense, it's when we try to live our own lives instead of allowing Jesus to live in and through us. The person who is born of God has the Lord's same desires and seeks the Lord's life instead of his or her own. Therefore, they cannot aim at the wrong target (hamartia).

> [12] *And he has confirmed his words, which he spoke over us and over our judges that governed us, by bringing upon us such a great evil: that such has never been done under the whole heaven as has been done upon Jerusalem.*

Why? They wanted to save themselves with their own works. We can only be saved by the Lords work, which must begin in us. The proof is tangible fruit. Today, great sectors that name the Lord do not consistently show forth the fruit of the Spirit. Individuals, great men or women of God, have shown this fruit throughout history.

I received an email listing some words of advice from a great preacher of many years ago in the United States of America named Charles Finney. These were good, but the recommendations will not save me. Why? Because when the life of God works in us, and when he transforms a person's heart, good things are born in our life. We don't need to make a list of sins and recommendations to be assured of fulfilling all things. The Jews have not been able to fulfill the law, and neither has anyone from this current age.

We must receive the Lord and allow his will to work in us. Our will must be to follow him through a change of nature because without this, we cannot fully obey God. The Bible tells us that whoever is led by the Spirit of God is not under the law (see Galatians 5:18). Why? The Spirit of God brings a new law (of life) that is superior to the old law of sin and death. It's the law of a new nature through the life of the Lord. Whomever the Spirit of God leads always surpasses the law, which is only a shadow and an example of the real thing. The person who is led by God's Spirit enters into the reality of the life of God.

The Lord Jesus wasn't interested in doing or fomenting the works of men. Apparently, he went against the letter of the law because he wasn't idle on the Sabbath since he was doing his Father's will. Even though the Lord Jesus did fulfill the true meaning of the law, many religious Jews couldn't see it, and this is why they sentenced him to death.

> [13] *As it is written in the law of Moses, all this evil is come upon us, and we never sought the face of the LORD our God, that*

we might be converted from our iniquities, and understand thy truth.

Sodom and Gomorrah were pagan cities, and Jerusalem was supposedly the city of God. But the "God" part was simply a façade. That's why Jesus said with nostalgia, as if he was contemplating the future, When the Son of man comes, shall he find faith on the earth? (Luke 18:8). He wasn't referring to the faith of those that say they believe in God but the faith of those that believe God and convert this into deeds (where faith and grace converge).

In the Bible, the word "earth" is sometimes symbolic of Israel and the church. Sadly, many of those who have true faith are not in the churches. If there were true faith on the earth (in the Holy Land) and in the church, terrible problems in the world and in the Middle East would decrease. Instead, they impose their own justice, but God's fruit of righteousness is rarely seen. Self-righteousness prevails.

> [14] *And the LORD hastened upon the chastisement and brought it upon us: for the LORD our God is just in all his works which he has done, for we did not listen to his voice.*

Because the Israelites didn't listen to God, he hastened his chastisement on Jerusalem. There were only a few centuries from the time of Israel's Golden Age with Solomon and David until the disgrace. I ask myself, "How are our modern nations doing in God's eyes?"

> [15] *And now, O Lord our God, who hast brought thy people forth out of the land of Egypt with a mighty hand and hast won for thyself a very clear name as appears unto this day; we have sinned, we have done wickedly.*

Daniel himself is the one praying this, a man who has (according to the Bible) a clean slate before God and before the world. We need more people like Daniel now. We need this in every single country because things are not going all that well anywhere.

> [16] *O Lord, according to all thy righteousness, let thine anger and thy fury be turned away from thy city Jerusalem, thy holy mountain: because for our sins and for the iniquities of our fathers, Jerusalem and all thy people is given in reproach to all that are about us.*

We can say the same thing about most of the so-called church of Christ on the earth.

¹⁷ Now therefore, O our God, hear the prayer of thy slave and his supplications and cause thy face to shine upon thy sanctuary that is made desolate, by the Lord.

The Lord made us desolate, but the Lord can cause his face to shine again over his true temple. If we are the people of God, we are the temple of God; we are his sanctuary, and we need God's face to shine again. If God's face shines on us, he will clean us, purify us, and transform us, but he will also kill our ego and our arrogance and destroy our own kingdoms.

¹⁸ O my God, incline thine ear and hear; open thine eyes, and behold our desolations, and the city which is called by thy name: for we do not present our supplications before thee confiding in our righteousness, but in thy many mercies.

Our self-righteousness is good for nothing, but the Lord, in his mercy, can place his righteousness in us; then his righteousness will flow on the earth.

¹⁹ O Lord, hear; O Lord, forgive; O Lord, hearken and do; defer not, for thine own sake, O my God: for thy city and thy people are called by thy name.

The "name" of God means the "nature" of God. The wrath of man doesn't work the righteousness of God. Any attempt on our part to impose God's righteousness by our own might will not work. God's righteousness will only function if it's done with God's strength. But he wants to place his strength in us. The Lord cannot put his strength in us if we don't desist from our own strength.

Notice the tone in which Daniel was speaking, being a righteous and clean man: it's similar to the Lord Jesus. He was a righteous and clean man that came to bear all our sins and the sins of his people.

²⁰ And whiles I was speaking and praying, and confessing my sin and the sin of my people Israel and presenting my supplication before the LORD my God for the holy mountain of my God;

Daniel confessed the sins of his people as if they were his own. In a similar way, the Lord Jesus came to carry our sins, our iniquities, our rebellions, and our ungodliness. What did he do with these? He took them to the cross (the Greek word stauros, or "stake") to nail them there and identify them with his death. He did this so we could have a new beginning in his life, leaving everything else behind.

> *21 I was even yet speaking in prayer, and that man Gabriel,
> whom I had seen in the vision at the beginning, flying swiftly,
> touched me about the time of the evening sacrifice.*

This chapter continues with Daniel's prayer until the Lord sends him an angel. This angel is sent at the very moment Daniel humbles himself to intercede for his people. Likewise, today the people of God have need for the heavens to open so that they may pray and intercede and receive a similar response.

The book of Daniel started with dreams given to a king who couldn't remember them. Then, Daniel began to have dreams and then visions of what God wanted him to see while he was yet awake. But now, what he had seen in a vision became reality when Gabriel touched him.

Who is Gabriel? One of the simplest translations of the name Gabriel is "man of God." Gabriel is an angel who represents the power and character of God.

In this hour, God wants to send his own men and women (those who truly belong to him) to go out and touch people who need to enter into God's reality. When God sends somebody, they are his angels or messengers, and he will back them up. If we go in God's true name (or nature), if God has truly sent us, and if they receive us, the Lord can touch them.

Daniel was touched at about the time of the evening sacrifice. Daniel was still troubled because the sacrifices had been suspended, and the temple was destroyed. But he remembered there was a sacrifice in the morning and another one in the evening. The morning sacrifice is a symbol of our Lord Jesus. The evening sacrifice symbolizes us as living sacrifices, willing to follow the Lord Jesus wherever he goes.

Daniel understood about the sacrifice, and God wants us to understand it too. The sacrifices are accomplished in Christ, but Christ (the Anointed One) is not only the Lord Jesus who came more than two thousand years ago; Christ is also a body of many members (anointed by the Holy Spirit) of which the Lord Jesus is the authority and the head, where the Spirit of Jesus Christ can flow throughout the whole body to cleanse and work in it (Ephesians 4).

> *22 And he caused me to understand and spoke with me and
> said, O Daniel, I am now come forth to cause thee to understand the interpretation.*

When the last chapter ended, Daniel didn't understand the vision of what was coming. Daniel didn't understand the war of the four winds in heaven against the beast here on earth. He didn't understand how men (like Adam, created in the image and likeness of God) could become a beast, degenerating into a state that could not be compared to any of the natural beasts on earth.

This is what our fallen race has done. We cannot understand Babylon's confusion. When Daniel was saying, unto us the confusion of face (vv. 7–8), that word "confusion" is the word for Babylon.

The Spirit of God had moved Cyrus and the kings of the Medes to have the temple of God rebuilt and to return God's sacred vessels to their rightful place. The Spirit of God is prophesying that there will be another "Cyrus." The Spirit of God will once again awaken the spirit of the "kings of the Medes."

There will be a different kingdom. We will see the restoration of the true temple of God on the earth, which is us, as living stones. God's "vessels" that had been profaned in the orgies of pagan drunkenness will be restored, and purity will return within the people of God. Many people have not yet understood this because they have not had God's touch, and they have not been yielding to God's true Spirit.

23 At the beginning of thy supplications, the word went forth,
. . .

Daniel may have prayed and interceded for a long time, but God sent the response when he first began to have this attitude. True intercession – true supplication – is not something that needs interminable repetition, because God sees the heart from the beginning.

23 . . . and I have come to teach it unto thee; for thou art a man greatly beloved: . . .

Beloved by whom? By God, because Daniel had a clean heart for what God wanted, and when God sees a clean people who have his same desires, he responds immediately.

23 . . . therefore understand the word, and understand the vision.

First, Daniel must understand the word that he heard and later the vision. Both must be understood. We need God's touch for this. God sent Gabriel for this purpose, but he can send whomever he wants to send. Gabriel came from the presence of God.

The problem we have now in the church is that many want to give touches, explanations, and understanding, but if they have not come from the presence of God, all they do is stir up more confusion from Babylon.

> [24] *Seventy weeks are determined [Heb. Cut] upon thy people and upon thy holy city...*

This is a judgment that God has determined, and it's going to be a cutting judgment that will separate the "new man" in the life of the Lord Jesus from the "old man" in his own life. The old man can try to fulfill the law by doing acts that appear religious, but only the new man has the divine nature, an inner change of nature (2 Peter 1:4).

> [24] *...to finish the prevarication and to conclude the sin and to make reconciliation for iniquity and to bring in everlasting righteousness and seal the vision and the prophecy, and to anoint the holy of holies.*

Seven Messages of Verse 24

There are about seven messages here. These seventy weeks are seventy weeks of years (a year for a day). The coming of the ministry of the Lord Jesus Christ is prophesied, and this is to do the following:

(1) *to finish the prevarication...* This has to do with the contamination of the holy and sacred things, so it will no longer be possible to do what they had been doing with the vessels of the temple of God (representative of God's ministers).

(2) *to conclude the sin . . .* According to John, whoever is born of God doesn't seek the wrong goals, but millions of people on this earth say they are born again, yet they continue living for themselves. So, what is this rebirth they have had? We live in a time when things have been modified by man, and man's things have been mixed with God's things. But the Lord says this corruption will collapse to its end, and he will give the true solution.

(3) *to make reconciliation for iniquity . . .* Iniquity is when someone sins, and instead of seeking purity, they hide it. It happened the first time when Cain hid his sin when God asked him if he knew where his brother was. Cain lied to God. Cain used this word when he said the consequences of his iniquity were too much for him to bear (Genesis 4:13).

Reconciliation is not "seeking middle ground." Reconciliation comes from the word that means, "to make right or straight." In order to straighten us out, a cleansing by the Lord Jesus Christ is necessary.

> [The] *ministry of reconciliation has been given to those who are a part of him, who participate in God's plan, deal with men and women who are contaminated and rebellious to cleanse them of their iniquity, and straighten them out with the same righteousness of our Lord Jesus.*[82]

(4) ... *and to bring in everlasting righteousness* ... Everlasting righteousness is not man's righteousness because the wrath of man does not work the righteousness of God. Everlasting righteousness is God's righteousness, and it can only flow where there is no prevarication, where sin is concluded, and where iniquity is reconciled.

(5) ... *and seal the vision and the prophecy* ... The realm of visions and prophecies is not safe. The devil has not been excluded from this realm. Therefore, sharp discernment is in order (1 Corinthians 14:29). Scripture states that all these things will end. Either they will be fulfilled, or the time of God's offer will come to an end (1 Corinthians 13:8–13). But there are three things that will remain forever: faith (that comes from the word fidelity), hope, and God's true love, which is charity. There are many today who move in visions and prophecy, yet they do not have the seal of God.

(6) ... *seal the vision and the prophecy* ... This is what Daniel was doing when he repented for his people. God gave Jeremiah the prophecy and Daniel the vision. Even though he didn't understand it, in tears and supplication before the Lord, he took his people's place and interceded and prayed until the vision and the prophecy were sealed, and God sent Gabriel to give the answer, the confirmation and the seal of God over what Daniel had heard and declaration of what was going to be.

(7) ... *and to anoint the holy of holies.* The Jews lacked this anointing. The priests lacked this anointing. The church has lacked this anointing. The realm represented by the holy of holies is where the presence of God is, and it's the only place where we can be transformed. The anointing of the holy of holies is the anointing that Gabriel had because Gabriel came from the presence of God. Gabriel touched Daniel with the heavenly anointing of the holy of holies, and this is the touch we need if we desire to enter into God's final purposes.

82　See 2 Corinthians 5:17–19.

> *[25] Know therefore and understand that from the going forth of
> the word to cause the people to return and to build Jerusalem*
>
> *. . .*

During King Darius's first year, Cyrus was ready to dictate a decree. He had not said it yet because if he had, Daniel would not be praying. God sent Gabriel to explain this to Daniel, saying something like, "Look, this is what's going to happen; the decree is going to go forth."

In another Scripture, the decree had gone out,[83] and the vessels were starting to be returned. The people went back and began to build the walls and the temple. God says that we are the stones that he wants to build,[84] and God can have the decree go forth to have the temple rebuilt (which is us) with the purpose of preparing a people for the return of the Lord Jesus (for he is coming back for a bride without spot or wrinkle or any such thing).[85]

> *[25] . . . unto the Anointed [Heb. Messiah] Prince, there shall
> be seven weeks, and sixty-two weeks, while the street shall be
> built again and the wall, even in troublous times.*

Seventy Weeks

We know the first phase of the reconstruction of the temple lasted seven weeks of years (that is forty-nine years). After another sixty-two weeks of years, the Lord came in troubled times and began his ministry, when he was around thirty, to fulfill the seven parts of this prophecy and to become the true temple. It was not the reconstructed temple that Herod later reformed. The natural temple was only an example and a shadow of the true temple, which is the Lord Jesus.

When Phillip, Andrew, Peter, and John were talking in the Gospels, they seemed to be saying, "We know the time has been fulfilled, and we are looking for the Anointed One and have found him."

Why? Because they knew that from Cyrus's decree to the Messiah's ministry, there would be sixty-nine weeks of years.

They didn't know the exact day in which the Messiah would appear, but they did know the year and approximate season. They were of the few who were aware. They knew the Messiah must appear then because this is what God sealed and confirmed with Daniel! Then came the part that the disciples were not able to understand at the time, but they

83   2 Chronicles 36:22–23; Ezra 1
84   1 Peter 2:5
85   Ephesians 5:27

understood later:

> ^{26} *And after the sixty-two weeks the Anointed One [Heb. Messiah] shall be killed and shall have nothing: (and the ruling people that shall come shall destroy the city and the sanctuary; whose end shall be as a flood, until at the end of the war it shall be cut off with desolation.)*

Who are the ruling people? They are the last kingdom (or empire) of the earth, which is Roman. The residues of the Roman Empire are the democracies we currently have. They revolve around things such as the Treaty of Rome.

Revelation 17:11 speaks of an eighth king (or kingdom) that had not come but will be there at the end. (Could this be America?) The spiritual battle for the hearts and souls of the people of the United States of America is being fought, and right now it isn't going well. We need to pray and intercede for our nation like Daniel did for his.

> ^{27} *In one week (they are now seventy) . . .*

When did this week begin? It began with our Lord's ministry at thirty years of age.

> ^{27} *. . . he shall confirm the covenant by many: and at the midst of the week he shall cause the sacrifice and the oblation to cease . . .*

The prophecy is revealed of how and when the redemption would take place. It was a prophecy of seventy weeks (a year for a day): seven weeks on one side, sixty-two weeks on the other, and one final week in which a division in the middle is established. Seven weeks of years make a total of forty-nine years in which the temple in Jerusalem is restored under the orders of Darius and Cyrus. Then there were sixty-two weeks of years when the city and the wall would be built in times of great distress until, at the end of these sixty-two weeks, the Lord Jesus turns thirty and begins his ministry, which gets cut off during the middle of the last week.

The disciples knew of the times. They would likely tell each other, "We know that it's time" (see Mark 1:15). They had counted the years, and they knew the prophecy pointed to that very year. They were very aware. Philip found Nathanael and said unto him, We have found him of whom Moses in the law and the prophets wrote: Jesus of Nazareth, the son of Joseph (John 1:45).

In John 1:37–51, we see the conversations between Andrew, Philip,

Nathanael, John, and Peter. The Lord called them, and they left everything to follow him. They had no clue as to what was going to happen because the prophecy said the return of the Messiah was going to be cut off during the last week. This part of history is clear among many Christian theologians.

However, the area where there is no clear agreement is in the last week. What happened during the second half of the last week after the Lord was crucified? It's clear that three and a half years followed with the ministry of the apostles, in which the Jews rejected their ministry completely. This is when they killed James and Stephen; then the Lord sent the Holy Spirit to Cornelius's house to begin what we know as the effusion of the Holy Spirit upon the Gentiles (Acts 10).

This was the entering in of the Gentiles, which is us, as wild olive branches grafted into God's special olive tree where Christ is the root and the sustenance. The natural unbelieving branches were cut off, and the wild branches that did believe among the Gentiles were inserted. Paul said the true Jew is the person who is circumcised in their heart,[86] and if the fact that the Jews rejected the gospel caused such a great opportunity for the Gentiles, how much more opportunity will the full restoration (which is also prophesied) cause? (See Romans 9 through 11.) We are living a natural restoration, but the spiritual restoration has not quite happened yet. There are Jews who have relearned Hebrew, but the vast majority of them do not have the Lord's life.

Sixty-nine weeks passed, but week seventy was a bit different. The sixty-two weeks and the seven weeks had been fulfilled, but Jesus, the Messiah, died in the middle of the last week (the seventh week). And with his death, he caused the sacrifice and the oblation (the present/offering) to cease. After his sacrifice and oblation, there was no need for animal sacrifices or oblations from us.

Many have understood about the sacrifice ceasing; after the Lord Jesus's sacrifice, it's no longer necessary to continue sacrificing lambs, calves, and rams because he showed us the way. He wants each of us to be a living sacrifice;[87] he wants us to take part in his death.[88] If we give up our own sovereignty to enter into his sovereignty, all our past is erased, and there is a new horizon for us. The problem is that many people want to enjoy the benefits of redemption without giving up their own way.

---

86   Romans 2:28–29
87   Romans 12:1
88   Romans 6:3

²⁷ . . . he shall cause the sacrifice and the oblation . . .

What is the oblation? In the Spanish translation, "oblation" is the same word for "present." The first use of the word "present" (in the Jubilee Bible) is when Cain gave the Lord a present (or offering). Cain's present was the work of his hands. He had worked and produced the fruit of the ground. He came to offer the fruit to the Lord; the fruit was grain that he had cultivated. This was not what the Lord wanted. For this reason, Cain was angry and killed his brother who had offered the firstborn lamb in sacrifice to the Lord.

Abel's choice of sacrifice meant he knew he needed to be redeemed and delivered; he could not do it himself because the only way to enter is in the Lord's life and authority. The Lord received Abel and rejected Cain because Cain offered the fruit of the labor of his own life. From then on, in the whole system of sacrifices, the present (or the work of our hands mistakenly translated as "grain offering") had to go hand in hand with a blood sacrifice, or the Lord would not accept it.

This provides an example and a shadow of 4000 years of the history of God's people: the work of our hands is not acceptable to the Lord unless we are under the blood, under the life and authority of the Lord Jesus, in a blood covenant. A blood covenant means a life for a life, and it works both ways.

The Lord Jesus came and fulfilled the sacrifice once and for all. This has been understood by some in the church, whether they are Catholic or evangelical or Orthodox or whatever, but the "present" part has not been understood. They have not understood that he has fulfilled the oblation (or the present), and now he wants to work in and through us so that we can be a present offered by him to God the Father.

If the Lord Jesus fulfilled the sacrifice, what is the fruit of the ground that the Lord offers alongside this sacrifice as the oblation? He said he was the grain of wheat that fell to the ground to die and grow and produce much more fruit: thirty, sixty, and one hundred for one. The Lord Jesus is the symbol of the "present" that man can cultivate, and the present the Lord Jesus offers his Father is us. He is the seed that has fallen in the ground to be multiplied (in us), and that present is a product of his hand and his ministry and not of our ministry.

²⁷ . . . he shall cause the sacrifice and the oblation to cease, . . .

These are no longer necessary. This is where there is a problem due to the offering and tithing system in many churches because now, we are the tithe; we are the offering; we are the living sacrifice; we are the present; and the one that accomplishes this is the Lord Jesus. He works in us and through us and offers it all to his Father. And as far as religion that does sacrifices and oblations, Jesus Christ (the Anointed Prince) has caused that to cease. No more religious ritual sacrifices from us are needed, no more presents. None of that counts. What counts is the sacrifice and the present/oblation prepared and offered by him. What he wants to do is to enter us into his sacrifice and oblation. This is the only way we can ever be accepted by God the Father.

The Lord Jesus wants to have communion with us so we can be in communion with his Father. We can then petition the Father directly and are able to ascend in sweet fragrance like the smoke of a burnt offering in which the sacrifice and the present went up in smoke toward heaven. This word "burnt offering" ("holocaust" in the original) relates to ascending and having the heavens open so God can listen and respond. The heavens were opened to Daniel.

The word "holocaust" is first used in reference to Jacob's ladder when the angels would ascend and descend. This unlocks a realm where the heavens are no longer "as brass." This is a prerequisite to God's dwelling place with his people and was fulfilled with the coming of the Lord Jesus.

But what did religious people do? Some have attempted to turn the new covenant into another old covenant. They sewed up the veil that was torn by the Lord's death. They restored a human hierarchy to replace God's priesthood of all believers. Again, they placed the people in a situation where they could not hear God's voice directly. They worked with their own hands to make new idols and offer their own sacrifices and presents.

When God didn't want to receive their presents, they killed those who, like Abel, had entered into the true sacrifice. The Spanish Inquisition killed multiplied millions and made it so that there was virtually no significant Bible distribution in the Spanish-speaking world until after World War II.

> [27] *In one week (they are now seventy) he shall confirm the co-*
> *venant by many: . . .*

When the Lord confirms the covenant, do you think it will really be confirmed? Could we be some of the many who have the covenant confirmed by them? Do you think we have God's seal, like Daniel had, not only on his own life but also over the intercession he was making so the decree would go forth?

Those with a heart for God began to count down the seventy weeks (of years) prophesied from the first forty-nine years until the ministry of the Lord; their prayer and intercession began with the foundation of Daniel (of a clean man's intercession).

Many important things will soon happen that will eventually lead to new heavens and a new earth. But God needs a people like Daniel.

[27] . . . he shall confirm the covenant by many: . . .

The promise to Daniel was not to confirm the covenant to many, but by many. The word of the Lord came to Jeremiah and said that in seventy years, the desolation would end. If God's people had continued to rebel, and things continued to go wrong, what if God had decided to postpone his promises and say, "Let's leave things the way they are for who knows how long?"

> *[27] ...he shall confirm the covenant by many: and at the midst of the week he shall cause the sacrifice and the oblation to cease, and because of the many abominations, desolation shall come, even until complete destruction shall be poured out upon the abominable people.*

The abominable people are Adam's race, the natural man in his corruption with his problem that will never get better but will always get worse. The only thing that ends this problem is the life of Christ. The Lord's presence either transforms us to his image and likeness, or when he returns it will destroy the man of sin completely.

There is another interpretation on the weeks of Daniel in which every week is a generation. The last week is possibly the last generation. Which one is the last generation? The last generation is the generation of Christ, and it's the generation that isn't going to die out. It isn't going to end until all is fulfilled. It's in the prophecy of Matthew 24 where the Lord Jesus explains the abomination of desolation or the prevarication that Daniel mentions in the holy place.

Today, the "holy place" of what ought to be the priesthood of all believers is in terrible condition. This is the place of intermediaries, a place of man's work with God's gifts, a place where man administers God's things. And it is full of prevarication (contamination). The Lord wants to restore the anointing of the holy of holies where the true presence of God is revealed.

The last week of Daniel is very controversial among theologians. Most evangelical scholars say that the chronogram was interrupted with

Jesus's death, and there will be another three-and-a-half-year period in the future when the rest of the events will occur at the end of the church age. Some say the entire seven years will be repeated. I'm not saying anything regarding this. It may or may not be.

The other interpretation many Protestants and some Catholics have is that those seventy weeks of Daniel kept going. They say that after the Lord Jesus's death, the next three and a half years were when the Jews definitely disqualified themselves. They think the seventy weeks ended about the time Stephen's death, and this is when God sent the Holy Spirit to Cornelius's household.

Restoration of Israel

In the natural realm, we have seen the restoration of Israel as a nation and of the Hebrew language. Presently, it isn't restored in the fullness of the life of Christ, but it's interesting that the Six-Day War happened in 1967, which appears to be a key year in Daniel's prophecies. This is the year where many lines of prophecy converge. The message of the Feast of Tabernacles among God's spiritual people also began to intensify from 1967.

Israel has its natural tabernacle (or dwelling place) again in Jerusalem. They are celebrating the Feast of Tabernacles again, even without full spiritual understanding. And Paul says if the rejection of the Jews to the plans and purposes of God opened the door so the gospel and salvation would reach the Gentiles, how much more will it be when they accept and receive their true Messiah? He sums it all in one phrase saying: life from the dead (Romans 11:15). In other words, the resurrection (which is the key to Tabernacles) is in the life of Christ, not in Adam's life.[89]

---

89   The Passover was fulfilled with the once and for all sacrifice of Jesus as our Passover Lamb. The day of Pentecost was fully come when the Holy Spirit was poured out upon the early church (Acts 2). I believe that we are presently experiencing the Feast of Trumpets as the end-time message of Tabernacles has been gathering intensity over the past several decades. If this is so, then the next event on the prophetic calendar, prior to the second coming and the fulfillment of the Feast of Tabernacles, is the prophesied corporate passage of the people of God into the realm of the holy of holies on the Day of Reconciliation (Yom Kippur) which is linked to the first resurrection (Revelation 20:4–6). The Day of Reconciliation was the only day of the year when the high priest could enter the holy of holies. Jesus is now our High Priest and our entrance into the realm of the holy of holies must be in his life, not in our own. In fact, the law states that anyone that does not afflict their soul and fast from their own works shall be cut off from the people of God on that day (Leviticus 23:23–32).

> [27] *. . . and because of the many abominations, desolation shall come, . . .*

This happens when man, in his natural inheritance from Adam tries to administer what is God's. And we are seeing desolation everywhere. We see this horrible desolation and terrible disgrace in Eastern Colombia with many abandoned church buildings in ghost towns. But many churches, virtually everywhere, are devoid of the presence of God and they don't realize it because God left them a long time ago; his presence is no longer there, but they keep functioning through their own efforts.

God says this will continue until complete destruction shall be poured out upon the abominable people. Salvation is not in our life; salvation is found in his life. Our life only produces abominations before God. The Bible even says that no one will ever be justified by keeping the law. The only way to be justified is by the shedding of blood. We have to be willing to leave our life (crucified with Christ), to place it in God's hands so that he is able to do what he wants with us and so that the life of Christ flows in us and through us. Abel symbolically did this, and God accepted the symbolic lamb, but it literally cost Abel his own life. The first abomination in human history was when Cain killed his brother Abel because he wanted to justify the work of his own hands.

Those of us who have wanted to follow Jesus have been exposed to our "brethren" who want to take our life because they want to be justified by their own works. They will attack those who are justified only by the life of the Lord Jesus.

The Lord Jesus made the sacrifice and the oblation (or present) to cease because now everything is complete in him. He started the work and will finish it, but he keeps inviting us in case we want to enter into his masterpiece. He continues being God Creator, and he wants to continue his creation in and through us. He plans on doing this until there are new heavens and a new earth in which righteousness dwells.

Let us pray:

Lord, we give you thanks for this clear picture and for giving Daniel a precise response. We ask, Lord, that we will be able to have the same attitude that Daniel had in order to be able to receive the touch of someone sent from your throne, to call us to partake of the anointing of the holy of holies, the place of your presence. Amen.

CHAPTER TEN

The Time of Fulfillment

Daniel 10

¹ In the third year of Cyrus king of Persia the Word was revealed unto Daniel, whose name was called Belteshazzar; and the Word was true, but the time appointed was long: and he understood the Word, and had intelligence in the vision.

God called Cyrus his "Messiah" in a prophecy in the book of Isaiah because an anointing came upon Cyrus that enabled him to fulfill God's will. Both Cyrus and Darius contributed toward rebuilding the temple. This tells us there will come a point (prophesied in the book of Daniel) when a time limit is established, and whosoever perseveres to the end will enter into God's full blessing once again.

The Jews waited with patience for their time in captivity to be fulfilled and later entered into a blessing. This is only a small example and a shadow of the real blessing that is about to begin.

When the "Word" was being revealed to Daniel, in Jerusalem they were beginning to rebuild the temple, and the vessels of the temple were being returned. The book of Revelation is the revelation of Jesus Christ. Many people have tried to guess the future with it, and Revelation does deal with the future, but the future is only worthwhile when it's in Christ. The person who doesn't find him doesn't have a future. The real timeline is the Lord himself.

David received the building plans for the temple by contemplating the beauty of the Lord as he came before the ark in the tabernacle of David.[90] This was God's intention so he could reveal his glory in a way

---

90   See The Tabernacle of David, Russell Stendal, Ransom Press International, Hollywood, Florida (2020).

we could understand. It's an example and a shadow of the true temple that was, and is, our Lord Jesus Christ. Now he wants to incorporate us as living stones into a much bigger temple. This is where we are headed.

A veil hung between the holy place and the holy of holies because fallen man is always excluded from God's presence. The Bible says that the veil is in the heart of the natural man, affirming that the Jews had a veil over their hearts, so when they read Moses, they couldn't perceive God's glory – they couldn't perceive Jesus the Messiah (2 Corinthians 3:15).

Many have done the same in the Christian church throughout centuries, and they continue with that veil. How long will they continue to be blinded to the truth?

The only way to enter into reason is how King Nebuchadnezzar did when he realized he was insane and looked up to heaven. This pleased the Lord, and he decided to make the king sane again. Nebuchadnezzar was a lot humbler after this, but his son didn't learn from him and lost the kingdom. This is how God has dealt with many people through centuries, and few have been able to learn these lessons from their ancestors. This is why some of the governments that we have now are not even a shadow of what they were before; everything accomplished by man is going to come down and God is going to do this "without hands." God is going to intervene directly, and that stone is going to hit the statue at its feet, and all the glory and the trajectory of the kingdoms of man (including our present democracies) are going to vanish like ash or dust with the wind.

> [2] *In those days I, Daniel, was mourning three weeks of days.*

The previous prophecy was of seventy weeks of years; this one talks of three weeks of days. It seems that their custom was to calculate time in this manner.

> [3] *I ate no pleasant bread, neither did flesh nor wine come into*
> *my mouth, neither did I anoint myself at all until the three*
> *weeks of days were fulfilled.*
> [4] *And in the twenty-fourth day of the first month as I was by*
> *the side of the great river, which is Hiddekel;*

"Hiddekel" means "arrow," and it's the same word for "Tigris" in another language. This great river flows through Iraq to the north of Babylon. This is one of the four rivers that flowed from the garden of Eden that were placed by God.[91]

---

91   See The River of God, Russell Stendal, Ransom Press International, Hollywood,

On the sacred Jewish calendar, the new year began on the first day of the seventh month of the agricultural calendar (celebrated as the Feast of Trumpets). On our calendar, this occurs in late September or early October, according to the phases of the moon. In Babylon, as well as in our calendar, the months can begin on any day. In God's calendar, the first month of the sacred calendar must begin on the new moon.

The message of the Feast of Trumpets was such that whoever didn't afflict their soul (turn their back on their own life) in anticipation of the advent of the Day of Reconciliation (Yom Kippur) would be cut off from the people of God (Leviticus 23:27–28). The Feast of Tabernacles began later on the fifteenth day of the seventh month and ended on the twenty-first day.

Daniel's Glorious Vision

What was Daniel doing? He was doing the opposite of what many people who only know the mindset of the Feast of Pentecost do. Many of these people don't know how to drink the water or how to eat delicacies of God's provision, and they attempt to hog God's gifts and blessings for themselves (for personal gain). They have no clue of the danger they're in because when God decides to take away the veil that is between the realms represented by the holy place and the holy of holies (in the true spiritual temple, which is his people), those who are not clean may not survive. It would be better to be outside with those of the law and the Gentiles. Those who say they're baptized by the Spirit and are part of this kingdom of priests that God has prepared from the beginning are in danger now if they have God's sacred things and have been using them their own way and seeking their own benefit.

Daniel wasn't doing this. God needs a people like Daniel today. We have come into the Feast of Trumpets, and the Day of Reconciliation is not far off. God is about to take the veil away and enter his corporate people into direct, face-to-face communication with himself.[92] Anyone who hasn't moved to the higher ground of the realm of represented by the holy of holies (which symbolizes the heavenly realm of the direct presence of God) will be in serious danger when this happens.

> [5] *and lifting up my eyes, I saw, and behold a man clothed in linens, whose loins were girded with very pure gold:*

In Revelation, the true bride of Christ (the clean body of Christ)

Florida (2019).
92   See Revelation 6:14; 11:19.

is dressed in fine linen, which are the good and righteous works of the saints that only God can do in and through us. The loins are the most important part because it is indispensable that our shame be covered.

In this case, the loins are not covered with leather, which is the mark of the prophet (the blood covenant); they are not covered with underwear made of the priest's fine linen (that has to do with Pentecost). His underwear is made of pure gold, and gold symbolizes God's nature.

From where did Adam and Eve fall? Why did they need leather girdles to cover their problem? They had lost the true covering. It was God's nature that covered them before.[93] This man that Daniel saw was covered by God's nature. He was sent from the presence of the throne of God, and this is what God wants for his people of Daniel today.

> [6] *his body was like the stone of Tarsis turquoise, . . .*

Tarsis is a transparent stone that shines with a penetrating yellow light.

> [6] *. . . and his face as a bolt of lightning, and his eyes as lamps of*
> *fire, and his arms and his feet like in colour to brilliant brass,*
> *and the voice of his words like the voice of an army.*

This is how God desires to have the body of Christ with the Lord Jesus at the head: and his face as a bolt of lightning.

Remember that the Word was revealed to Daniel. When the Lord Jesus came, he was the Word in flesh, blood, and bones. Now the revelation of this glorified Word is going to come to a body of Christ with many members.

What does God want? He wants a clean people. He wants to take a remnant from Pentecost, from this whole church system, and enter them into Tabernacles, into God's true presence. He wants to take a remnant out of an extremely corrupt environment, where they groan and cry out because of all the prevarication and corruption they see (and God seals them because they cried out). The ones who are sealed are candidates to enter into the realm of the presence of God and be kept under his wings; this is the security that we have in the new day that is coming.[94] Note that there are no wings mentioned in the holy place. Only in the holy of holies. This is the realm of Psalm 91.

I prefer not to fight about superficial details of the end times, or about the three and a half years, among other things, because these issues create many differing theories. God will develop all these things the

---

93   See Genesis 3:21.
94   See Ezekiel 9:4; Revelation 7:3.

way he wants to. But I dare say this: what is coming will be terrible for the person who is unclean and does not have God's presence inside of them and God's protection surrounding them. It's going to be great for those who are found with God's presence. This is what Scripture refers to when it says that the day of the Lord is great and terrible (Malachi 4:5).

> *⁶ . . . and his face as a bolt of lightning [this picture is also in Revelation 10] and his eyes as lamps of fire, and his arms and his feet like in colour to brilliant brass, and the voice of his words like the voice of an army.*

He is the Lord of many armies (or hosts), but there is a special army that will receive the kingdom and the inheritance, which, in the highest sense, is himself.

The apostle John (who had a special friendship here on earth with Jesus), Daniel (a man with no record of wrongs according to Scripture), and Saul on his way to Damascus (later Paul, the apostle) all had a similar thing happen to them when they saw this person, which is the revelation of the Lord Jesus united with his true body.

> *⁷ And only I, Daniel, saw that vision: for the men that were with me did not see the vision; but a great fear fell upon them, and they fled and hid themselves.*

What does Scripture say will happen in that day when the sixth seal is opened? It says every person that dwells upon the earth, great or small, will run and hide when the heavens (or veil between the earth and God) is rolled up like a scroll (Revelation 6:12–17). The Bible also describes Daniel, Paul, John, Joseph, and Elisha, who are all figures and examples of the true body of Christ, united with the head. This is the same picture that is found in Revelation 1 and 10. Scripture says of that day, *Rejoice ye heavens, and ye that dwell in them. Woe to the inhabiters of the earth and of the sea!* (Revelation 12:12). For those who dwell in the presence of God, it will be a great day to be alive. For those who dwell in the religious realm of the earth (up to now veiled off from the direct presence of God) or in the sea of lost humanity, it will be terrible.

> *⁸ Therefore I was left alone and saw this great vision, and there remained no strength in me, for my strength was turned into dismay, and I retained no strength.*

It says further on in the book of Daniel that God cannot fulfill his final purpose *until the scattering of the power of the holy people shall be finished*

(12:7). It isn't by our strength, not by our arm; it's when we learn that God can truly work in our lives.

The Feast of Pentecost is about the gifts of God and the baptism of the Holy Spirit, but God doesn't stop us from adding what we think is good. The first feast (of Passover) is where God tells us what is wrong and offers redemption. In the second feast, he offers to give us of his Spirit, but we are faced with a choice between putting to death the deeds of the flesh by the Spirit so that we may live (in the life of Christ) or using the provision of God for personal gain.

Some begin by trying everything out that seems good in their own eyes. Like the apostles who fished all night and caught nothing, we attempt to do good. However, unless we find God's true presence, this is impossible. The disciples were not successful until they saw Jesus on the shore and heard and obeyed him.

The only way to be productive in Passover and Pentecost is when we have been sent directly from the throne of God. This is only possible if we have entered into the presence of God, and God's presence has overthrown us and taken away our own strength.[95]

This happened with the Pharisee Saul who was converted and later referred to as Paul the apostle.[96] It happened with many heroes of the faith. Abraham had to come to this moment. Job passed from a realm of only hearing to a realm where he could see God's glory. The same happened with Isaiah, John, and the rest of the apostles.

If we don't enter into God's presence, we cannot enter the kingdom and the inheritance that God has for his sons. But this is a realm where entrance is not obligatory, or out of fear, or earned by our own merits.

We can enter into Passover or Pentecost if we accept the plan of God (and Jesus Christ is the plan of God). But the only way to enter into Tabernacles is to be conformed to the plan of God. This not only requires our disposition but for the sword of the Word of God to be active in our ears. If the Lord doesn't work and enter us in, we cannot come in.

---

95   The feasts of God may represent the path of an individual believer, but they are also prophetic of God's overall plan for his people over the ages. Passover was implemented as the children of Israel left Egypt and the Day of Pentecost came near the beginning of the early church. The Feast of Trumpets is preparing God's people for the first resurrection (when some will reign with Christ, and some will be cut off) and the full celebration of the Feast of Tabernacles will come when Jesus returns in person and overtly demonstrates his kingdom. This also ties in with the wedding supper of the Lamb.

96   Saul/Paul is known as Saul (meaning "desired") in Scripture up until Acts 13:9 and from then on is mentioned exclusively as Paul (meaning "small").

> *⁹ Yet I heard the voice of his words, and when I heard the voice*
> *of his words, then was I placed into a deep sleep on my face,*
> *and my face was toward the ground.*

Yet again, before the presence of the Lord, Daniel's face fell toward the ground; he didn't fall over backward as occurs in many places today. Some people in Scripture fell backward before the Lord's presence. In Isaiah 28, the drunkards of Ephraim fell backward.

> *Judas went to the garden of Gethsemane with the mob to imprison the Lord Jesus. Jesus asked, Whom seek ye?*

> *They responded, Jesus of Nazareth.*

> *The Lord said, I Am, and they all fell backward (John 18:3–7).*

Many people believe it is a big deal to fall over backward. This happens with rebellious people before the presence of God, and it may have happened to many of us. But in the Scriptures, every single time the presence of God encounters a clean person, they fall on their faces, on their knees. It greatly troubles me to observe places where everyone falls over backward and no one falls on their face before the Lord.

A Touch From God

> *¹⁰ And, behold, a hand touched me and caused me to move*
> *upon my knees and upon the palms of my hands.*

A touch from God was necessary even to kneel before the true presence of the Lord.

> *¹¹ And he said unto me, Daniel, O man greatly beloved, pay*
> *attention to the words that I shall speak unto thee, and stand*
> *up upon thy feet: for I am sent now unto thee. And as he was*
> *speaking this with me, I was trembling.*

Daniel needed a touch from the Lord to kneel or crawl on all fours like an animal before the Lord's presence. A special word was required to stand before the Lord like a man. In the process of corruption, man has been losing his humanity and becoming more and more like a beast.

The representations God gave of man's "sublime" governments were horrible, fierce beasts, of which the last is outside of nature as we know it. It is a beast mixed with iron and bronze, transformed into a destroying machine to destroy and trample whatever was left.

This is the picture that God has of our present democracies where men make their own laws, judge accordingly, and trample on anything that's left.[97] Nothing ever seems to be left over; there are always deficiencies in our present governmental system.

At least thousands of years ago, Babylon was represented as the statue's head of gold. There was treasure, reserves, provision, and abundance, but most people were the king's slaves. However, he cared for them because they were his.

Notice the misery today. Even at great cathedrals, there are homeless people in terrible condition, sitting outside the doors begging as in Jerusalem many years ago. These people have lost a sense of belonging and must defend themselves at all costs in a very cruel world.

> [12] *And he said unto me, Fear not, Daniel: for from the first day that thou didst give thy heart to understand and to afflict thy soul before thy God, thy words were heard, and I am come because of thy words.*

Feast of Trumpets

From the first day. The first day was on the Feast of Trumpets (the first day of the seventh month). The message of the Feast of Trumpets is that whoever doesn't afflict their soul, desist from their own life, or refuse to enter into the true fast as prescribed by God in Isaiah 58 cannot be delivered when the Day of Reconciliation comes; which is the moment of entering into God's presence because we cannot be straightened out (or reconciled) in our own life.

There is no reconciliation in our life. For every person that shall not afflict themselves in that same day, . . . the same person will I destroy from among his people (Leviticus 23:29–30). Reconciliation is in his life. (See Leviticus 23:23–32.) Daniel understood this, and from the first day, from the Feast of Trumpets, God sent the reply.

There is a spiritual war mixed in with natural things because God, from his side, can see through the veil. We cannot see very well into the spiritual realm behind the veil from our side,[98] but that veil doesn't impede the Lord's eyes.

From the first day, God had sent the response, but the response came at the end of the Feast of Tabernacles. God is saying that a revelation of the Word is coming that is a revelation of the Lord Jesus Christ.

The picture in Daniel is the same as the picture in Revelation 10, and

---

97   Daniel 7:7; Revelation 13
98   1 Corinthians 13:12; Hebrews 10:20

that of the prophet Isaiah and all the other prophets. It's the picture of a people of which Isaiah says, Behold, I and the children whom the LORD has given me are for signs and for wonders in Israel from the LORD of the hosts, who dwells in Mount Zion (Isaiah 8:18).

Those who show off with their gifts saying, "Lord, Lord, in your name we did many wonderful works," run the risk of the Lord telling them, I never knew you; depart from me, ye that work iniquity (Matthew 7:22–24). Why? Because they had God-given gifts and were using them at least partly for their own benefit. It isn't that the Lord didn't know who they were; it's that God doesn't recognize them as his sons, capable of receiving the kingdom as an inheritance.

> [12] . . . *for from the first day that thou didst give thy heart to understand and to afflict thy soul before thy God, thy words were heard, and I am come because of thy words.*

God is willing to send a response to some of us when we have responded to the message of the Feast of Trumpets in the same manner that Daniel did. As Daniel desisted from his own life, so we need to be reconciled to the Lord's life.

> [13] *But the prince of the kingdom of Persia withstood me twenty-one days: and behold, Michael, one of the chief princes, came to help me; and I remained there with the kings of Persia.*

All this has a celestial side and a natural counterpart. Here on earth, according to Scripture, God sent strength to Cyrus, who placed Darius the Mede in charge of Babylon (instead of the king of the Chaldeans). But on the unseen spiritual side of things, there was a prince of the kingdom of Persia who continued to oppose God, and Gabriel was delayed twenty-one days. But, in the end, it all helped demonstrate the plan of God because the fullness of the revelation of the Word of God – of the Lord Jesus, as he is – comes at the end of the Feast of Tabernacles.

In historical terms, the Passover (the Jews under law) lasted close to fifteen hundred years; Pentecost (the church under grace) has lasted about two thousand years. Tabernacles is prophesied to last one thousand years. Scripture also says that for God, one thousand years is as a day, the day of the Lord (this is the seventh prophetic day, the seventh millennium that I think could begin 6000 years from the fall of Adam, which is the foundation of the world system under Satan that is based on lies instead of truth).

> [14] *Now I am come to make thee know what shall befall thy peo-*

*ple in the latter days, for there shall still be vision for several
days.*

It appears that God has decreed seven thousand years of history upon the human race, until there are new heavens and a new earth. It also appears that he has decreed that after six thousand years of history of fallen man under the prince of this world (the devil), the great and terrible day of the LORD[99] will arrive on the scene in which the stone cut without hands will crash into all of man's systems and kingdoms, ending them and magnifying the Lord.[100]

This is a hit that will be made within a time frame in which the Lord will gather all those who have been faithful during the six thousand years of abominations done in the times of men and resurrect those who he has chosen to reign with Christ in the day of the Lord (see Revelation 20:4–6). But the greatest test is coming.

It's one thing to be faithful in adversity but quite another thing to be faithful in prosperity. If we place a person who has residues of self in a position of authority such as in a farm, a business, or a radio station, in time, that person may magnify himself or herself. This happens with kings and presidents. Some people have been faithful to the Lord in a kidnapping, in jail, or other types of persecution, but they go to America, the land of prosperity, and many have not been able to deal with that prosperity.

Prosperity is able to water and fertilize all the seeds in a garden in such a way that the bad and the good are both stimulated. These thousand years, even with the first resurrection, are going to be very interesting. This is why the devil will be set free for a short while at the end of the thousand years to see who wants to join him against the people of God and magnify themselves, because only righteousness will dwell in the new heavens and new earth.

Scripture says that even the heavens that we have now are not clean in his eyes. It says that there will be a tremendous war in the heavens and that the things on this earth affect the war in the heavens (Matthew 18:18).

Gabriel and Michael

Daniel afflicted his soul when he responded to the message of the Feast of Trumpets. This produced an answer from heaven via the most su-

---

99   Joel 2:11, 31; Malachi 4:5
100   Daniel 2:34–35, 45 coincides with Revelation 11:15–19.

blime (and powerful) creatures of the heavenly hosts. Gabriel came but couldn't do it alone, so Michael helped him.

It seems that there are only three angelic beings named in the Bible: Gabriel, Michael, and Lucifer (who fell). We need to understand this picture clearly. When Daniel afflicted his soul and gave his heart to understand, all of God's forces of heaven were mobilized in his favor! The opposition was so strong it took twenty-one days for this heavenly mission to be fulfilled on earth.

This is a living parable, an example for us, as we are entering into reality at the end of our present age. If clean people like Daniel are in favor, the corrupt are against it. Michael (one of the chief princes, whose name means "who is like God") is proof that God has princes who are like him, representing him as he is. When Gabriel came (meaning "mighty valiant one of God"), it was the picture of the vision of who the Lord is. Notice its effect on Daniel. The Lord wants a people like this.

> [14] *Now I am come to make thee know what shall befall thy people in the latter days, for there shall still be vision for several days.*

Which are the latter days? When Daniel was involved, approximately three and a half prophetic, one-thousand-year days had passed since creation, and the latter days were the three and a half remaining days to complete the seven days of the prophetic week. In Daniel 12, these are described as *a time, times, and a half* (12:7).

> [15] *And as he was speaking such words unto me, I looked toward the ground and became dumb.*

Daniel, one of the wisest human beings of all time, with the ability from God to interpret visions and many other things, didn't say, "Oh, so the flaming eyes mean this, and these other things mean that . . ." No, he became dumb! Speechless.

> [16] *And, behold, one like the similitude of the son of man touched my lips; then I opened my mouth and spoke and said unto him that stood before me, O my Lord, by the vision my sorrows are turned upon me, and I have retained no strength.*

Something similar had happened to Daniel in various occasions. When King Nebuchadnezzar saw Daniel, he said that he was like God. When the three boys were in the fire, the king saw someone there with them who represented the Lord. In a determined realm, Daniel had represented the Lord like this, but on this side of the veil.

Remember, the ark of the covenant was on the other side of the veil, and it had certain things in it, and this was from where God spoke. The seat of reconciliation was upon the ark of the covenant. (This was incorrectly translated as the "mercy" seat, because it is not directly related to mercy.) It's the seat of reconciliation, and it's mercy for a person like Daniel, but it's total destruction for a person who isn't clean. All this is under the wings of the two cherubim.

Michael is referred to in the New Testament as the archangel (Jude 1:9), and Gabriel is called "that man Gabriel" in Daniel and is twice referred to as an angel in the New Testament (Luke 1:19, 26). There is some circumstantial evidence that has led some to believe that Gabriel and Michael are cherubim but the Scripture does not seem to directly spell this out. Ezekiel describes the cherubim as being living creatures having up to four faces (including the face of a man) and associates them directly with the glory of God.[101] At any rate, we can clearly deduce that the presence of either one of them is awesome.

> [17] *For how can the slave of my Lord talk with my Lord? for as for me, for in that instant I had no more strength in me, neither was there any breath left in me.*

At this moment, Daniel didn't know if he was going to live. Many believe the rapture is going to be a soft thing that is going to get carnal Christians out of here and deliver them smoothly to the presence of the Lord. What happened to Daniel will likely happen to those of us who do "well" in this "rapture."

> [18] *then there came again and touched me one like the appearance of a man, and he comforted me,*
> [19] *and said, O man greatly beloved, . . .*

This is the third time the term "greatly beloved" is used in the book of Daniel. Daniel was dedicated to loving God, and he chose to do God's will. Daniel was an example of what the Lord Jesus did and what we will do if we enter by the true and only way.

Peace

> [19] *. . . O man greatly beloved, fear not: peace be unto thee,*

In God's kingdom, peace comes when God gives the order. It isn't nego-

---

101 Ezekiel 10

tiable. We cannot come as rebels and give in a little so that God will give in a little and come to a supposed reconciliation; this is false peace. True peace is when the Lord gives the order. Daniel hears, *peace be unto thee.* Jesus also said, *my peace I give unto you* (John 14:27). If God doesn't give the peace, there is no peace because his presence imposes peace. When an angel arrives, it's a perfect representation of God from the other side of the veil, from the realm of the Spirit that we cannot perceive with our natural eyes.

> [19] *peace be unto thee, be of good cheer, and be well. . . .*

Be well, because he was dying.

> [19] *. . . And as he spoke unto me, I was strengthened and said, Let my Lord speak; for thou hast strengthened me.*

Before, Daniel didn't have the strength to receive the Word. This is a Word capable of doing in anything that remains of our own life; we must be touched and strengthened and encouraged by God in order to receive it.

> [20] *Then said he, Knowest thou why I have come unto thee? Because now I must return to fight with the prince of the Persians; and when I am gone forth, next the prince of Grecia shall come.*
> [21] *But I will interpret unto thee that which is written in the scripture of truth: and there is no one that holds with me in these things, but Michael your prince.*

It appears that Michael has special jurisdiction over the people of God.

Let us pray:

Heavenly Father, we ask you to remove the veil in our hearts that keeps us from experiencing your presence and perceiving your glory. Please open our eyes to the truth, so that we may perceive you as you really are, so that the glory of your presence might destroy any residue of anything displeasing to you that remains in us. Amen.

Chapter Eleven

Kings of the South and North

Daniel 11

[1] *And in the first year of Darius the Mede, I stood to encourage and to strengthen him.*

Gabriel was fighting a Persian prince, but at the same time, he was there to strengthen Cyrus and Darius (who had replaced the kingdom of Babylon) that the order might come forth to move the people of God out of Babylon and give them the opportunity to rebuild the temple, the city, and walls of Jerusalem.

For a long time now, many of God's people have been in bondage again, and God has used it to form our character, just as he did for Israel during many years of slavery in Egypt. But the time came to leave Egypt. Such a time has come now for us to come out from under the confusion of men and man's governments, even out from under men who appear to have been called of God if they have imposed their own government.[102] Even King Saul started with a calling from God, but his pride pulled him down.

God has a group he has been preparing in the "desert" who are: like the remnant that left Babylon to travel through the wilderness back to Jerusalem, like David and his four hundred or six hundred, like Gideon and his three hundred, and like the seven thousand of Elijah and Elisha who did not bow before Baal. God has people like Ezekiel's men who cried out when they saw the abomination in the temple. God sealed and marked them and took them out of there. He hid them in the mountain, and he is that mountain because the stone that destroys the image grows and becomes a mountain that fills the whole earth until there is no more

---

102 Revelation 18:4

room among the people of God for anything else but him.

Neighboring Kingdoms

² And now will I show thee the truth. Behold, there shall yet be three kings in Persia, and the fourth shall obtain far greater riches than they all; and by his strengthening himself with his riches he shall stir up all against the realm of Grecia.

³ And a valiant king shall stand up, that shall rule over a great dominion and do according to his will.

⁴ But when he is reigning, his kingdom shall be broken and shall be divided by the four winds of heaven, and not to his posterity, nor according to his dominion by which he ruled; for his kingdom shall be plucked up, even for others beside those.

⁵ And the king of the south, [this Hebrew word is identified with the people of God] and of his principalities, shall make himself strong; and he shall exceed him and make himself powerful; his dominion shall be a great dominion.

This passage goes on and on about the conflict between the king of the north and the king of the south all the way to the time of the end. Remember that the original use of this terminology in Scripture described the ten tribes that became so apostate that they eventually became worse than some of their pagan neighbors as the kingdom (or king) of the north and the kingdom of the south described Judah (along with residues of Simeon, Benjamin, and Levi) who continued to worship at the temple in Jerusalem, although they had bouts of legalism (and also some idolatry), even when captured by Babylon, at least a substantial remnant never lost their spiritual identity and heritage. God's people, however, throughout history have had a penchant for "marrying" into that which is represented by the king of the north and for making unholy alliances.

⁶ But at the end of some years they shall join themselves together; for the king's daughter of the south shall come to the king of the north to make an agreement, but she shall not retain the power of the arm; neither shall he stand, nor his arm; for she shall be given up and those that brought her and he that begat her, and those that were for her in this time.

⁷ But of the new shoot from her roots shall one stand up upon his throne and shall come unto the army and shall enter into the fortress of the king of the north and do in them according to his will and shall prevail:

This all seems to describe some of the intrigue between the Medes and the Persians versus Alexander the Great. It begins as a historical recount, yet transitions into realms that are very difficult to coincide with human history by dividing it into only two kingdoms, the king of the north and the king of the south.[103] This is confusing unless you understand that spiritually there are only two sides (or kingdoms) and that those who are supposed to represent God and be the good guys (the south) have a very strong tendency to become contaminated by the bad guys (the north), and those of the "north" have many differing factions that don't always get along.

In the old Spanish, it is literally translated as "the king of the north and the king of the 'noonday' (mediodía in Old Spanish; negeb in Hebrew)." The noonday, or south, is linked to the southern kingdom of two and a half tribes that continued to worship God in Jerusalem, while the northern kingdom of ten tribes became spiritually indistinguishable from their pagan neighbors and eventually lost their spiritual identity as tribes of Israel. In prophecy, the north wind can represent adversity and tribulation, while the south wind represents blessing and prosperity.

Many kingdoms and governments have had their noonday. The United States of America is now in its noonday. Never in the history of the world has there been prosperity like this.

The king of the north came and repeatedly attacked. The king of the north and the king of the south proposed a marriage and gave a daughter in alliance (a humanistic solution for ending the war), but it didn't work out. Why? Why has this conflict lasted from the time of Daniel until now? History majors – whether they study church, political, or economic history – know there have always been conflicts; students memorize the dates of all the battles and revolutions.

Jesus summarized it by saying that every house or city divided

---

103 This is because even though here upon the earth there are apparently many kingdoms. Satan is the prince of all the kingdoms of this fallen world. However, his people and his kingdoms are in continual war and strife among one another. This is why Jesus said, Every kingdom divided against itself is brought to desolation (Matthew 12:25). On the other hand, from the spiritual realm there are only two sides described here as the king of the north and the king of the south. To further complicate matters, the king of the south, who is aligned with the people of God, is not always pure and clean. This is why the entire scenario eventually leads into a time of trouble (also known as Jacob's trouble) such as never was until there were people until now (Daniel 12:1).

against itself will not remain (Luke 11:17). The devil, who is the prince of this world, has never united the world. He can't even unite the kingdom of the north. Some seek the things and pleasures of this world, and others discipline themselves in tremendous austerity. These two tendencies always clash.

As the book of Daniel gives us snapshots of these clashes, they resemble what happened with Greece, Persia, the Muslims, the Crusades, the church, etc. We can clearly identify some points.

> *8 and even their gods, with their princes, with their precious vessels of silver and of gold, shall be taken captive in Egypt; and for some years he shall maintain himself against the king of the north.*

Egypt is a symbol of the legalism and slavery, and confusion reigns when people make laws they cannot fulfill. Thus, Egypt (meaning double black) can be a symbol of the people of God under law.

> *9 Thus shall the king of the south enter into the kingdom and return to his own land.*
> *10 But the sons of that one shall be stirred up and shall assemble a multitude of great armies and shall come in great haste, and overflow and pass through and turn and come with wrath unto his fortress.*

This sums up human history.

> *11 Therefore the king of the south shall become furious and shall come forth and fight with him even with the king of the north; and he shall put a great multitude into the field, but all that multitude shall be given into his hand.*
> *12 Therefore the multitude shall be filled with pride, his heart shall be lifted up, and he shall cast down many thousands, but he shall not prevail.*
> *13 And the king of the north shall put another multitude greater than the former . . .*

Throughout the history of Israel and the church, every time the people of God thought they had the kingdom and they would prosper, a tremendous king (or alliance) came from the "north" and devastated them (as time went on the Vikings, the Huns, and the barbarians came from the north against Rome to the south). Even in the United States of America, with its immense prosperity, Bin Laden came, and with three airplanes, he destroyed the Twin Towers and smashed into the Pentagon on 9/11. Who would have thought?

The godly heritage of the United States is diminishing because the devil is dominating almost every part of society. The terrorists are inspired by the devil, but some of them think it's God. Many Americans believe God is on their side (and it never occurs to them to question whether they are on God's side). We see the difference from our history books when we look from God's perspective. Everything is found here:

> *14 But in those times many shall stand up against the king of the south, and sons of robbers of thy people shall raise themselves up to establish the vision, but they shall fall.*

The word "times" here in the book of Daniel can refer to thousands of years. When God's people take refuge in Egypt (prophetically symbolic of the bondage of legalism) things can rapidly degenerate into sons of robbers taking advantage of everyone like in the days of young Moses. These "Pharaohs," who set themselves up as intermediaries to control the people of God, attempt to establish the vision, but they always fail because God's people must individually be in direct contact and fellowship with God in order to be victorious.

> *15 So the king of the north shall come and cast up a mount and shall take the strong cities, and the arms of the south shall not withstand, neither his chosen people, neither shall there be any fortress that can withstand.*
>
> *16 And he that comes against him shall do according to his own will, and there shall be no one that can stand before him, and he shall stand in the glorious land, which by his hand shall be consumed.*

This seems to describe events such as those surrounding the different Greek kings that dominated the Mideast until the Roman conquest.

> *17 He shall then set his face to come with the strength of his whole kingdom and shall do upright things with him, and he shall give him a daughter of his women to persuade her, but she shall not stand, neither be for him.*
>
> *18 After this he shall turn his face unto the isles and shall take many, but a prince shall cause him to cease his affront and shall even turn his reproach upon him.*

> ¹⁹ *Then he shall turn his face toward the fortresses of his own land, but he shall stumble and fall and not appear again.*
> ²⁰ *Then shall succeed in his throne a taker of taxes who shall be the glory of the kingdom, but within few days he shall be broken, neither in anger, nor in battle.*

The Romans were definitely takers of taxes, and some of this sounds like it could be referring to men such as Julius Caesar and successive Caesars.

> ²¹ *And a vile person shall succeed in his place, to whom they shall not give the honour of the kingdom: nevertheless he shall come in with peace and obtain the kingdom by flatteries.*
> ²² *And with the arms they shall be overflown of a flood before him and shall be broken; yea, also the prince of the covenant.*

The Lord Jesus died in the midst of the intrigues of these human governments after the Romans took over Jerusalem. In front of the backdrop of the empires of this world, the moment in which the prince of the covenant is broken happens almost without anyone noticing. This produced greater consequences and a delayed effect as the gospel was preached throughout the known world.

> ²³ *And after the union made with him he shall work deceit and shall rise and shall overcome with few people.*
> ²⁴ *With the province in peace and in abundance, he shall enter and do that which his fathers have never done, nor his fathers' fathers; he shall distribute prey and spoil and riches to his soldiers; and against the fortresses he shall forecast his devices, even for a time.*
> ²⁵ *And he shall stir up his forces and his heart against the king of the south with a great army; and the king of the south shall move to the war with a great and mighty army, but he shall not prevail, for they shall betray him.*
> ²⁶ *Even those that ate his bread shall break him, and his army shall be destroyed; and many shall fall down slain.*
> ²⁷ *And the heart of both these kings shall be to do evil, and at the same table they shall speak lies; but it shall not prosper, for the time appointed is not yet come.*

Over the years, the makeup and alliances forming the kings of the north and of the south have sometimes shifted, but eventually corruption seems to always prevail.

> *²⁸ Then he shall return into his land with great riches; and his heart shall be against the holy covenant; and he shall do exploits and return to his own land.*

And so church history (east and west) is littered with events such as inquisitions and crusades.

> *²⁹ At the time appointed he shall turn toward the south, but the latter coming shall not be as the former.*
> *³⁰ For the ships of Chittim shall come against him; therefore he shall be grieved and return and have indignation against the holy covenant: so shall he do; he shall even return and have an understanding with those that have forsaken the holy covenant.*

From this point on, the death sentence for the prince of this world began. Two or three witnesses in heaven will sit in judgment to sentence him forever; this is where we all come in. Verse 31 is the next reference point where we can approximate a time:

> *³¹ And arms shall be placed on his behalf, and they shall pollute the sanctuary of strength and shall take away the daily sacrifice, and they shall place the abomination that makes desolate.*

This literally happened to the Jews in AD 70, and again in approximately AD 678 in the church. Historically speaking, we know the abomination that makes desolation occurs when man thinks he is God. The daily sacrifice is the sacrifice that the Lord Jesus did; it's sufficient for us if we dwell in him.

But a corrupt system arose where the Lord's sacrifice was not considered to be enough. We were told to add our own works to Christ's sacrifice, giving rise to indulgences, compulsory religious acts, and other requirements. At this time, the world entered into a long period, historically, that even secular historians have called the Dark Ages.

> *And from the time that the daily sacrifice is taken away until the abomination of desolation, there shall be a thousand two hundred and ninety days. (Daniel 12:11)*

As mentioned previously, Pope Agatho seems to have been the first to say that he was the Vicar of Christ on the earth, and if we count 1290 years from the year AD 678, when it appears that the pope declared himself infallible, we come precisely to the Six-Day War in June of 1967.[104] Many

104 See chapter 8.

things have happened since the Six-Day War; the holy place, the place and the realm of the priesthood of all believers, has become more and more contaminated and dominated by false spirits, and the true remnant has been left outside the camp or is in the process of leaving. A new message has been birthed outside of the camp with anointing from the holy of holies. It was not common to hear messages with the anointing of Tabernacles before the Six-Day War – only the anointing of Passover or Pentecost. So, we have a point of reference in Daniel 11 from verse 20 to 22 where it refers, more or less, to the Lord Jesus's first coming. In verse 31, it likely refers to those such as Pope Agatho, AD 678, and successors who have been "desolate" of the true presence of God.

It looks as though our present age (2000 years of grace) could have begun when the Lord Jesus entered the second stage of his life, where he presented himself in the temple at the age of twelve to voluntarily submit to the imperfect authority that God had placed in his life: Joseph and Mary. These next eighteen years were a symbol of the age of the church. The number eighteen goes hand in hand with "lilies" and every other symbol of Pentecost. If this began here, then Pope Agatho did what he did exactly in the year 666 of the age of the church, and this could be at least part of what Revelation 13:18 is referring to. It's also possible that this scenario could apply to a select remnant that God is preparing ahead of others who are coming along behind and need a good example to follow.

In Revelation, it isn't the outer court that gets trampled, as is mistranslated in many Bibles; it's the inner court, the holy place, that is tread under foot forty-two months. Forty-two months are the same as 1260 days, depending on how the months are counted.

> *But leave out the court which is within the temple and measure it not, for it is given unto the Gentiles, and the holy city shall they tread under foot forty-two months.*

> *And I will give my two witnesses, and they shall prophesy a thousand two hundred and sixty days, clothed in sackcloth. (Revelation 11:2–3)*

God's Restoration

God is restoring something, but he is not restoring Pentecost. He's returning to the true dimensions (see Ezekiel 40–47). We must understand that the tabernacle of David had no furniture, only the ark; in other words, it didn't have provision for an intermediary priesthood conducting symbolic rituals. It was set up to portray the priesthood of all believers. This is where David could come and contemplate the beauty of the Lord in preparation for building the true temple of living stones (of which, the plans for Solomon's Temple were just a shadow).

This is what God offers to each one of us. You cannot enter in by simply reading a message from Russell Stendal. These messages are of limited use, like jump-starting your car that has a dead battery. If you don't fix the alternator, if your car doesn't generate its own energy, if you don't have direct contact with God, and if God isn't in contact with you, you will not enter in. You will be in the same predicament as the foolish virgins (Matthew 25:6–13).

If we grab hold of the Lord, as is common in Passover or Pentecost, this is not the same level of security as when the Lord himself takes hold of us. This happened to Daniel. The Lord came and touched him, and spoke to him, and brought him up from being on his face as though dead, from being on four feet like an animal until he stood him on his feet like a man. The revelation of Gabriel and Michael almost killed Daniel; then the Lord spoke to him.

Can you imagine what the revelation of the Lord Jesus in all his glory is like? Can you imagine what God wants to do with us? He desires a complete transformation.

There are examples of this in nature, like the worm that crawls around eating and suddenly ends up trapped in a cocoon until it comes forth as a beautiful, colorful butterfly flying high above the other worms. If we didn't know the story, we would compare the butterfly with the worm and say, "No, it isn't the same creature." This is similar to the metamorphosis that God wants to do in us. It goes beyond what we can imagine.

> *But as it is written, That which eye has not seen nor ear heard neither has entered into the heart of man is that which God has prepared for those that love him. (1 Corinthians: 2:9)*

It cannot enter into the heart of man; it can only enter God's heart and flow from his heart. God wants to place his heart in us.

> *[32] And with flatteries he shall cause to sin those that violate the covenant, but the people that do know their God shall be strong, and do exploits.*

There are people that do know their God; they have existed even during the darkest days of history.

³³ And the wise among the people shall give wisdom to many,
yet they shall fall by the sword, and by fire, by captivity, and
by spoil, for some days.

Since the time of Daniel, it has been about two and a half prophetic days (close to 2500 years) . . . some are still falling; the number of those who have been martyred or "beheaded" to be under the headship of the Lord of Lord's and King of Kings is being fulfilled.

³⁴ And in their fall, they shall be helped with a little help, . . .

We've received a little help during this time, but only enough to live each day. Hebrews 11 describes this. The prayers of God's people under tremendous tribulation in these past few "days" have been stored up in heaven. Revelation 13, 14, and 15 describe how these vials filled with the wrath of God will be poured out in a moment upon the world system.

³⁴ …but many shall cleave to them with flatteries.
³⁵ And some of the wise shall fall to be purged and cleaned and
made white, even to the time of the end because even for this
there is time appointed.

Many people have gone through difficult experiences because of their faith in the Lord and have come through purged and cleaned and made white. For this purpose, God has allowed many injustices. It's necessary for these things to happen, but woe unto those who cause them.[105]

³⁶ And the king shall do according to his will, . . .

Which king? In our ego, we all feel like kings, and the pride of the natural man will continue full steam ahead.

³⁶ . . . and he shall exalt himself and magnify himself above
every god and shall speak marvels against the God of gods
and shall prosper until the indignation is accomplished, for the
determination has been made.

This speaks of someone promoting the systems of this world that are like beasts. In the book of Daniel, there are four beasts and seven heads; in Revelation, there is one beast with seven heads. At the same time, Scripture says the four winds of God are waging a war against the great sea, and the beasts come out of the sea of lost humanity (Daniel 7:2–3).

God is looking for those who submit themselves to his dealings and let him correct them. The Lord wants to come in and kill the nature of

---

105 See Matthew 18:7; Luke 17:1.

the beast that is inside each one of us. He wants to put an end to the false prophet (or false spirit) who comes as an angel of light to deceive us. The Lord wants to displace the spirit of antichrist that wants to dwell in us instead of God's Spirit. We are to be the temple of God.

I'm not saying that there may not be clearer and more personified manifestations of this, and that in the time of the end there may not be literal times to count the days as they are, and so on. I'm not denying that all this could happen, but the most important thing is that we understand that this battle must be won in us. (It seems that a literal fulfillment of these days has already happened twice in history to the Jews: once in AD 70 with the destruction of Jerusalem, and also with the Holocaust caused by Hitler in the early 1940s.)

> *37 Neither shall he care for the God of his fathers, nor the love of women, nor care for any god, for he shall magnify himself above all.*

So now we have celibacy among other things.

> *38 But in his place shall he honour the god of fortresses, [Ala Mahozim] a god whom his fathers did not know; he shall honour it with gold and silver and precious stones and with things of great price.*

These fortresses (called temples, churches, cathedrals, or even mosques) have been built virtually everywhere, even though we are the true temple. People have spent much of their resources building these religious fortresses. Evangelical people are not exempt from this. They can be more fanatical about constructing their buildings and making their own religious fortress than anyone else.

> *39 And with the people of the strange god that he shall know, he shall make strong fortresses, increase their glory; and cause them to rule over many, and shall divide the land for gain.*

Becoming territorial, they organize clergy meetings and send missionaries. Some say politics is their area, etc. They divide the land for gain (the land can be symbolic of the people of God), not to mention the actual boundaries of their parishes and dioceses.

> *40 But at the end of the time the king of the south shall lock horns with him, and the king of the north shall raise up a storm against him with chariots and with horsemen and with many*

> *ships, and he shall enter into the lands and shall overflow and*
> *pass over.*

The United States, Israel, and possibly some of their allies are now the king (or kingdom) of the south, even though they may not be in total agreement in every area. The king of the north is working hard and with much austerity. Sometimes he mobilizes in the jungles or in other countries, such as Iran and North Korea. China (allied with Russia) is gaining terrible strength, and this is all heading for a tremendous collision. Many European nations seem to be sitting on the fence while the pope moves ever closer to the king of the north. Here is a question that may be expedient to ask ourselves: are the United States, Israel, and their allies locking horns with China, Iran, Russia, and their allies? Will this develop into the end-time conflict prophesied by Daniel that will trigger the direct intervention of God? Will this lead to the time of trouble such as never has been until now?

> [41] *He shall come to the glorious land, and many provinces shall*
> *fall, . . .*

We could also say that many churches will fall. Every church will fall, except for the true church (and we are the church if we are in a right relationship with God). There is a natural picture of this taking place in natural Israel. But the fundamental true part of Israel is the spiritual side because a genuine Jew is someone who has a circumcised heart (Romans 2:29). God wants there to be many true Israelites in natural Israel, but many true Israelites are also scattered throughout churches in the whole world. I think there are even more scattered outside of any of these fortress structures.

There is about to be a head-on collision between the two sides, and woe to the lukewarm! Some, who have enough of God for the enemy to target them but have cooled off, are in a middle stage. They represent a threat to the world system, but they don't count on God's full protection or the anointing of Tabernacles. So, they will be in great danger.

> [41] *He shall come to the glorious land, and many provinces shall*
> *fall, but these shall escape out of his hand, even Edom and*
> *Moab and the first of the sons of Ammon.*

This is a tremendous enigma because these are the nations that caused Israel the most trouble. These nations also have remote family ties with the people of Israel. They had their own covenants, and God passed them through the destruction prophesied in the Old Testament.

The same thing happened to the nation of Israel. God said that if those who are supposed to enter in do not, if the first invited guests of the feast do not enter, he will look for other guests (see Matthew 22).

It's true that Scripture says that God loved Jacob and hated Esau (who was the founder of Edom), but this is also a picture for us. The first time we are born, God hates the "old man" in us, but he loves us as true sons when we are born a second time from above.

But God is not prohibiting Edom, Moab, or Ammon to go to the feast. If the people of "Israel" do not want to go in first, God will let anyone in who meets his conditions. The only thing you have to do to enter the feast is to wear the clothes (wedding garment) that he designates (come under his authority) and eat the food that he provides (feed on the pure, uncontaminated Word of Tabernacles).

> *And he said unto me, Write, Blessed are those who are called unto the marriage supper of the Lamb. And he said unto me, These are the true words of God.* (Revelation 19:9)

If God puts his covering over us, if he nourishes us, he will make us clean, even if we are from Edom (the builders of their own kingdoms) or from Moab (who come from their own spiritual fathers). It will not matter if we're from Ammon (who were the first to represent democracy). God can cause us to be born again into his nature if we renounce having our own kingdoms. We need to renounce our own spiritual fathers and submit to God the Father. We need to renounce democracy and favor instead theocracy, where God is in charge instead of men or the people.

> [42] *He shall stretch forth his hand to the lands, and the land of Egypt shall not escape.*
> [43] *And he shall take over the treasures of gold and of silver and of all the precious things of Egypt, of Libya, and Ethiopia where he passes.*

This war that is coming is going to do away with many things, but there are other things that are going to remain firm because they are built in a realm where they cannot be shaken. What happened with Edom, Moab, and the sons of Ammon has happened to us: we have been in what we thought was the church, but it turned out to be another kingdom. We have been under someone we thought was the authority, but they turned out to be an earthly authority and not our heavenly Father. And we have been where we thought the covering was good, but it came from man's democracy.

If we have volunteered to receive God's judgment, we will not be hurt when judgment falls upon the rest of the earth. But whoever is still there, rejoicing in the laws that they themselves made, or soaking in this world's noonday sun under the heavy hand of modern Pharaohs (as is represented by Egypt, Ethiopia, and Libya), will be swept away in the new day that is coming.

> [44] *But tidings out of the east and out of the north shall trouble him; therefore he shall go forth with great fury to destroy and to kill many.*
> [45] *And he shall plant the tents of his palace between the seas, in the desirable mountain of the sanctuary; and he shall come to his end, and shall have no one to help him.*

This is when the stone cut without hands[106] is going to crash into the kingdoms of this world. Revelation 11:15 says all this will be reduced and collapse. It shall all be broken to pieces and carried away by the wind like chaff from the threshing floor, and our Lord's true kingdom will rise in a visible way because right now it's in our hearts, not of this world, and therefore invisible to the natural man.

Let us pray:

Lord, forgive us for thinking we were under the right covering when we were actually under the covering of man-made democracies and worldly systems, rejoicing in the systems made by human hands. Make us clean, and teach us how to live for the right kingdom, an eternal one. We surrender to your authority and your covering, asking that you place your nature within us. Amen.

---

106 Daniel 2:34, 45

Chapter Twelve

A Time of Trouble

Daniel 12

¹ And at that time shall Michael stand up, the great prince who is for the sons of thy people, and it shall be a time of trouble, such as never was since there were people until now, but in that time thy people shall escape, all those that are found written in the book.

This is the time of Jacob's trouble (see Genesis 32). I wonder if this is the same time that Revelation 12:7–10 takes place? It certainly seems possible.

Entering In

Are we written in the book? God says it is possible to be erased from the book (Psalm 69:28). One theory is that we are born already written in God's book, but those who disqualify get erased. That doesn't ring entirely true to me, but I am confident that everyone who is genuinely born again from above is definitely registered in God's book. They are citizens of the heavenly Jerusalem.

I also know that no matter how rebellious a person is, it's possible for them to respond to the feast to which God is inviting everyone (Revelation 19:9). God said anyone can come: the lame, the dumb, the maimed, even those who are good and those who are evil (Luke 14:15–24; Matthew 22:1–14).

The only requirement is to receive his covering and eat his food. The only one who is cast out is the person without a wedding garment (who, therefore, did not want to be under God's authority). Entering and partaking of God's feast is easy, but some people complicated it with their religious requirements.

> *² And many of those that sleep in the dust of the earth shall be awakened, some for eternal life, and some for shame and everlasting confusion.*

"Those who sleep in the dust of the earth" could refer to the ones who are in Hades, but I believe this lines up perfectly with Matthew 25:1–13 and Jesus's parable about the bridegroom and ten virgins. The earth is a reference to the people of God. Adam was made from the dust of the earth.

Both the wise and the foolish virgins were asleep when the (trumpet) call went out announcing the arrival of the bridegroom. Five virgins entered into eternal life, but the other five found shame and everlasting confusion.

Many who call themselves God's people today sleep in the dust of the earth in the sense that they are completely asleep in the Adamic nature and clueless as to God's end-time plan and purpose. It is high time to wake them up.

> *³ And those that understand shall shine as the brightness of the firmament; . . .*

Many people think it's important to understand Bible prophecy and the book of Daniel. God is giving us more clarity because now is the time to unlock things we couldn't understand before. But even if we could understand every detail, this would not be the most important thing. The most important thing is that we are understood in heaven.

When Daniel gave his heart and afflicted his soul, he was heard that same day in heaven, and God sent the answer, which required the mobilization of the two chief princes of the heavenly hosts. This is worth it.

> *³ . . . and those that teach righteousness to the multitude as the stars in perpetual eternity.*

Notice in Scripture, "eternity" refers to quality; the word "perpetual" means "ongoing, forever." Whatever is eternal is forever because God is forever. His life is eternal, not because it's forever but because it's of a quality different from ours. Eternal life is not our corruptible life that lasts forever. Eternal life is God's incorruptible life, to which we can enter, producing true righteousness ("righteousness" and "justice" are the same word in Hebrew).

God wants people who teach true righteousness to the multitude to be as the stars in perpetual eternity. Abraham was to have two kinds offspring: some like the sand of the sea, and others like the stars of heaven (Genesis 22:17; 26:4). Those who are like the sand of the sea will have problems in the time of trouble at the great day of the Lord. Some, like the stars, will be above the circumstances.

The book of Daniel ends with Daniel receiving a revelation given directly from God. He was not able to understand most of this because it wasn't the time. It was sealed until the time, and that time is now, and we can receive it because it's about to be fulfilled.

Seal the Book, Shut Up the Words

⁴ But thou, O Daniel, shut up the words, and seal the book until the time of the end: many shall pass by, and knowledge shall be multiplied.

He told Daniel to seal the book until the time of the end. He said that when the prophecy is fulfilled, after the end of the days prophesied (which I understand to be a day for a year), thou shall go to the end and shalt rest, and thou shalt raise up in thy lot [or in thine inheritance] at the end of the days (Daniel 12:13).

Many years have passed, and knowledge has multiplied. We are at the time of the end of the age of man and the beginning of the great day of the Lord. We are in a transition. I don't know if this transition will be unnoticed at first by the world's historians, as has happened in other past crucial moments when God was going to do something especially important.

When God was going to begin the Passover, he took the people of Israel out of Egypt. The Egyptians remained with their problems, but few noticed that God was doing something new with his people (who went around in circles in the wilderness for forty years while the unbelieving generation died off and God prepared a new generation to enter the promised land).

It took forty years of preparation in the desert until God caused them to enter into the promised land. Then God made the inhabitants of Jericho tremble.

God marked a time that was not easily noticed by the historians and theologians. This was when Jesus entered the temple as a twelve-year-old boy. His parents were frantic looking for him, but he was astounding the "wise" men (Luke 2:40–52). However, he went back with Mary and Joseph (who didn't seem to understand what was taking place) and remained eighteen more years at home.

This is similar to what has been happening in the church for the last two thousand years. It has been two thousand years with "Mary" and "Joseph," and depending on our attitude, it has either been good for us or not. Jesus increased in wisdom . . . and in grace with God and men. The Lord is looking for a people who are understood before God and before men.

> ⁵ *Then I Daniel looked, and, behold, another two who stood, one on this side of the bank of the river, and the other on that side of the bank of the river.*

Hiddekel[107] is a river of God that means "arrow." In Revelation 6:2, a white horse appears, and the one riding the horse has a bow and is ready to shoot. In Daniel 12:5 there is one on each side with the main thing happening in the middle of the river.

God wants to call us unto holiness, and he wants to "shoot" us with his truth. He wants to take us in his current, and God's true river soon gathers depth so we cannot touch the bottom, and we lose control completely. God brought Daniel to this point. (See Ezekiel 47.)

> ⁶ *And one said to the Man clothed in linens, who was upon the waters of the river, When shall be the end of these wonders?*

This is the end of the terrible fight God has against the natural man: the four winds of heaven against the sea, against the monsters and the beasts, and against the systems of this world. Some, who were our friends, are not our friends anymore.

David, who was part of the army of Israel, killed the giant, and soon everything was in his favor. But after the confusion with jealous Saul, he found himself marching with the Philistines against Israel. What happened? (See 1 Samuel 28 and 29.)

We have lived similar experiences because the things of God center on the attitudes of the heart. When we see things from God's perspective, it turns out some of our enemies are not so big, and some are not as bad as we thought they were, while some of our friends are not as good as we thought they were.

God brings out what is in the heart of each person. In David's army of God that eventually defeated all the enemies of the people of God, mighty men of Gath from the army of the Philistines rallied to David and helped him to deliver Israel. You can read the list of David's mighty men at the end of the second book of Samuel.

---

107 Daniel 10:4

> *⁷ And I heard the Man clothed in linens, who was upon the*
> *waters of the river, who raised his right hand and his left hand*
> *unto heaven, . . .*

This is a similar picture to Revelation 10.

> *⁷ . . . and swore by the living one in the ages that it shall be for*
> *a time, times, and a half; . . .*

This doesn't mean three and a half years because this is the living one in the ages that it shall be for a time, times, and a half. He is the same God that began Passover with the people of Israel, the same God who began the church in Pentecost for these times, and he is the same God who is going to have the day of the Lord. He is going to divide time once and for all, and at the end of the day of the Lord (referred to as a thousand years in Revelation 20), there will be new heavens and a new earth. He is not just a living God for three and a half years; the Living One in the ages is Jesus Christ, and he continues for all time.

The translation leaves something to be desired when it says and a half a time because in the original, it can also mean "the division of time." This means that first the remaining "time" of the Jews still needed to end, followed by the "times" of the Gentiles, and now, the day of the Lord is going to mark the division of time forever.

> *⁷ and when the scattering of the power of the holy people shall*
> *be finished, all these things shall be fulfilled.*

Some people, including close friends, didn't like my translation of this verse. They begged me to change it. At first, one wouldn't think that part of one verse would have such high implications, and if I wanted to avoid conflict, I would gladly change it.

Let's read it again: and when the scattering of the power of the holy people shall be finished, all these things shall be fulfilled.

What is keeping these things from being fulfilled? God must take his "holy people" to the end of their own efforts because as long as we insist on putting our two cents into the things of God, certain prophecies that have to be fulfilled cannot be fulfilled in and through us. That is why God has developed his plan the way it is: so that we desist. This is difficult because each one of us seems to think that we know more than God. So, this has to happen. There are a lot of seemingly good things from which people don't want to desist. They like their plans for spiritual warfare. They prefer to march to who knows where, pray for who knows what, and evangelize the world their way – among other pet personal projects that each person has.

They might say, "I'm going to pay my tithe at a certain a place, and God will give me back one hundred percent of what I gave." Often, many of them were not even investing in God's kingdom; they were investing in an impostor's kingdom. In order to invest in God's kingdom, we would need to be directed by the Holy Spirit. Those who would legalistically follow tithing according to the Old Testament, many times, forget to tithe to the widow, the orphan, the "priest," the "Levite," and also the poor, the stranger, and others. They don't read those verses in the Word. Scripture says that after three years, the tithe that was saved must be taken out and released to celebrate a great feast. (We must remember that the letter of the law kills, but the Spirit gives life.)

> *At the end of three years thou shalt bring forth all the tithe of thine increase the same year and shalt lay it up within thy gates. And the Levite, who has no part nor inheritance with thee, and the stranger and the fatherless and the widow who are within thy gates, shall come and shall eat and be satisfied, that the LORD thy God may bless thee in all the work of thy hands which thou doest. (Deuteronomy 14:28–29)*

> *When thou hast made an end of tithing all the tithes of thy fruits the third year, which is the year of tithing and hast given it unto the Levite, the stranger, the fatherless, and the widow, that they may eat within thy gates and be filled; then thou shalt say before the LORD thy God, I have brought the consecrated things out of my house and also have given them unto the Levite and unto the stranger to the fatherless and to the widow, according to all thy commandments which thou has commanded me; I have not transgressed thy commandments, neither have I forgotten them. (Deuteronomy 26:12–13)*

If we add up all the different types of tithes in the Old Testament, we see it amounted to much more than ten percent. God says those who are led by the Spirit always surpass the law, and those led by the Spirit are not under the law. In the new covenant, the right hand must not know what the left hand does (Matthew 6:3).

> *[8] And I heard, but I did not understand; then I said, O my Lord, what is the fulfillment of these things?*

You may very well find yourself in the same situation regarding these verses. Unless the Lord reveals it to us, it isn't possible for any of us to understand these things.

Daniel heard well. God said the fulfillment couldn't come until the end of the scattering of the power of the holy people. This was terrible. They were expecting another king like David who would overtake the kingdoms of this world by force. Many in the Christian and Catholic Church believe they must control the systems of this world. But God is not after the White House, or the Vatican, or any other symbol of the power of this world. Those powers will all topple. God will do something different with a very different kingdom.

After Daniel asked God questions about some pretty amazing things, he wanted to know about the fulfillment of these things. God gave his reply:

> *⁹ And he said, Go thy way, Daniel, for these words are closed up and sealed until the time of the fulfillment.*

Time, Times, and Division of Time

This man clothed in linens in verses 6 and 7 is no other than the Lord, and Daniel called him "Lord." At the end of Daniel's life, the Lord himself began to give him direct revelation, but he also told Daniel there were some things that needed to remain sealed until the time of the fulfillment. When will this happen? It will be for a time, times, and a half. In Hebrew, this literally means a "time," "times," and the "division of time."

Because of the difference they see before and after this event, most people believe the division of time began when Jesus was born. Thus, our history is divided into before Christ (BC) and after Christ (AD).

Although this is a most important event that changed history forever, it is not the real division of time. A greater time is coming when the stone cut without hands will hit all the empires of this world in their "feet," and all man's schemes will fade away. The kingdom of God will enter with power. In that day, his mountain will not only be the highest mountain; it will be the only mountain. This will truly divide the time.

Prophetically, the word "time" refers to the number of days in the week in representation of the millenniums. Six days, or six thousand years, are prophesied in which man works, but after that comes the day of rest: the seventh day. This corresponds to the seventh millennium, or the day of the Lord. This is a day when no man will be allowed to carry his own burden or do any servile work because everything will be the Lord's. (This is symbolically portrayed in Leviticus 23:23–32).

Our Lord Jesus did most of his miracles on the Sabbath. Why did he choose this day? Why not some other day? Why did they get so angry with him for this? How was it in the creation? Did God make man for the Sabbath, or did he make the Sabbath for man? The Lord resolves all these questions by saying he is Lord of the Sabbath! (Mark 2:27–28).

What was missing when Daniel heard this prophecy? The "time of the law" was yet to be fulfilled, and the "times" of the fifth and sixth days were to come after this. The "last days" are the three last days of the week of which the two "times" represent the two thousand years, which are the "times" of the Gentiles followed by the day of the Lord, the seventh day.

According to this prophecy, "the division of time" comes after "the time of the Jews" (or the remaining time of the law) and after "the times of the Gentiles." If we calculate accurately (because there may be errors in the calendar), we are near the end of the times of the Gentiles and close to the division of time when God will impose his kingdom (see Appendix). The systems of this world will receive a final blow from which they will never recover.

If there is a "time" after the two "times" and after the division of time, or half a time, is this the time of the fulfillment mentioned in Daniel? The time of the fulfillment is when time gets divided. It begins with the day of the Lord, the seventh millennium, the thousand years, which corresponds to the Feast of Tabernacles.[108]

> [10] *Many shall be purified and made white and purged, but the wicked shall get worse; and none of the wicked shall understand, but the wise shall understand.*

Daniel received understanding and wisdom from God, but God also understood him. When Daniel asked for an explanation, God responded immediately and sent Gabriel to explain it to him. Michael, one of the chief princes, apparently spent twenty-one days fighting alongside Gabriel so Daniel could receive the response. Likewise, Gabriel said that from the moment Daniel opened his heart to understand, the response came.

---

108 We know that more than six thousand years (six prophetic days) have gone by since the creation of Adam. However, we don't know exactly how long the world system has been active under the prince of this world (Satan). We do not know exactly when Adam and Eve fell and were banished from the garden of Eden. We know that their sons, Cain and Abel, were born after the fall (outside the garden) and that they came to maturity and Cain killed Abel. We also know that God granted them a replacement son for the line of Abel, named Seth, who was born when Adam was 130 years old and that the line of Christ goes through Seth (see Appendix).

Brethren, if God is opening these words now, it's because we are close to the time of the fulfillment, the thousand years of the last prophetic day, the day of the Lord.[109]

> [10] *Many shall be purified and made white and purged, . . .*

This is through all the injustice and persecution that true Christians have gone through for so long.

> [10] *. . . but the wicked shall get worse; and none of the wicked shall understand, but the wise shall understand.*

The corruption of the natural man will get worse, but those who allow the Lord to sow his life in them will understand. In Spanish, this verse translates this way: "those who are understood shall understand." Those that are understood in heaven and understood here on earth are going to understand. Some of us are beginning to understand.

> [11] *And from the time that the daily sacrifice is taken away until the abomination of desolation, there shall be a thousand two hundred and ninety days.*

Daniel 12 says that 1290 days must be counted from that point, and as previously mentioned, when we count 1290 years from Pope Agatho, we come to AD 1967, to the Six-Day War. Let's review briefly: if the law was given on Mount Sinai about the year 1488 BC, then fifteen hundred years under law would be fulfilled about the year twelve of our present age. Age twelve is when Jesus went to the temple as a boy to confirm his covenant and decided to continue to submit voluntarily to Joseph and Mary, even though he knew that they were an imperfect authority; but God had placed them in his life. From that point, 666 years later (in AD 678), it appears that a man, seated in a temple of marble and stone that he thought was the temple of God, was declared the Vicar of Christ (as God), instead of us being the temple of God and the Lord of heaven sitting on the throne of our life through the Holy Spirit who is the real vicar of Christ.

Even if this was not the exact date, at some point not too far away, they removed the daily sacrifice of a victorious life of praise unto God and began offering unending bloodless sacrifices. This ritual was instituted under the false premise that we all must sin in word, thought, deed, and by omission every day. (Of course, if someone came into victory in

---

109 We must also bear in mind that just as a day is as a thousand years in the eyes of the Lord, a thousand years can also be one day (Psalm 90:4; 2 Peter 3:8).

Christ against all odds, then they could always beatify them after death and make them an object of worship for everyone else!)

Some used the mass, and others used the Holy Communion. Please do not misunderstand; many of us have attended these masses and communions with good intentions, and the Word is very clear. If we are sealed by God, and if we are his, even if we drink "any deadly thing" it will not hurt us (Mark 16:18). If you must go to one of these places, and they feed you something, it will not harm you as long as you're in God's will.

But God has allowed some of us to be there, front row and center, when the cape was removed and all the people fell over backward, and we were the only ones left standing. Whoever has God's seal cannot receive any other mark, so we can go wherever God sends us, and nothing will affect us. The fire didn't affect the three Hebrew boys. We don't have to fear the false fire in these people if we have God's true seal. The person who is not sealed is in danger anywhere that isn't clean.

God's seal comes when we convince him to seal us and separate us. He's even willing to seal those who groan and cry out because of the abominations they see. From the Six-Day War in 1967, the abomination that causes desolation is definitely in the holy place (of the realm of charismatic, ecumenical renewal) and now, in many, if not most of these places, the spirit they say is the Holy Spirit is some other spirit.

> [12] *Blessed is he that waits and comes unto one thousand three hundred and thirty-five days.*

What is going to happen after 1335 (prophetic) days? If we calculate this from the year 678 AD, by the year 2012, we are in it. What is going to happen when the two thousand years are fulfilled if they began from the year AD 12? Is this the end of our present age? Does this lead into a period of transition? We don't know exactly what is going to happen.

Note the word "blessed." This means that whoever is intact and clean when reaching this point will come into the true blessing that God will begin once again: a blessing for his people, a blessed people.

What happened to Daniel was a shadow in comparison to the reality that is now upon us. Jeremiah prophesied that the Babylonian captivity would last seventy years. Daniel interceded, and God sent the answer. Two very powerful angels were mobilized (who were leaders of the heavenly hosts), and Darius gave the order to restore Israel. It took, however, another forty-nine years until the temple and the wall of Jerusalem were rebuilt under Ezra and Nehemiah.

How long will it be before there be a corporate new creation man?

How many years will it take? Isaiah prophesied that an entire nation will be born at once (Isaiah 66:8).

There have been many attempts to make a new man. The Marxist revolutionaries who wanted to make a new society soon realized that without a new man, they couldn't make their new Colombia. They attempt to make a new man, but to no avail because no doctrine, creed, external force, or ideology can change the human heart. If we have been transformed by the power and presence of Christ, we know what a new man is. We know that God can make a new man, and he's doing it.

The new man will inherit all things, not the old man. Entering into the day of the Lord will be similar to when Cyrus gave the order to restore Jerusalem. Some wanted to return. Those who left Babylon with the vessels of God had to go through many dangers. But they began to build. Now it will be without the sound of a hammer or iron tool. This will not be as before because it isn't the old man working by the sweat of his brow; it's the new man by the Spirit of God, in perfect rest from his own efforts, doing God's will. It's the people of Daniel, where God is once again the judge discerning good and evil. God is now going to decide what is good and what is evil. This new kingdom will be built in spite of the dangers and enemies of the people of God. Look at what's going to happen:

> *¹² Blessed is he that waits and comes unto one thousand three hundred and thirty-five days"* [*a year for a day*].
> *¹³ And thou [Daniel] shall go to the end and shalt rest, and thou shalt raise up in thy lot [or in thine inheritance] at the end of the days.*

At the end of how many days? Of 1335 days (a year for a day)? Or at the end of the days of the age of grace? One example where we can see this is Matthew 24. Another is in Revelation:

And I saw an angel come down from heaven, having the key of the bottomless pit and a great chain in his hand (Revelation 20:1). Chaining the devil up is no problem when God gives the order. Just one angel can do it.

And he laid hold on the dragon [notice it doesn't say they laid hold on the dragon], the serpent of old, which is the Devil and Satan and bound him a thousand years and cast him into the bottomless pit (Revelation 20:2–3). What bottomless pit? This sounds remarkably similar to the same jail (Hades, or Sheol, or Abyss) that he used to run before.

> *. . . and shut him up and set a seal upon it, that he should*

deceive the Gentiles no more, until the thousand years should be fulfilled; and after it is necessary that he be loosed a little while. And I saw thrones, and those who sat upon them, and judgment was given unto them; and I saw the souls of those that were beheaded for the witness of Jesus and for the word of God and who had not worshipped the beast neither its image neither had received its mark upon their foreheads or in their hands; and they shall live and reign with Christ the thousand years. (Revelation 20:3–4)

Those who came out from under their own headship are now under the headship of Christ. This would include those such as Daniel.

But the rest of the dead did not live again until the thousand years were finished. This is the first resurrection. Blessed and holy is he that has part in the first resurrection; on such the second death has no authority, but they shall be priests of God and of the Christ and shall reign with him a thousand years. (Revelation 20:5–6)

Daniel is going to take his place. He used to manage everything for two of the world's greatest empires, which, according to God's vision, were cleaner than our present-day governments (of iron and clay mixed). Daniel had run Babylon and oversaw the construction of the some of the wonders of the ancient world. However, none of this is mentioned in the Bible because it isn't Daniel's true inheritance.

God has a blessing, a true blessing, for those who have chosen to live his life instead of their own. This blessing has been found by individuals, not only throughout the age of grace but also throughout the age of the law. God is promising a blessing for all his people who have Jesus Christ as their head.

Jesus Christ will return whenever God the Father decides. Will his people come into the fullness of his blessing and break the curse? Yes. I believe Jesus will return in person according to Luke 24 and other Scriptures.[110]

The list of the heroes in Hebrews 11 indicates that some of them didn't even have a roof. They were persecuted, tortured, and killed, and

---

110 It is very interesting to note that the Lord Jesus himself said that he didn't know when; only the Father knows the day and the hour. There are indications he will return when he finds the fruit he is looking for on earth. This is what the Song of Solomon says. When his clean people are bringing forth the fruit he desires, he will come back (Song of Solomon 6:11–13).

yet they didn't receive the fullness of their inheritance. This inheritance is the true Daniel, which is Christ. He is on the other side of the veil, which means Tabernacles and the holy of holies, and we cannot enter in our old carnal life.

We are to be dead to sin[111] and alive in Christ. This is the message of the Feast of Trumpets. It's the message Daniel heard when he cried out to God for understanding and afflicted his soul (turned his back on his own life and ceased from his own works).[112] He desisted from nourishing his own life, and God sent the answer that same day. Because of this, Cyrus and Darius gave the order to rebuild Jerusalem.

We are now coming to the end of the Feast of Trumpets. How many of us will deny ourselves and desist from our own works and allow the Lord to live his life in us?[113]

I'm going to bring up one more secret to end this chapter. In Daniel's time, only two faithful captains were available in heaven to bring God's reply to Daniel: Gabriel and Michael, who commanded the loyal heavenly hosts because Lucifer had rebelled. Gabriel said that Michael was the only other prince that was in his favor. It is very likely that these are the two cherubim that cover the realm represented by the holy of holies that has a very special anointing (Daniel 9:24).

But now, because of our Lord's work of redemption, he went to the devil's jail and took captivity captive. He cast Satan out of his empire of death.[114] Now he holds the keys of death and of Hades (Revelation 1:18). Therefore, if we are his when we die, we will go directly into the presence of the Lord instead of being locked up in Hades. We are confident, I say,

---

111 Romans 6:2, 11; Ephesians 2:1, 5; 1 Peter 2:24

112 Note that this message applies to every individual as well as to the entire body of Christ.

113 Some would paraphrase this message with the phrase "death to self." This, however, is not exactly biblical (because we may have an old self and a new self). The Scriptural terminology includes being "dead to sin" (dead to all wrong goals or desires) and gives the requirement that if we are to follow Christ, we must "deny our self and take up our cross" (Matthew 16:24). There have been many strange happenings at convents, religious orders, and in Christian communities perpetrated by those who would attempt to extinguish the unique individuality that God has created in each of his children by preaching an extreme (and unscriptural) message of death to self that lends itself to confusion. When we deny our self, take up our cross, and put to death the deeds of the flesh by the Spirit (Romans 8:13) until we are dead to sin, the life of Christ within us will enhance our personality as God perfects each living stone for a very special and unique place in the body of Christ, which is his temple (Ephesians 4:14–16).

114 John 12:31, Hebrews 2:14

and willing rather to be absent from the body and to be present with the Lord (2 Corinthians 5:8).

Paul himself said he had gone to the third heaven (he didn't know if in body or in vision) and heard unspeakable words, which it is not lawful for a man to utter (2 Corinthians 12:4). All I want to say is that now there are many overcomers. There is a great cloud of witnesses of all times[115] who are undoubtedly cheering us on. And the heavenly hosts have the angels, but there is also our Lord Jesus who is above all powers and principalities,[116] for he has ascended far above all the heavens[117] and is seated on the right hand of God[118] with all power and authority with many brothers and sisters who have overcome, beginning with righteous Abel. The number that God needs to set up his righteous government in heaven and in earth is being completed.[119]

The jail of Hades is full; the devils are being defeated. The Lord is upon the river of God's purposes with a witness on each side, which represent his true body (some are in heaven and some on earth). He shall soon appear on a white horse,[120] and the armies of heaven shall follow him. Many more in heaven favor him now than when this happened with Daniel. May he open our eyes![121]

Let us pray:

Lord, we give you thanks. We ask you, Lord, that our desire might not be to only know a few things. We give you thanks for the understanding and the revelation that you have given us. But allow us, Lord, to be understood before your throne and before those who are lost in the world around us. Amen.

---

115 Hebrews 12:1
116 Colossians 2:15
117 Ephesians 4:10
118 Hebrews 10:12
119 Revelation 6:11; 20:4–6
120 Revelation 19:11–14
121 See 2 Kings 6:17

Part II

Prophecies
of David, Haggai, Zephaniah, and Zachariah

The Morning Star and a Prophecy of David

Death and Resurrection of Jesus

Matthew 27

⁵⁰ But Jesus, when he had cried again with a loud voice, gave up the spirit.

⁵¹ And, behold, the veil of the temple was rent in two from the top to the bottom; and the earth did quake, and the rocks rent;

⁵² and the graves were opened; and many bodies of the saints who slept arose

⁵³ and came out of the graves after his resurrection and went into the holy city and appeared unto many.

The Lord's death removed the separation that existed between the holy place and the holy of holies. Remember, behind the veil within the holy of holies was the ark of the testimony of the presence of God. Two cherubim and the seat of reconciliation were on top of the ark, from where God spoke. The high priest was only allowed to enter once a year, and he had to be clean, having done everything God's way. Any strange person or high priest who was not clean and went in could pay with their life. He had to come in with the blood. This is where the priest would listen to God: one high priest for all the people.

The Lord Jesus's mission was to break this division so we could once again have access to the presence of God the Father. This is what Adam and Eve lost when they were excluded from the garden and the cherubim were placed at the entrance of Eden with a flaming sword. The cherubim were embroidered on the veil that separated the holy place from the holy of holies. This veil was torn in two, from the top to the bottom, when Jesus died. According to Romans 5:10, the death of Jesus reconciles us with God, but it also says we shall be saved by his life.

His death opens the way for us once again, but if we are going to enter in, it has to be in his life, and not in our own. This requires being born again from above.[122] That's why the high priest had to come in with blood; this is why there was a scapegoat and all the other symbols. But the Lord Jesus came to convert the symbols into reality for us. Unfortunately, the human priests didn't take long in sewing the veil up again, in paying false witnesses to say that it was not the angel of the Lord who removed the stone from the empty tomb and other conspiracy stories.

The resurrection of Jesus was different from anything that ever happened before. When Lazarus was resurrected, he appeared bound hand and foot with grave clothes. But no one had to unbind the Lord Jesus when he resurrected.

The Lord had been bound in sheets with the same rituals, but the angel of the Lord removed the stone. Even though the linen clothes were there, the Lord was not. Matthew says that when Jesus was resurrected, some of the people who were closest to him doubted when they saw him.

They doubted because he was transformed. It's clear in 1 Corinthians 15:35–50 that it is one body that is sown and another that is raised up. The bodies of flesh and blood that we have on earth are corruptible; after the resurrection, Jesus remains incorruptible.

In Matthew 28:7, the angel told the women to go and tell the disciples the Lord Jesus was risen from the dead. But according to John 20:14–16, Mary Magdalene had an encounter with the Lord and didn't recognize him until he called her name.

Some saw him and only doubted until he spoke because they recognized his voice. The Lord Jesus says his sheep follow his voice and don't get confused or follow a stranger's voice (John 10:27). He was talking about mature sheep; it isn't the word used for lambs.

Further in the Scriptures when they encounter the Lord Jesus, he doesn't say, "Go and tell my disciples…" Look at what he says in Matthew 28:10: Then Jesus said unto them, Be not afraid; go tell my brothers that they may go into Galilee, and there they shall see me (emphasis added). Jumping ahead to verse 16 it says, Then the eleven disciples went away into Galilee, into the mountain where Jesus had appointed them.

What does this mean? First, the Lord Jesus had called them to be disciples; then he had called them apostles. Near the end of his ministry in the Gospel of John, Jesus said they were his friends if they did whatever he commanded them and that as his friends, he had made all things that he had heard from his father known unto them (John 15:13–15).

Now, after the resurrection, the Lord called them his brothers.

---

122 John 3:3, 5; 1 Peter 1:23

Because of Jesus's death and resurrection, we can participate directly in his nature (as members of his own family), to follow him and enter the kingdom of heaven like children, in humility. To participate in the divine nature that Peter speaks of in 2 Peter 1:4, we must be willing to die to the old man (to selfishness), die to sin, die to pride, and die to our arrogance.

Jesus overcame the grave, but only after he gave up his life first. The "morning star" refers to the Lord Jesus and to what he did, a link first found in Psalm 22, which is dedicated to the Overcomer. There has been some modern confusion as to the value of the original word (some have translated it as referring to the chief of the choir or the head of the musicians). In the translations of the early Reformation this is not the case. David dedicated this Psalm to the Overcomer along with another fifty-four Psalms (fifty-five total).

Psalm 22

To the Overcomer upon Aijeleth Shahar [the morning star], A Psalm of David.

It begins with the last words that the Lord spoke while he was on the cross.

> [1] *My God, my God, why hast thou forsaken me? why art thou*
> *so far from helping me and from the words of my cry?*

The Lord Jesus quoted Psalm 22 when Scripture says, he gave up the spirit. Jesus wasn't killed. The Jews didn't kill him and neither did the Romans. They nailed him to the cross, and they had every intention of killing him, but Scripture says he laid down his life for us.[123] He not only laid down his life, but he had the power to take it again.[124]

Psalm 22 goes on with a description of his death on a cross and later says:

> [12] *Many bulls have compassed me: . . .*

These are religious men who operate according to the flesh.

> [12] *. . . strong bulls of Bashan [religious bulls] have beset me*
> *round about.*

---

123 In this we have known the charity of God because he laid down his life for us; we also ought to lay down our lives for the brethren. (1 John 3:16)

124 Therefore does my Father love me, because I lay down my soul that I might take it again. No man takes it from me, but I lay it down of myself. I have power to lay it down, and I have power to take it again. This commandment I have received of my Father. (John 10:17–18)

The sons of Ephraim fattened their animals at Bashan. They had sought out their inheritance before crossing the Jordan River, which symbolizes death. Many in today's churches want their inheritance on this side of death, on this side of burying the old man. And God allows this to a point.

In Numbers 32, two and a half tribes of Israel told Moses, in effect, when he got mad at them, "We're going to go fight for our brothers, and then we'll go back." But they wanted to fatten their cattle (cater to their flesh), and their offspring ended up worshipping Baal with their fat bulls.

God allows those who seek to have their flocks on "this side of the Jordan" to do so. All of them say they will fight so the kingdom of God comes, but this can get corrupted in practice. By the time the Lord came in person, this state of affairs was so bad, they failed to recognize him; they rebelled against him, surrounded him, and crucified him.

> *[14] I am poured out like water, and all my bones are out of joint: my heart is like wax; it is melted in the midst of my bowels.*
> *[15] My strength is dried up like a potsherd; and my tongue cleaves to my jaws; and thou hast brought me into the dust of death.*
> *[16] For dogs have compassed me: the assembly of the wicked have inclosed me: they pierced my hands and my feet.*

David wrote all this approximately one thousand years before Christ.

> *[17] I may count all my bones: they look and stare upon me.*
> *[18] They part my garments among them and cast lots upon my vesture.*
> *[19] But be not thou far from me, O LORD: O my strength, haste thee to help me.*
> *[20] Deliver my soul from the sword; my life from the power of the dog.*
> *[21] Save me from the lion's mouth and from the horns of the unicorns.*

When the body of Jesus was sealed in the tomb, the devil thought he would be able to imprison his soul in the Sheol of death. This is similar to what symbolically happened to Daniel. When Daniel was thrown in the lions' den, they placed a stone and sealed it. However, the one who didn't sleep that night was King Darius.

It didn't go well for those who sent Daniel to the lions' den. The next morning, when the king took Daniel out, he put them in instead. The devil thought he could trap the Lord Jesus in death, and Scripture implies that the devil will go through the same thing; it seems the devil will be incarnated in a human form, and he will die, and death will imprison him for a thousand years (Revelation 20:1–3). Very interesting.

²² *I will declare thy name unto my brethren; . . .*

When Jesus came out in resurrection, he said, Go tell my brothers (Matthew 28:10). His natural brothers entered after Pentecost. But it's clear that the brothers he was talking about here were his eleven remaining disciples.

According to the Gospel of John, he came and breathed on them and told them to receive the Holy Spirit (John 20:22). The breath (or Spirit) of Jesus grew and got more and more intense until the day of Pentecost when the Holy Spirit saturated all those who were together an in one accord.

True Baptism

It's important to understand how God works: first, one can receive a touch of God through someone who has God's Spirit; second, God will anoint those who convince him that they desire to be under his government and direction with his Holy Spirit so that we may become his witnesses. And we are his witnesses of these things, so is also the Holy Spirit, whom God has given to those that persuade him (Acts 5:32).

Matthew 28 ends like this: Go ye therefore and teach all nations, baptizing them in [Greek, into] the name of the Father and of the Son and of the Holy Spirit (v. 19).

Baptizing into the name of the Father, the Son, and the Holy Spirit is the same as baptizing into the Holy Spirit. God's name refers to his nature, and the Father, the Son, and the Holy Spirit all have the same nature. It's the same as baptizing into the name of Jesus because Jesus also has that same nature. The Lord Jesus has God's nature; however, he came in Adam's flesh and likeness but with God's life inside, and he overcame. He is one hundred percent man, but he is also one hundred percent God, and he is the only mediator between God and men.[125]

After the resurrection, the Lord Jesus told his disciples that he has all the power, all the authority in the heavens and the earth, because he is seated at the right hand of his Father. The right hand symbolizes power

---

125 For there is only one God and likewise only one mediator between God and men, the man Christ Jesus. (1 Timothy 2:5)

and authority (Matthew 28:18). What is he doing with that power now? He's mediating a new covenant to place his life in us[126] to enable us to follow him, and he is the Way for fallen humanity to return to God the Father. He will clean us from all that is corruptible, by the Holy Spirit. Thus, as Scripture says, when we see him, we shall be like him.[127]

Go ye therefore and teach all nations, . . . The nations refer to the Gentiles, the unconverted, those who do not have circumcised hearts. Because all the kingdoms of this world will eventually collapse, and the Lord commands us to teach the unconverted.

. . . baptizing them . . . Notice it doesn't say baptizing them in water like John the Baptist did. There has been a misunderstanding for nearly two thousand years. The symbol of the water is good, but the symbol is not reality. The symbol is a beautiful example of dying to the old man and resurrecting in the novelty of new life. In the early church, those who responded to the gospel with water baptism received the Holy Spirit. And the only one who can baptize us into the Holy Spirit and fire is Jesus (Matthew 3:11).

But sometimes water baptisms can take place without Jesus being involved. Then people are not baptized into the name of the Father, the Son, and the Holy Spirit. They are not submerged into God's nature. Then the Holy Spirit doesn't start to flow from the depths of their being.

Everyone understood the wonders of God in their own language on the day of Pentecost. That was how three thousand people were converted the first day (Acts 2). It's likely that the early Jewish believers were baptized in water, but they were also baptized into the Holy Spirit.

In that time, many Jewish customs were being practiced. Not only were they baptizing in water, they were also killing lambs and goats and bullocks in the temple. In the council of Jerusalem described in Acts 15, they told the Gentile believers to keep themselves from pollution of idols, from fornication, from things strangled, and from blood. Notice they didn't mention getting baptized in water, paying tithes, or keeping the Sabbath day. Later, Paul said he didn't come to baptize but to preach

---

126 As all things that pertain to life and to godliness are given us of his divine power, through the knowledge of him that has called us by his glory and virtue, whereby are given unto us exceeding great and precious promises, that by these ye might be made participants of the divine nature, having fled the corruption that is in the world through lust. (2 Peter 1:3–4)

127 Beloved, now we are the sons of God, and it is not yet made manifest what we shall be; but we know that if he shall appear, we shall be like him; for we shall see him as he is. (1 John 3:2)

Christ.[128] Men have erred regarding rituals and have lost the reality behind the rituals in many cases.

The true baptism into the name of the Father, the Son, and the Holy Spirit cannot be done with water (because water is only a symbol). Remember that Scripture says there is only one baptism (Ephesians 4:5) The one who does this is the Lord Jesus, and he can work through anyone he chooses.

In the first century, the apostles laid their hands on people who were being baptized into the name of Jesus so they would receive the Holy Spirit. Then, when a canny businessman named Simon (who used to practice magic) realized people could receive the Holy Spirit by the laying on of hands by the apostles, he wanted to buy this power with money. Over the centuries, those who have desired to buy position and power in the church have been described with the word "simony," in reference to this Simon (Acts 8:9–24).

Returning to Psalm 22:

22 I will declare thy name unto my brethren; in the midst of the congregation I will praise thee.

Declaring the name of the Lord is to declare his nature. It's possible to do this with the baptism of the Holy Spirit and fire. Once the Lord had spoken to his brethren (his disciples) as they congregated, as he sent them out in the name of his Father, he breathed on them and said, receive ye the Holy Spirit (John 20:22). But, immediately prior to his ascension, the first assignment he gave them was to return to Jerusalem until they received power from on high (Luke 24:49).

The original Greek word, dunamis, is not an exact translation of our English word, power; this word translated into Old Spanish is potencia. What is the difference between potencia and power? The word potencia is used in aviation. The potencia of an airplane is the crankcase that encloses the crankshaft that is bolted to the propeller. This is where the crude power of the explosion of the gas is harnessed and controlled. The power that is administered by the propeller is under perfect control by the pilot, who can modify it according to the need by use of the throttle. It isn't an unbridled power.

The power God placed in his disciples is the same power he has placed in many throughout the age of grace. It isn't God's perfect will for

---

128 For Christ sent me not to baptize, but to preach the gospel, not with wisdom of
   words, lest the cross of Christ should be made void. (1 Corinthians 1:17)

people to desperately seek to improve their own situation in this corrupt world by using God's gifts and provisions for personal gain. Therefore, the anointing of the Holy Spirit is also a test. Jesus promised that those who are faithful with little will receive more, and those who are unfaithful will eventually lose what little they have been given.

The power the Lord Jesus manifested was capable of everything, but he was always subject to the will of his Father.

The Lord Jesus didn't want to drink that last cup; he didn't want his hands and feet to be nailed to the cross. He said that if he chose, he could request more than twelve legions of angels to rescue him. But having all that power (potencia), he accepted the will of his Father in heaven and followed a path no one wanted to follow (this path is called the way of the cross).

Scripture says a few women watched from afar (Mark 15:40; Matthew 27:55). Matthew observed and recorded what he saw (but he apparently was even farther away). John, however, stood under the cross in the place of maximum danger.

Before the Lord Jesus gave up the Spirit, he told John to take care of Mary (John 19:25–30). The Lord's true witnesses are willing to give their lives for him with no regard for themselves. It doesn't matter if you are killed or not; what matters is that your heart is willing.

Revelation says John was a faithful witness;[129] the word "witness" is the same word used for "martyr." He was probably the only witness (faithful martyr) among the original apostles who, according to tradition, died of natural causes.

> [22] *I will declare thy name unto my brethren . . .*

God wants to place his nature in us, and he does this through the baptism of the Holy Spirit and fire, which is the same as being baptized into the name of the Father, the Son, and the Holy Spirit. John the Baptist said, I indeed baptize you in water unto repentance, but he that comes after me is mightier than I, whose shoes I am not worthy to bear; he shall baptize you in [Greek, into] the Holy Spirit and fire (Matthew 3:11).

The Lord Jesus left his apostles (sent ones) on earth, and he still has some of his sent ones[130] here as a vital part of the body of Christ to con-

---

129　Revelation 1:5

130　Today many use the term "missionaries" instead of apostles. True missionaries, or apostles, are sent by God. Today there can be confusion as to who has actually sent out a given missionary. Was it God? Or was it a human institution, denomination, or self-proclaimed authority?

tinue fulfilling the mandate of teaching and baptizing into the name of the Father, the Son, and the Holy Spirit. This is not a ritual. The apostles would lay their hands on a person, and then people would notice the evidence of the Holy Spirit in that person.

The baptism in the Holy Spirit is not a Babylon- or Egypt-style brick factory where everyone gets passed through the pre-baptismal course or the "life in the Spirit" course. It's clear in Acts 5:32 that God gives his Holy Spirit to those who persuade him. Other translations say, "to those who obey him." But that is not entirely correct because first of all, it isn't the word used in the original, and second, we cannot fully obey God without the Holy Spirit.[131]

The word "persuade" relates to the root word "to have faith." The purpose of our faith is to persuade God that we desire to submit to him and depend on him until his faith operates in us. We can persuade him, but then he will come in and convince us. He comes in like fire to do away with everything corruptible in our lives so we can know the Father. The fire of correction is revealed later as the fire of God, the Father's love for us as his legitimate sons who receive his correction and his blessing.

> *23 Ye that fear the LORD, praise him; all ye the seed of Jacob, glorify him; and fear him, all ye the seed of Israel.*

Who is Jacob? Jacob is an "Israel" who has not been completely converted but is in the process of conversion. Israel is God's name (or nature) placed into Jacob. This happened at a time of extreme crisis when Jacob and his entire family were about to be destroyed by an enraged Esau who was on his way to meet them with four hundred men (Genesis 32).

> *24 For he has not despised nor abhorred the affliction of the poor in spirit; neither has he hid his face from him, but when he cried unto him, he heard.*

I believe the Lord Jesus continued reciting (and living the reality of) Psalm 22 but that the writers of the Gospels were only able to hear the first phrase because it was what he said right before he gave up the Spirit. Nonetheless, he entered the devil's jail, or empire of death (Hebrews 2:14–15) in the underworld of Hades, broke the jail, and came out with the keys of death and Hades. He cast the devil out of the underworld (John 12:31), led captivity captive, and ascended on high with all that were his (Ephesians 4:7–10). He was now twice the owner of us and of

---

131 And we are his witnesses of these things, and so is also the Holy Spirit, whom God has given to those that persuade him. (Acts 5:32)

all creation because he created everything from the beginning and now because he purchased us with his own blood (Psalm 68:18; 24:1; 1 Corinthians 10:26; 1 Peter 3:18–22; Revelation 5).

> 25 *My praise shall be of thee in the great congregation; I will pay my vows before those that fear him.*

Could it be that the Lord Jesus preached the rest of the psalm, which he started to recite as he died, to the multitude of imprisoned souls who were his, like Abraham, Isaac, and Jacob who were awaiting redemption? It appears that he also preached to the disobedient.[132] Soon, everyone saw people who had died walking the streets of Jerusalem. Rocks rent, graves opened, and the earth shook with his death (Matthew 27:51–54). The Lord remained approximately forty days on the earth before he ascended (Acts 1:3). The religious people paid the soldiers a lot of money so they wouldn't tell any of it. And Scripture says the love of money is the root of all evil (1 Timothy 6:10).

> 26 *The poor shall eat and be satisfied: those that seek him shall praise the LORD; your heart shall live for ever.*

He was telling this to his own.

> 27 *All the ends of the earth shall remember and turn unto the LORD; . . .*

The Lord Jesus left that place with all authority.

> 27 *. . . and all the families of the Gentiles shall worship before thee.*

Revelation 5 says a sealed scroll had been written on, within and without, but no one was found worthy to open it until the Lamb who was slain was found worthy. Now, Jesus is beginning to open the seals, and those seals relate to ownership over us and the earth. God's plan is not for us to remain in the old Adam, full of corruption, saying we have to sin by word, thought, deed, and omission every day, and the only thing we can do is cry out, "I'm guilty; it's all my fault."

The Lord came to abolish sin and guilt to make us free. Once we have

---

132 For the Christ also has once suffered for sins, the just for the unjust, that he might bring us to God, being put to death in the flesh, but made alive in spirit, in which he also went and preached unto the imprisoned spirits, which in the time past were disobedient, when once the patience of God waited in the days of Noah, while the ark was being made ready, wherein few, that is, eight souls were saved by water. (1 Peter 3:18–20)

that freedom, we can choose whether or not we will use the gifts of the Spirit of God under the control and discipline of our heavenly Father, or if we will go wildly after our own personal benefit.

Judas was the first of the false apostles, but the New Testament mentions many more. And after closing the New Testament, who knows how many false apostles have come!

> *28 For the kingdom is the LORD'S, and he shall have dominion over the Gentiles.*
> *29 All those that are fat upon the earth shall eat and worship; all those that go down to the dust shall bow before him; and no one can keep his own soul alive.*

The only one who can revive the soul is the Lord. Not only is the Lord Jesus a living soul, but he is also a life-giving Spirit (1 Corinthians 15:45).

> *30 A seed shall serve him; it shall be accounted to the Lord for a generation.*

The generation of Christ is active today: the generation of the brethren of our Lord Jesus Christ, the generation of the body of Christ, the generation of the morning star.[133]

> *31 They shall come and shall declare his righteousness unto a people that shall be born, that he has done this.*

Immediately before he died, Jesus said, It is finished. The truth of this finished work of redemption should be applied and effectuated in each believer by faith. It is by grace and faith (Ephesians 2:8).

Grace is the undeserved power of God to convert us, to transform us. But faith relates to our dependence on him. (The faith of Jesus relates to his total dependence on his Father.) Faith alludes to convincing him we want to depend on him so he will place the fire of his Spirit in us, thereby baptizing us into the name of the Father, the Son, and the Holy Spirit.

His faith can come into us and change our desires. After our desires are pure and righteous, he can grant us the desires of our heart, which will also be the desires of his heart. These desires will be the same as the desires of the heart of our heavenly Father. This is the work of the Holy Spirit.

In the book of Numbers, a false prophet named Balaam said a few great truths. This prophet was false, but not because his prophecies were

---

133 This is also known as the forty-second generation, according to Matthew 1:17.

false. He had committed to saying only what God told him. Balaam was false because his heart was false;[134] he was seeking money and his own personal benefit with the gift that God had given him. Nonetheless, look at what Balaam said:

> *I shall see him, but not now; I shall behold him, but not near by; there shall come a Star out of Jacob, and a Sceptre shall rise out of Israel and shall smite the corners of Moab and destroy all the sons of Seth. (Numbers 24:17)*

He announced judgment, and the prophet himself was destroyed afterwards in the battle (Joshua 13:22). "Moab" means "of his own father." He was referring to those who do not want to accept the discipline of the heavenly Father, those who have their own (spiritual) father.

The part about the sons of Seth is more serious. This comes from Genesis 5. Scripture begins with Adam and ends with Christ because the generation of the body of Christ (forty-second from Abraham) comes after the generation of Jesus (forty-first), and there are no more generations in the Bible from that point on (see Matthew 1:1–17).

> *This is the book of the descendants of Adam. In the day that God created man, he made him in the likeness of God; male and female created he them and blessed them and called their name Man, in the day when they were created. And Adam lived one hundred and thirty years and begat a son in his own likeness, after his image, and called his name Seth. (Genesis 5:1–3)*

According to Scripture (and according to his flesh), the Lord Jesus Christ came from the line of Seth. But we just saw that Numbers 24:17 says there shall come a Star out of Jacob, and a Sceptre shall rise out of Israel and shall smite the corners of Moab and destroy all the sons of Seth. The first chapter of Matthew, containing the genealogy of the Lord Jesus, ends saying: Jacob begat Joseph the husband of Mary,[135] of whom was born Jesus, who is called Christ (Matthew 1:16).

We must bear in mind that "Christ" is now made of many members of which the head of this body of Christ is the Lord Jesus. Scripture says the Lord Jesus was born because the Holy Spirit came upon Mary before she and Joseph had an intimate relationship. However, according to the

---

134 2 Peter 2:12–16; Revelation 2:14

135 Note that according to Scripture husband and wife are one flesh (Genesis 2:24; Matthew 19:5).

genealogy of Jesus, Joseph was the husband of Mary,[136] and he appears in the place God gave him because God the Father gave him the responsibility of raising his Son. So, he placed Joseph in the genealogy.

In reality, Jesus came to destroy the line of Seth; he came to defeat the old, corrupt man in Adam (by crucifying the flesh) to open a plan of salvation in the generation of Christ. Therefore, the end of Psalm 22 says, A seed shall serve him; it shall be accounted to the Lord for a generation (v. 30). Not Adam's seed; Adam's seed will end.

The natural man born of Adam will not live forever because eternal life is only found in the Lord Jesus Christ. It's a lie from the devil to think everyone is going to live forever. It isn't true that some live forever with the devil and others live forever with God. Scripture says, the soul that sins, it shall die (Ezekiel 18:4, 20). The second death in the lake of fire is eternal death (Revelation 20:12–15; 21:8).

According to Scripture, the first death doesn't kill the soul. The soul is destroyed only in the second death, which is the lake of fire (see Matthew 10:28). No one is presently in the lake of fire (that is the ultimate hell), not even the devil or his fallen angels.

He will first spend a thousand years in what used to be his own jail (in the abyss or bottomless pit also known as Hades) where he had imprisoned the souls of the dead until Jesus cast him out of the underworld and took possession of the keys to death and Hades.

> [And] *when the thousand years are expired, Satan shall be loosed from his prison and shall go out to deceive the Gentiles which are upon the four corners of the earth, Gog and Magog, to gather them together to battle; the number of whom is as the sand of the sea. And they went up on the breadth of the earth and compassed the camp of the saints about and the beloved city; and fire came down from God out of heaven and devoured them. And the devil that deceived them was cast into the lake of fire and brimstone, where the beast and the false prophet are, and they shall be tormented day and night for ever and ever. (Revelation 20:7–10)*

This is eternal death, and the torment goes on for ever and ever.

Those who enter into eternal life are those who have produced good fruit. This is only possible if God has worked in and through us. Scripture

---

136 In other words, Joseph and Mary (after the birth of Jesus) as husband and wife became one flesh (Genesis 2:24; Mark 10:7–8). This is the legal basis upon which Joseph is in the genealogy of Jesus.

says the tree that does not produce good fruit will be cut off. The tree that will be cut off is Adam's tree, Seth's tree. The tree that gives good fruit is the tree of Christ. After his first coming, the incredulous branches were cut off, but the believing Gentiles were inserted along with the remnant of believing Jews that remained in the good olive tree of Christ.

To be unbelieving and to be disobedient are the same thing. If you believe in the doctor, you will take the medicine and do what the doctor says. You receive no benefit to believe that the doctor is a doctor with all qualifications and degrees if you do not obey him. The apostle John observed the final judgment: whosoever was not found written in the book of life was cast into the lake of fire (Revelation 20:15).

The Morning Star

> [But] *the path of the just is as the light of the morning star, that shines more and more until the day is perfect. (Proverbs 4:18)*

Before the day of the Lord and the Sun of righteousness is born (Malachi 4:2), the morning star will rise in our hearts if we respond to the gospel.

> [We] *have also the most sure word of the prophets, unto which ye do well that ye take heed, as unto a light that shines in a dark place, until the day dawns and the morning star arises in your hearts. (2 Peter 1:19)*

The wise men that came to worship the baby Jesus followed a special star. The Bible says they were wise, they followed the light of the star, and the light led them to baby Jesus. It doesn't mention any missionaries or apostles arriving in their land first; they searched for the light and found the Savior.

Scripture says we should not condemn or judge. We don't know what God has done in many instances. Paul said that in the times of ignorance, God overlooked many things, but now he has sent his Son and is calling all men everywhere to repentance (Acts 17:30).

In the midst of many promises to the overcomer in Revelation 2, verse 28 says: And I will give him the morning star.

What is this morning star? First Corinthians 15:46 says the spiritual is not first, but the natural; the Lord can teach us many lessons using the natural realm around us. Paul even says in Romans 1 that those who are in paganism without God are without excuse because observing creation makes it obvious there is a Creator.[137]

---

137 Because that which is known of God is manifest to them; for God has showed it

Man is not evolving toward a superhuman race, as some people say; man didn't evolve as a monkey and is not on his way to becoming superman. Man came from a creation – which, prior to the fall, God said was very good – and is heading the opposite direction, evolving toward becoming a beast.

Scripture calls an out-of-control man without God a beast. That is the reality of the situation. Man thinks he is refining his form of governing, and God predicted all the way back in the book of Daniel that the present governments would be more degenerate and corrupt than the ones that existed millennia ago. Instead of being compared with gold or silver or even brass, the feet of the image that God revealed to Daniel were made of iron and baked clay which broke into pieces when smote with the stone cut without hands (Daniel 2:31-45).

Cancer and genetic problems seem to be on the rise. The human race is declining, but the generation of Christ is going from glory to glory toward perfection. And in God's vocabulary, "perfection" implies a seed that can reproduce life. The same word is also translated as "maturity."

According to the Bible, many people have demonstrated perfect hearts. Job is described as perfect before God; so was Daniel and also Joseph in Egypt. David had a perfect heart toward God, etc.

But some say, "Joseph must have failed in something; Scripture says that when that great sum of wheat was stored, Joseph lost count because it didn't have a number, so how could Joseph be perfect? He didn't even know how much wheat he had stored up during the time of abundance."

And others say, "David got into a terrible problem with Bathsheba and Uriah." People who think this way have not read the Chronicles of God very well. David's sin doesn't come up because God forgave, washed, and cleaned it. David stands firm in the life of Christ, not in the life of David. Saul's mistakes are recorded in the Chronicles of God, but not David's. The Holy Spirit left Saul who didn't even realize when the Spirit of God left him. David cried out to God in repentance, and God didn't take the Holy Spirit from him.[138] The process of restoration was very costly; he lost four sons, and blood never left his house (someone was always getting killed). David even had to flee from the throne for a

---

unto them. For the invisible things of him, his eternal power and divinity, are clearly understood by the creation of the world and by the things that are made so that there is no excuse; because having known God, they did not glorify him as God, neither were thankful, but became vain in their imaginations, and their foolish heart was darkened. (Romans 1:19–21)

138 Psalm 51

while, but God purified and restored him and closed his life in victory.

This is the victory God has for all of us, depending on our attitude – not on the circumstances, but our response to them. If we convince God we want to be clean and under his government, that we desire to feed exclusively on what he says, he can cause us to overcome. That is his specialty.

Kidnapped for the Lord

In 1983, I thought God might give me a great reward because I was making many sacrifices as a missionary for him. I went to the jungles and mountains and did what I could for God. A few things worried me: tests would come and many of the so-called works we did for God didn't remain firm.

The narcotics temptation came, and most who were supposedly converted went to cultivate drugs. Upon the heels of this, the guerrillas came, and most Christians fled. The large missions organizations eventually removed virtually all of their foreign missionaries from eastern Colombia. Many pastors were killed and their church buildings burned down or turned into community centers. I asked God to send the gospel to the guerrillas. And one fine day, after six months of praying almost every day with great intensity, they kidnapped me. I reacted, and I fought to escape, but they tied me up in the jungle.

After thirty-seven or thirty-eight days of being stuck in this adventure, something happened to me. I had not seen the sun or the moon or the stars for a long time because we were under tall, thick triple canopy jungle that covered the entire sky. I slept in a hammock the guerrillas had hung for me with a mosquito net on top and a big black tarp over that for protection from the rain.

Under these conditions, I received a revelation from heaven. It had been raining while I slept when suddenly a bright light woke me up. I thought one of the guerrillas was shining a flashlight directly into my eyes. I was mistaken. The light was the morning star, and it was unlike any star I had ever seen.

Under those immensely thick trees, there was a little hole. And through that hole, at precisely 3:00 a.m., exactly on the day that (if I am not wrong) was the beginning of Feast of Tabernacles that year, the star shone on me. Maybe because I had not seen the sun, moon, or stars for so long, but the star looked like it was one fourth of the size of the moon. It was a focused light, like an immense white laser that passed by and penetrated the mosquito net, which was made of a material that caused the light to be focused into distinct rays. This woke me like an electric shock.

I asked the guard for the time, and he said it was three in the morning. I was restless and thinking, and I said, "No, look again, and tell me exactly what time it is."

He said, "It's 3:00 a.m." I told him I had to get up. He handed me my shoes. I was tied and without shoes to keep me from escaping because they thought I was extremely dangerous. I got up while watching the star, and when I did, I bumped my head on the black plastic hung over the top of the hammock. This contained several gallons of water which poured on top of my head. My shower at three in the morning made the guerrilla laugh.

I stood looking at the star until it disappeared from the little hole within the trees. The guard told me I had to go back to bed. I lay back down again and was almost asleep when bam! the star shined on my face again.

I asked the guerilla again for the time, and he said it was four in the morning. I told him I needed to know exactly what time it was. He responded that it was 4:00 a.m.

I told him I needed to get up again, and he handed me my shoes. I got up, and then splash! I bumped my head once again against the black plastic and got drenched with water. I had goose bumps all over because I had emptied that plastic and had made sure no water remained, and it had not been raining.

I contemplated that beautiful star. It was fascinating. Nothing else could be seen. The star was huge, and I observed it through another hole that was higher up than the first time I had seen it. There were two holes, and everything else was completely covered. Everything lined up for the morning star to shine on my face at exactly three and four in the morning.

I looked at the little hole beneath where I had seen the star at three in the morning (an hour before), and there was another little red star shining through that was following the first star.

I began to weep right there, and the guerrilla didn't understand why. He was concerned and kept trying to reassure me. I kept looking until dawn, and the sun eventually came out. It passed through the same two holes. The moon had passed through the same two holes also. Everything that day happened in that same plane.

For a time, I thought maybe it had been something special that only

I had seen. But after I was released from the guerrilla camp, I bought a Japanese watch. It was a Seiko that came out in a unique edition. It showed the orbits of the planets. The date could be switched to any time of any year and show where the planets had been relative to the sun and the earth and one another.

I put the date of when these events happened to me, and the planets all lined up. I switched the watch through all the years, two hundred years back and two hundred years forward (which was the full time span that the watch would give), and they never lined up like that again.

I went to the Smithsonian Institute in Washington where they have a record of all the celestial events that happen. It turned out that there was an event where the planets lined up, and the earth got very close to Venus.

I learned that when the planets lined up, not only was Venus lined up with the Earth, but Mars also came after the other one. The orbit of all of them made them look very close and near the earth. On top of that, on the date of my experience, we were exactly in equilibrium on the earth between the inclination that it makes in winter and summer. We were in the fall equinox.

The people at the Smithsonian said the last time that exactly this happened was perhaps in the time of King David. Many people had gone to see the event, which could best be seen two degrees north of the Equator. That was approximately where I was during my time of the kidnapping.

The Sign of the Morning Star

As it turned out, when I left the day I was kidnapped, I had taken the wrong weapon with me; I had left the Bible at home and had taken the five-shot .38 revolver instead. After thirty-eight days, the Bible arrived at the camp because the guerrillas had begun to negotiate with my family, and so my mother was able to send me a Bible. They had taken the gun away from me on the first day of captivity. The morning after I received the Bible, I opened it as the day dawned. I didn't feel like an overcomer, but I asked the Lord to convert me into an overcomer because I knew that God promised the morning star to the overcomers. So, I opened my new Bible for the first time, precisely here in Revelation 22, and I began reading the following verses: I, Jesus, have sent my angel to testify unto you these things in the churches. I AM the root and the offspring of David and the bright and morning star (v. 16).

He is the bright star, the Star, not the stars. He is the star the wise men followed; he is the star that will come from Jacob; and he is the morning star.

And the Spirit and the bride say, Come. And let him that hears say, Come. And let him that is thirsty come; and whosoever will, let him take of the water of life freely (v. 17). God wanted to show me something, and he poured water on my head twice that same morning so I didn't get it wrong.

God is going to do something completely new. The day of the Lord is coming. It will be a great day for many, but a terrible day for others. The stars (of those using God-given gifts for personal gain) will fall, the sun (of the prosperity of this world) will darken, and the moon (of religion without a personal relationship with Jesus Christ) will turn into blood (Matthew 24:29; Mark 13:25; Joel 2:31; Acts 2:20; Revelation 6:12), but whosoever shall call on the name of the LORD shall escape (Joel 2:32).

Those who are trying to draw people to themselves are going to come down. The misrepresentation we see now, all this clowning around with the name of God, will end. The wars in the name of God and in the name of religion have been terrible, and they still continue. The Word says the sun of this world with its attraction for the things of this world will become black as sackcloth (Revelation 6:12).

> ^{Arise,} *shine; for thy light is come, and the glory of the LORD is risen upon thee. For, behold, the darkness shall cover the earth, and gross darkness the peoples: but the LORD shall arise upon thee, and his glory shall be seen upon thee. And the Gentiles shall walk to thy light, and the kings to the brightness of thy birth. (Isaiah 60:1–3)*

Scripture says when the peoples are in gross darkness, the morning star will come. It will rise first in our hearts before the fullness of the new day dawns. All the things of this world are going to come down. The morning star is the Lord Jesus Christ, and the Shulamite was convinced of this by the end of the Song of Solomon. Her inheritance was him, and his inheritance was her.[139] Just as the morning star arose, the little red star followed on exactly the same path. This is the path that the Lord Jesus walked, and it is the same path for us too.

> ^{Immediately} *after the tribulation of those days shall the sun be darkened, and the moon shall not give her light, and the stars shall fall from the heaven, and the powers of the heavens shall*

---

139 Song of Solomon 2:16; 6:3; 7:10

be shaken, and then shall appear the sign of the Son of man in heaven, and then shall all the tribes of the earth mourn, and they shall see the Son of man coming in the clouds of heaven with great power and glory. (Matthew 24:29–30)

What will the sign be? The disciples asked the Lord, "Tell us, when shall these things be? and what shall be the sign of thy coming and of the end of the age?" (Matthew 24:3). What sign will there be before the day of Lord, before his day of righteousness? The sign will be the morning star, the body of Christ shining with the truth and righteousness of Jesus.

The morning star is very real in the natural realm, but it's also the body of Christ, a people of God here on the earth that is not a dull light like the moon's reflection from the sun. It isn't a moon that waxes and wanes between revivals. The church has sometimes been so off track, it's like the moon when it gets between the earth and the sun, making a complete eclipse with no light at all passing. The church's years of misrepresentation previously caused dark centuries known as the Dark Ages.

How does this happen? By reason of the fights because the "moon" became blood; because of the "erratic stars" trying to attract everyone toward themselves; because of the "waterless clouds"; and furthermore, because of the "spots and blemishes" on the agape feasts of the Lord (Jude 1:11–13).

But the Lord Jesus will have a bride, without spot or wrinkle, which will shine with the same light of Christ (Ephesians 5:27). He promises a moon that shall shine like the sun and never wane (Isaiah 60:20). Isaiah predicts that this moon will shine like the sun with all of the Lord's glory. Then the Sun of righteousness will shine seven times greater, giving us light of seven days in one.[140]

A great number of the Psalms are written to the Overcomer. There is only one Overcomer. The only One who has overcome is the Lord Jesus Christ, but he wants to overcome in us, making us overcomers. He wants to take us out of the realm of religious symbols and place us in the reality

---

140 Moreover the light of the moon shall be as the light of the sun, and the light of the sun shall be sevenfold as the light of seven days, in the day that the LORD binds up the breach of his people and heals the stroke of their wound. (Isaiah 30:26)

For, behold, the day comes that shall burn as an oven; and all the proud, and all that do wickedly shall be stubble; and the day that comes shall burn them up, said the LORD of the hosts, that it shall leave them neither root nor branch. But unto you that fear my name shall the Sun of righteousness be born, and in his wings he shall bring saving health; and ye shall go forth and jump like calves of the herd. And ye shall tread down the wicked; for they shall be ashes under the soles of your feet in the day that I make, said the LORD of the hosts. (Malachi 4:1–3)

of his life.

His love is different from our love. His life is different from our life. His life is eternal life, not only because it lasts forever and never had a beginning, but because it has another higher quality. He came that we could have life and life in abundance, another kind of life (John 10:10).

In the midst of all the problems with Jacob, God changed his name (nature) into Israel in the midst of his pilgrimage on this earth (this happened at the time of Jacob's trouble). We can feel his life by the Holy Spirit and not only feel it, but if we submit to our heavenly Father's correction, he can convert us into multipliers of the life of Christ.

Imagine all those coming to an end who are using his gifts to attract people to a place, to form a circus, to get money, or to promote some man-made doctrine or organization. What will happen when those "stars" stop shining as in any dawn? God gives us the example almost every day. When the skies clear, the last star that remains in the sky is the morning star, and then the new day dawns.

> ^{Immediately} *after the tribulation of those days shall the sun be darkened, and the moon shall not give her light, and the stars shall fall from the heaven, and the powers of the heavens shall be shaken, and then shall appear the sign of the Son of man in heaven, and then shall all the tribes of the earth mourn, and they shall see the Son of man coming in the clouds of heaven with great power and glory. And he shall send his angels with a trumpet and a great voice, and they shall gather together his elect from the four winds, from one end of heaven to the other. (Matthew 24:29–31)*

The Lord Jesus Christ is not coming back for a spotted, wrinkled, messed up bride that flees from trouble and who must be helicoptered (or raptured) off of the battlefield. Song of Solomon says she shows herself forth as the morning, fair as the moon, clear as the sun, and imposing as the standard-bearer of the army (Song of Solomon 6:10). Other translations say, "as terrible as an army with banners." But the original speaks of the standard-bearer. This is a reference to Christ.

In ancient times, the standard-bearer could also be in charge of the trumpet. This is how the army was controlled. They didn't have radios or any modern form of communication. At the appropriate sound of the trumpet, the standard went forward, and everyone went forward, and if it drew back, everyone fell back. The one who controlled the standard and the trumpet controlled the army, and Scripture says this woman is as imposing as the standard-bearer.

After being persecuted and in retreat, the woman (representing the people of God) is nourished by God for a time and times (the time of the Jews and the times of the Gentiles). Then the great dragon loses its wings (its ability to operate in the heavens) and is cast unto the earth. The woman receives the wings of the great eagle to fly above the circumstances and gain access to the heavenly realm.[141]

The Song of Solomon implies that whoever would challenge her challenges the power of the heavenly host; it's as if they had directly challenged the Lord Jesus who has all power and authority (Song of Solomon 6:10; 8:5) because she no longer does her own will but uses her freedom to do the will of her beloved.

At the end of the Song of Solomon, in chapter 8 where the Lord is the one who is speaking to his wife, in some translations it's inverted, but in the original it says this: Thou, she that dwellest in the gardens (Song of Solomon 8:13).

Our ancestors were kicked out of the garden of God, but now we have access once again. Ezekiel speaks of a priesthood with access to the presence of God and another priesthood that does not (Ezekiel 44:10–16). Those among the priesthood of all believers (including intermediary clergy) that exists now, that can hide behind a veil and do abominations in the holy place, is going to be swept away. God is going to finish with two witnesses: one is himself (the husband, the Lord) and now the other witness is her (the bride). And two or three witnesses are needed for any matter involving life or death.[142] And the devil will be condemned and imprisoned for a thousand years and then cast into the lake of fire (the second death) with all his followers.

Thou, she that dwellest in the gardens, the companions hearken to thy voice (Song of Solomon 8:13). She can now give orders to the "companions"; she can give orders to the servants in his house. What used to be a little Shulamite girl burned by the sun (burned by the world), a peasant who followed the footprints of the sheep and of the true pastors with her little flock of female goats, became the daughter of a prince married into his royal family as queen (Song of Solomon 7:1). She represents the bride of Christ.

---

141 And when the dragon saw that he was cast unto the earth, he persecuted the woman who brought forth the man child. And to the woman were given two wings of the great eagle that she might fly from the presence of the serpent into the wilderness, into her place, where she is nourished for a time and times. (Revelation 12:13–14)
142 Deuteronomy 19:15; 1 Timothy 5:19

The companions hearken to thy voice; cause me to hear it, Song of Solomon 8:13 continues. The Lord told his disciples he wanted friends. After his death and resurrection, he called them brothers. He said whatever we asked the Father in his name would be granted. The problem is that he has not had a corporate people who have truly and consistently represented his name, but he will. Then she will be the highest representation of the morning star.

Let us pray:

Lord Jesus, we ask not only to be able to understand your revelation, not only to receive it, but Lord, that we could truly be your brothers, your bride, part of your body, blood of your blood, born of blood and of water (of your life and of your word). Just as Eve came out from Adam's heart, from Adam's side, we ask that we could also form part of what has come out of your heart all these years. We ask, heavenly Father, for your correction, your discipline, along with your love and tenderness as part of the preparation of this great morning star that will shine when there is no more light anywhere else on the earth. Amen.

CHAPTER FOURTEEN

The Time Is When the Lord Says: Haggai's Prophecy

The word of the Lord came by the hand of Haggai at about the same period as Zechariah, son of Iddo the prophet; it appears that he was contemporary to the second half of the book of Daniel.

Haggai's Message

Haggai 1

¹ In the second year of Darius the king, in the sixth month, in the first day of the month, came the word of the LORD by the hand of Haggai the prophet unto Zerubbabel the son of Shealtiel, governor of Judah, and to Joshua the son of Josedech, the high priest, saying,
² Thus speaketh the LORD of the hosts, saying, This people say, The time is not yet come, the time to build the house of the LORD.
³ Then came the word of the LORD by the hand of Haggai the prophet, saying,

Each prophet is different. This says the word came by the hand of the prophet Haggai; the Lord may have dictated it, but Haggai wrote it down. The message came to the prophet, and the prophet delivered.

In the second year of Darius the king refers to the period after the experience that Daniel had in the lions' den; it was after king Darius was convinced of who the Lord was and after he ordered a decree to be published everywhere exalting the greatness of the God of Daniel. King Darius, son of Ahasuerus, could also have been known, after the death of his father, as the Ahasuerus of Queen Esther (as mentioned, Ahasuerus is a title, not a personal name). His spirit had been awakened by the Lord[143] and his heart dealt with so that he would be in agreement with the order of King Cyrus (his superior) to allow the return of the vessels of the temple and the rebuilding of the house of the Lord. Cyrus the Persian apparently left Darius the Mede in charge of Babylon while Cyrus continued his world conquests (after having given the decree to return the vessels of the Lord to Jerusalem and for a remnant to rebuild the temple).

The message of the Lord, prophesied by Haggai, is directed to Zerubbabel the son of Shealtiel, governor of Judah. "Zerubbabel" means "sprout from Babylon."

The people of God thought they had lost everything in the Babylonian captivity. However, the Lord brought forth a "sprout from Babylon."

"Shealtiel" means "I have asked of God." Daniel was asking God to fulfill Jeremiah's prophecy. He did this with humility, repenting for the sins of his people.

Daniel asked the Lord to clarify the message, so this is why the Lord sent the prophet Haggai with the revelation of the Word concerning a declaration about the reconstruction of the house of God. These words involve us in the end of the times because Scripture says that we are the temple of God where the Holy Spirit dwells, and God desires to place the fullness of his Spirit in a corporate temple built of living stones.[144]

Haggai's story is a picture for us. In the natural realm, a man named Zerubbabel was rebuilding Jerusalem, but this has an implication toward our time. When the glory and the purity in the early church became contaminated and all but vanished (after six centuries or so), another kind of Babylonian captivity took place; confusion began to dominate the people of God. Small resurges occurred sporadically from time to time.

Haggai also directed his message to Joshua the son of Josedech, the high priest. In Hebrew, "Joshua" is the same as "Jesus" in Greek; "Josedech" means "the Lord is righteous." The Lord is now directing this same message to a remnant who have come out of man's systems of confusion as a sprout from Babylon;[145] our high priest (Jesus) is in heaven

---

143 Jeremiah 51:11

144 See 1 Corinthians 3:16; 6:19; 2 Corinthians 6:16; John 2:21.

145 Zerubbabel, meaning "sprout from Babylon," was in charge of rebuilding Jerusalem and the temple. There is an interesting parallel here with the Lord Jesus.

And he [Joseph] came and dwelt in a city called Nazareth, that it might be fulfilled, which was spoken by the prophets, that he [Jesus] shall be called a Nazarene (Matthew 2:23). A Nazarene is a resident of Nazareth, meaning "branch or sprout."

with all power and authority to implement this new covenant.

Throughout many long centuries, the new covenant (that has been implemented on an individual level) has been isolated in many materials (or living stones) scattered in their confusion by men who have tried to do good things in the work of God. But they have not succeeded collectively, nor will any of them ever be able to accomplish it. This is what the Lord is referring to (as we advance through this chapter) when he speaks of men who dwell in their own houses (in their own sects, denominations, or groups) while his house is deserted. His house is to be a house of prayer for all nations (or denominations).

> *⁴ Do you have time, all of you, to dwell in your panelled houses, and this house is deserted?*

This question remains today when we speak of purity of heart, when we speak of perfection before the Lord, when we speak of fulfilling the prophecies in Scripture. Most churches and ministries build their own houses, and they are comfortable. So how are things going? They say those prophecies are not to be fulfilled now; they say it isn't time for the Lord's true house. In order to celebrate the Feast of Tabernacles, the people of God were to each leave their own house, farm, or village and walk to where God would indicate. When they all came together, they were to live in booths or tabernacles made of branches.[146]

> *⁵ Now therefore thus hath the LORD of the hosts said; Consider your ways.*
> *⁶ Ye have sown much and bring in little; ye eat, but ye are not filled; ye drink, but ye are not satisfied; ye clothe yourselves, but you are not warm; and he that is a hireling receives his wages in a bag with holes.*

The will of man is mixed in with the will of God in men's houses, and we will never find lasting satisfaction there. Only those who hunger and thirst for righteousness will be satisfied (Matthew 5:6). The Lord commands us to be righteous, and even to be perfect, as our heavenly Father is perfect (Matthew 5:48). He said the people who make their own houses have sown much but bring in little; he said that those who eat there are not filled; those who drink there are not satisfied, etc. He said that the covering, the clothing, provided there doesn't give warmth and, therefore, doesn't really cover; he says that he that is a hireling receives his wages

---

Therefore, a nickname for Jesus was the Nazarene (the branch, or the sprout).
146 Leviticus 23:39–42; Deuteronomy 16:13–15; 31:9–13

in a bag with holes.

The good shepherd gives his life for the sheep, but the hireling flees when there is danger.[147] In the same manner, the houses of worship and denominations of men are full of hirelings who will not give their lives for the sheep, and the sheep know it. That is why many continually wander from place to place (from church to church and from one group to another). These sheep have a continual need that is never completely satisfied.

> *7 Thus hath the LORD of the hosts said, Consider your ways.*

God's Mountain

Our ways are man's ways of doing things. The Lord wants us to do things his way. His way is that we go up to the mountain. The Lord is speaking of the mountain of his holiness,[148] a "mountain" where everything is done exclusively for him and in a manner that is pleasing to him.

> *8 Go up to the mountain and bring wood and build the house; and I will place my will in her, and I will be glorified, said the LORD.*

When God deals with us, we are the wood, the stones, and all the materials that the Lord will use to build the house.

> *9 Ye look for much and find little; and when ye lock it up at home, I shall blow upon it. Why? said the LORD of the hosts. Because my house is deserted, and ye run each one of you unto his own house.*

Whatever is not founded on the rock, which is the Lord, will fall when the winds, the storm, or the tests come (Matthew 7:25–27). This will happen to those who build their own houses (their own groups, sects, or denominations) when the Lord says that his true house is deserted.

"Deserted" doesn't mean the house is empty; it means that instead of God's house, there is a desert; there is nothing. The Lord says we are the temple or the house, and if nobody is there, then there is nothing.

---

147 I AM the good shepherd; the good shepherd gives his life for the sheep. But the hireling, who is not a shepherd, whose own the sheep are not, sees the wolf coming and leaves the sheep and flees; and the wolf catches them and scatters the sheep. The hireling flees because he is a hireling, and the sheep do not belong to him. (John 10:11–13)

148 Used multiple times in Psalms.

> [10] *Therefore the rain of the heavens over you is held back, and the earth has held back her fruits.*
>
> [11] *And I called for a drought upon this land and upon the mountains and upon the wheat and upon the wine and upon the oil and upon that which the earth brings forth and upon the men, and upon the beasts and upon every labour of hands.*

The work of the hands of the natural man doesn't receive God's blessing, even when he does things for God. God's blessing is like the rain, and when there is no rain, when there is no blessing from God, there is only desert. This is true in the spiritual as well as in the natural. We live in a time of a lot of movement, a flurry of activity and of "works." And each pastor speaks of the "work" that they are doing, of how many sheep they congregate in their work and how many pay their tithe, etc. For the Lord, many of these "works" are not his house because he considers them to be man's house.

Many are in a spiritual drought; the revelation of God isn't flowing, and this dryness reaches the mountains. Mountains denote power and purpose and authority. Each mountain is dry because each leader decided to have his own kingdom; they have decided to make their own religious fortress.

This ensures drought upon the wheat (the message that is sown), upon the wine (the life that is being shared), upon the oil (the anointing), and upon everything the earth produces. In the highest sense, we are the earth, and the Lord wants to sow in us.

> [11] *. . . and upon the men, and upon the beasts and upon every labour of hands.*

The Lord doesn't accept the work of our hands if we aren't joined to him. The Lord didn't accept the work of Cain's hands because Cain didn't understand the true sacrifice; he didn't understand that the blessing isn't found in our own lives but in the life of the Lord.

Abel understood this and didn't come with the futile work of his own hands but with a blood sacrifice (Genesis 4:3–7). This indicated he knew that man, in his natural state, cannot please God with his own works. A change of life is required; the death of the old man is required to have the resurrection of the new man. This message is directed to the new man, to the sprout from Babylon under the ministry of Jesus, our everlasting High Priest of the order of Melchisedec.

> [12] *Then Zerubbabel the son of Shealtiel, and Joshua the son of*

Josedech, the high priest, with all the remnant of the people, heard the voice of the LORD their God and the words of Haggai the prophet, as the LORD their God had sent him, and the people feared before the LORD.

The Lord sent a message by the mouth of the prophet, and when the message came, they paid attention. They heard the voice of the LORD their God and the words of Haggai the prophet. The Lord sent a ministry; he sent a prophetic message like the message we are preaching, and the people heard God's voice directly. Since the Exodus, the people of God had lost this ability – from the moment that the Ten Commandments were established.

Before the Ten Commandments, the people of God told Moses they didn't want to hear God's voice because they didn't want to die (see Exodus 19 and 20). They wanted Moses to go up the mountain and return with the message. That's how they obtained Ten Commandments on stone tablets instead of having the law of God written on their hearts and in their souls.

Much time passed, and many disasters occurred before the Babylonian captivity. The people had not wanted to hear the Lord's voice during that time, but in this message that came through Haggai, a small remnant that had come out of Babylon heard the voice of the LORD and of the prophet. The Lord continues to do the same now; he sends his prophetic message, but he also wants to speak directly to each heart.

Ambassadors of the Lord

¹³ Then spoke Haggai the ambassador of the LORD in the embassy of the LORD unto the people, saying, I am with you, said the LORD.

Haggai came as the ambassador of the LORD. He also spoke in the embassy of the LORD. It's one thing for an ambassador to speak with his government in his embassy or to speak to a certain people concerning his embassy, but it's another thing for people to listen to the ambassador in his own embassy (which is legally part of his own country). In this verse, the Lord refers to Haggai as his ambassador, and the place where the message is given as in his embassy.

Today the Lord has "ambassadors" that speak from his "embassy." It's different when the Lord sends someone to seek the lost with a determined message (like he sent the apostles) than when the Lord's true people seek him in his own embassy, where they can be assured that not only what they hear but everything that happens is from the Lord with absolutely no interference.

¹³ *Then spoke Haggai . . .*

Haggai names himself many times in this chapter. "Haggai" means "born on a feast day," and the Feast of Trumpets announces the Day of Reconciliation. This all leads to the Feast of Tabernacles (or ingathering), which was the most important feast. It's also highly probable that the Lord Jesus Christ was also born on a feast day; Haggai, Daniel, David, and many other prophets project an image and a shadow of what the Lord Jesus would and will accomplish in his first and second comings. Jesus's first coming fulfilled the Passover and led to the day of Pentecost being fully come. His second coming will fulfill the Feast of Tabernacles. So, the Lord Jesus not only came to fulfill the feasts, but it's likely he was also born on a feast day (probably the Feast of Trumpets). Look at the reaction Haggai's message produced!

> ¹⁴ *And the LORD woke up the spirit of Zerubbabel the son of Shealtiel, governor of Judah and the spirit of Joshua the son of Josedech, the high priest, and the spirit of all the remnant of the people; and they came and worked in the house of the LORD of the hosts, their God,*
> ¹⁵ *in the twenty-fourth day of the sixth month, in the second year of Darius the king.*

The Lord woke up their spirit. One of the last things that Jesus did (when he ascended after his resurrection in his first coming) was that he opened their understanding so they might understand the scriptures (Luke 24:45).

In Haggai, he woke them up before the remnant began the work in the house of the Lord. Many people today have a capacity for the things of God but are sleeping (Matthew 25:5).

Some say, "It isn't time for the people of God to come together as one and have a glorious manifestation of the presence of God here on earth; that's surely for another time and another place; we'll probably be perfect in heaven, but can't do it here."¹⁴⁹

---

149 Over the last fifty years or so the word "ecumenical" (meaning "in the family") has come into vogue among members of highly structured denominations who are desperately seeking unity. I fear that many have not realized that there are only two possible families that Christianity may come together in. There is the family of Adam, and there is the family of the Lord Jesus Christ.

The Lord will respond the same way he did to the remnant in the times of Haggai with a message like this: "Look at what's happening; you're making many houses (of worship); you're in a flurry of religious activity, but what happened to the wheat? What happened to the wine? What happened to the oil? What happened to the message? What happened to the life of the Lord? What happened to the true anointing? Where are you?"

Men work hard with little results. They may move multitudes or put on a tremendous performance, but where are the transformed lives?

What happened in Haggai began the first day of the sixth month. On the twenty-fourth day of the same month, God woke up the spirit of the governor of Judah, the high priest, and the remnant of the people.

They had spent centuries without the Lord awakening the spirit of a collective group. Occasionally, he awoke the spirit of one or two people, but in this book he woke up the spirit of the leaders and the remnant to do the will of God.

Haggai 2

¹ In the seventh month, in the twenty-first day of the month . . .

Three and a half weeks later. This is seven weeks after the ministry of Haggai began. Leviticus 23 speaks of the Feast of Tabernacles and says this feast began on the fifteenth day of the seventh month and lasted seven days. Therefore, the twenty-first day of the seventh month is the last day of the great Feast of Tabernacles.[150] Remember, Haggai is the prophet "born on a feast day."

God has a collective prophet (under the testimony or headship of Jesus) that will also be "born" on the day of the feast.

> *¹ . . . the word of the LORD came by the hand of the prophet Haggai, saying,*
> *² Speak now to Zerubbabel the son of Shealtiel, governor of Judah and to Joshua the son of Josedech, the high priest, and to the remnant of the people, saying,*

Return to Work

Once again, the Lord is sending a message, but the spirit of the people

---

150 But in the fifteenth day of the seventh month, when ye have gathered in the fruit of the land, ye shall keep a feast unto the LORD seven days; the first day shall be a sabbath, and on the eighth day shall also be a sabbath. (Leviticus 23:39)

is already awake when the message arrives. Sending a message to those who are asleep is different than sending one to those who are already awake.

> ³ *Who is left among you that saw this house in her first glory? and how do ye see her now? Is she not as nothing before your eyes?*

When this moment arrived, many wept. Some wept out of awe because they were once again building the foundations of the house of God, and others wept because what they were now doing was nothing compared to what had been lost (Ezra 3:12).

In the same way, many people look back, having the writings and the description of the glory of the early church, and we know we are not experiencing anything compared to that. Because of this, many people want to return to the last great revivals, or as it was in the days of Azuza Street, or the Great Awakening in England, or the Reformation, or Saint Augustine, or Saint Jerome, or even the days of the apostles. However, the Lord is telling us that even though we have small beginnings with this sprout from Babylon, the glory of this latter house will be greater than of the former (Haggai 2:9).

> ⁴ *Yet now be strong, O Zerubbabel, said the LORD; and be strong, O Joshua, son of Josedech, the high priest; and be strong, all ye people of this land, said the LORD, and work; for I am with you, said the LORD of the hosts:*

God doesn't command us to be strong in our own life pursuing our own agendas. He doesn't command us to be strong in constructing our own houses, even if we build them in the promised land, even if we build within the realm that we think is the new covenant. Many "houses" have been built, but the ministry of Haggai was so that the people would stop looking at what they were doing in the name of God and so that they would return to the true work. The true work requires God, but it also requires us to be spiritually awake and aligned with him. It requires us to put in our complete effort, but it also requires the Lord's complete effort.

> ⁴ *. . . I am with you, said the LORD of the hosts:*
> ⁵ *The word that I covenanted with you when ye came out of Egypt and my Spirit is in the midst of you: do not fear.*

The word that I covenanted refers to the word that came when they were leaving Egypt, which was a word that the people of Israel said they could not keep listening to because they would die. Therefore, they received it on stone tablets, and those tablets had to be hidden a bit later on in the ark of the covenant, in the holy of holies beyond the reach of the people because no one could fulfill them. That word and those commandments were for the future.

The commandment didn't say, "Do not kill." It said, "Thou shalt not murder" (future tense). But they spent much of the next fifteen hundred years killing themselves, and they even murdered the Lord Jesus when he came to live among them.

God promises a new covenant written on the tablets of our hearts and in our souls. We have known all this; the church has always known this. But the Christian church (Orthodox, Catholic, even evangelical and Protestant) organized by men has also had a nasty history of killing each other. Some of the worst wars in the last two thousand years have been done in the name of God. Even today, many Christians who throw up their hands in horror when the dastardly deeds of some of their religious ancestors are mentioned will think nothing of doing in the reputation of anyone who shines the light of the truth onto the work that they have supposedly been doing for God.

> ⁵ *The word that I covenanted with you when ye came out of*
> *Egypt and my Spirit is in the midst of you: do not fear.*

We have the Scriptures that God finished compiling near the beginning of the church age. Our English word "church" is an unfortunate adaptation of pagan origin (ekklesia in Greek can be much better translated as "congregation" and literally means "those who are called out.") When God began taking Gentiles out of the systems of this world, he used this word ekklesia to refer to every congregation (that for the first two centuries met almost exclusively in private homes). Therefore, in the New Testament many different congregations are mentioned, but Scripture is clear that there is only one body (Ephesians 4:4).

There are sixty-six books that we call the Bible, but those who use them without the Spirit end up in bondage to terrible legalism (that can cause many people to react into lawless licentiousness at the drop of a hat, particularly at the change from one generation to another).

Sometimes people say only an elite group with much humanistic education can interpret Scripture. This is why they left it for so many years in Greek and Hebrew (or later in Latin) without the common people having access to it in their own language. Even now, those who interpret Scriptures with their own understanding are making many sects with different beliefs. The Word, according to his covenant with us, along with his Spirit is in the midst of his awakened people because the letter kills, but the Spirit gives life.[151] Coming out of Egypt means coming out of bondage, coming out of legalism, coming out from under the hyper control of the modern day Pharaohs who would continue to enslave the people of God and deny them their liberty in the Spirit.

> [6] *For thus hath the LORD of the hosts said: Yet even once, and I will shake the heavens and the earth and the sea and the dry land;*
> [7] *and I will shake all the Gentiles; and the desire of all the Gentiles shall come: and I will fill this house with glory, said the LORD of the hosts.*

The history of this house shows its humble beginnings in the days of Zerubbabel, but it's also where the Lord Jesus Christ came in person, seeking the state of his Father's house. Sadly, he found it had been turned into a den of thieves instead of a house of prayer for all nations. Now we are the temple of God. When the Lord returns, how will he find us? Will he find a den of thieves, each one looking for their own benefit from the sacred things of God? The Lord Jesus is coming back for a bride without spot or wrinkle or any such thing that he can fill with the fullness of his glory.[152]

When the Lord came the first time, the earth shook! But in the second coming, both heaven and earth will shake! This is how we know this message is talking about the Lord Jesus's second coming, and the first coming was only a partial fulfillment in the temple (still made out of literal stones) before the Jewish people. God says this second fulfillment will shake the heavens and the earth and the sea and the dry land; and I will shake all the Gentiles; and the desire of all the Gentiles shall come: and I will fill this house with glory, said the LORD of the hosts.

There was no moment similar to the glory of God filling King Solomon's temple at the house that Zerubbabel, Josedech, and the remnant constructed (1 Kings 8:11). The glory of God that entered into the

---

151 Forasmuch as ye are manifestly declared to be the epistle of Christ ministered by us, written not with ink, but with the Spirit of the living God; not in tables of stone, but in fleshy tables of the heart. . . . Who also has made us able ministers of the new testament, not of the letter, but of the Spirit; for the letter kills, but the Spirit gives life. (2 Corinthians 3:3, 6)

152 That he might present her glorious for himself, a congregation, [Gr. ekklesia – called out ones] not having spot or wrinkle or any such thing, but that she should be holy and without blemish. (Ephesians 5:27)

house Zerubbabel constructed was the Lord Jesus himself many centuries later. On the day of Pentecost, when God's Spirit came upon a remnant of about one hundred and twenty in the upper room (who were all of one accord), it quickly spread the very same day to three thousand;[153] the porch of Solomon at the temple may have been the site of this occurrence. Today, we are the true house that God wants to fill with his glory.

Throughout the centuries, individuals have had incredible experiences with the Lord, but now the Lord promises to place *stone upon stone* (Haggai 2:15). Another picture of this is in Ezekiel 37 in the valley of dry bones where all the dry bones revive; each bone is joined where it should be, and a great army is formed. When Jesus returns, there will be a first resurrection (Revelation 20:4–6) as he *comes with ten thousands of his saints to execute judgment on all and to convince all that are ungodly among them of all their ungodly deeds which they have unfaithfully committed and of all the hard words which the unfaithful sinners have spoken against him* (Jude 14–15). This is when he puts the finishing touches on his house (1 Peter 4:17).

> [8] *The silver is mine, and the gold is mine, said the LORD of the hosts.*
> [9] *The glory of this latter house shall be greater than of the former, said the LORD of the hosts, and in this place I will give peace, said the LORD of the hosts,*

If we are the house, if the Lord plans to place the fullness of his glory in us, if he intends to link each of us correctly to the rest of the house, and if this is where he will place his peace, the Lord's peace must begin one by one in our hearts and extend out from there.

> [10] *In the twenty-fourth day of the ninth month, in the second year of Darius, the word of the LORD came by the hand of Haggai the prophet, saying,*

Is It Time?

Three months, three weeks, and three and a half days had passed since the beginning of the ministry of Haggai the prophet. This date refers to bases being laid again in the house; it relates to the foundation of the house. No blessing exists before the foundation of the house is laid; the blessing comes after it's in place. We know what that foundation is. Paul tells us that no other foundation other than Jesus Christ crucified can

---

153 Acts 2

be laid (1 Corinthians 3:11). This means that we are to be crucified with Christ, dead to sin, dead to the deeds of the flesh, and that he is to be alive in us. Then the hidden mystery of God is revealed, and it's Christ in you, the hope of Glory (Colossians 1:26–27).

> [11] *Thus hath the LORD of the hosts said; Ask now the priests concerning the law, saying,*
> [12] *If one bears holy flesh in the skirt of his garment, and with his skirt touches bread or pottage or wine, or oil or any food, shall it be made holy? And the priests answered and said, No.*
> [13] *Then Haggai said, If one that is unclean by a dead body touches any of these, shall it be unclean? And the priests answered and said, It shall be unclean.*
> [14] *Then Haggai answered, and said, So is this people, and so is this nation before me, said the LORD; and so is every work of their hands, and all that they offer here is unclean.*

This is dealing with a startling situation that I believe is prevalent in the history of the Christian church. This is when the people allegedly depend on the work of the Lord Jesus on the cross without being cleansed by the reality of this work. Some want to handle truth one way, and others want to handle it another way. Some say that during the mass, the elements (the wine and the host) are literally converted into the blood and flesh of Christ. Others prefer to use crackers and grape juice; they say it is a symbol of the body and the blood of Christ.

If what is unclean by a dead body touches something, everything is made unclean, according to the law. If the presence of Jesus by the Holy Spirit is missing from our gatherings, then the elements of "communion" cannot on their own bring clean life. These things (even if they are holy) cannot sanctify anyone (only Jesus can sanctify us by the Holy Spirit). The way we do things, the way man manages the things of God for his own benefit, has no way of sanctifying anyone; rather, a little leaven will corrupt the whole lump.

It is quite easy to end up with everything dead, everything contaminated, everything unclean because we've touched everything with our own interests and our own unclean life. We have not been able to receive the true blessing. Some have obtained the blessing as individuals (maybe even as families or fellowships), but an entire congregation or denomination, such as a house or church, has rarely ever been able to maintain the clean blessing of the Lord from generation to generation.

> *¹⁴ Then Haggai answered, and said, So is this people, and so is this nation before me, said the LORD; and so is every work of their hands, and all that they offer here is unclean.*

The Lord is saying that the vast majority of these holy communion suppers in the evangelical church, or masses in the Catholic Church, or Jewish Passovers – however good the intentions may be – are in the same condition as the people of Israel when they returned to reconstruct Jerusalem. Nothing worked, and the true life – the true anointing, the true message – was not, and is not flowing if all that they offer is unclean. In order for us to be a clean and living sacrifice, sin and guilt must be dealt with God's way.

> *¹⁵ And now, I pray you, consider in your heart from this day forth, from before a stone was laid upon a stone in the temple of the LORD:*
> *¹⁶ since these things were: when one came to a heap of twenty measures, there were but ten; when one came to the pressfat [wine vat] to draw out fifty vessels out of the press, there were but twenty.*

Twenty measures are symbolic of grace; ten are symbolic of law (man has a penchant for turning the New Testament back into law). Fifty vessels are symbolic of the power of the Holy Spirit in Pentecost; twenty means that even when we fail, God doesn't fail and continues to hold out his mercy and grace to those who repent.

> *¹⁷ I smote you with the east wind and with mildew and with hail in all the labours of your hands, yet ye did not turn to me, said the LORD.*

If God's people do not repent (individually and corporately) there will always be a shortage, and God's people will always need to be persuaded in order to give the tithes and offerings. They must be threatened, and even then, there is never enough. At the time when the people of Israel were in the desert constructing the tabernacle, Moses told them not to give any more because they had already donated more than was needed to finish the task (Exodus 36:5–7).

Many churches today are like the democracies, like the monster in the book of Daniel that destroys everything with its iron teeth. It tramples the leftovers, leaving nothing for anyone, and the need never ends. The strategy of asking and trying to obtain the things of this world never ends.

God didn't tell Haggai, "In this new work of the house of God, we're going to need a lot of gold; we're going to need a lot of silver. We have to get all the people to give because if they don't give, we can't start the work."

God began a different way. He began by saying, The silver is mine, and the gold is mine. He said, in effect, "Pay attention. Up until now you've done things your way. You have a priesthood and some sacrifices and offerings where you think that the "flesh" is sacred. You think you have the sacred things of God, but everything is unclean; you've contaminated everything by your own life because everything you minister is death. Your sacrifices don't sanctify anything; but wait, because new foundations must be established before placing stone upon stone. After the clean foundation is laid today, everything will be different."

> [18] *Consider now in your heart from this day forth, from the twenty-fourth day of the ninth month, even from the day that the foundation of the LORD'S temple was laid, put your heart into it.*

He didn't say, "Bring your gold and your silver here. Bring your precious stones, your offerings, and your tithes." He didn't say any of this. He said, "Put your heart into it, and you will see this work." The Lord wants us to give him our heart; he wants us to put our heart into what he's doing (not the other way around).

> [19] *Is not the seed yet in the barn? Not even the vine, nor the fig tree, nor the pomegranate, nor the olive tree, has blossomed yet, . . .*

We don't really have anything tangible in hand of eternal value that can be offered other than our hearts.

> [19] *. . . but from this day will I bless you.*
> [20] *And the word of the LORD came the second time unto Haggai in the twenty-fourth day of the month, saying,*

The word of the Lord came to Haggai and told him to speak to Zerubbabel two times. Only three months and twenty-four days had passed since the beginning of his ministry, and they began their work.

> [21] *Speak to Zerubbabel, governor of Judah, saying, I cause the heavens and the earth to shake,*

Why? Because whatever ye shall bind on earth shall be bound in the heaven; and whatever ye loose on earth shall be loosed in the heaven (Matthew 18:18). Please note that the causing of the heavens and the earth to shake ties this prophecy to the day of the Lord and to the second coming.

> *22 and I will overthrow the throne of the kingdoms, and I will destroy the strength of the kingdom of the Gentiles, and I will overthrow the chariot and those that ride in them; and the horses and their riders shall come down, each one by the sword of his brother.*

As long as the "Gentiles" (individuals, families, tribes, congregations, or nations) do not have circumcised hearts, they will not be able to please God, no matter how they may try. In the end, many of those who remain unclean will do each other in.

> *23 In that day, said the LORD of the hosts, I will take thee, O Zerubbabel, my slave, the son of Shealtiel, said the LORD, and will make thee as a signet ring; for I have chosen thee, saith the LORD of the hosts.*

The kingdoms of those who made their own houses will topple. The strength of the kingdom of the Gentiles, of the unconverted, of the chariot, of man's machinery (the religious machinery, without mentioning the political and economic machinery) will vanish. The Lord says, I will overthrow the chariot and those that ride in them; and the horses (those who operate according to the flesh). As in the days of Gideon, those that ride in them; and the horses and their riders shall come down, each one by the sword of his brother.

In that day . . . In the new day of the Lord; this new day begins suddenly, while everyone is saying, "It isn't time." Then God comes on the scene and sends the message, even though men say it isn't time; God says, "Now is the time." The remnant that is symbolized by Zerubbabel (shoot out of Babylon[154]) will be like a signet ring. They will represent the authority of God upon the earth. Less than four months passed from when God said it was time until they placed the new foundation of the house of God.

> *23 In that day [in the day of the Lord that is about to dawn on us], said the LORD of the hosts, I will take thee, O Zerubbabel, my slave, the son of Shealtiel, said the LORD, and will make*

---

154 "Zerubbabel" can also be translated as "contrary (or repugnant) to confusion."

> *thee as a signet ring; for I have chosen thee, saith the LORD*
> *of the hosts.*

This remnant will give orders in the name of the Lord. This happened with the Shulamite in the Song of Solomon; she ended up worthy of all authority; she ended up with the power to run the army; she ended up speaking, and his companions would listen to her, and even her husband would listen to her. Why? Because her heart was one with his heart just as Jesus's heart is one with his Father (Song of Solomon 8:13; John 17)

Who will be as a signet ring? Zerubbabel and this remnant (or sprout from Babylon). The Lord will place them with the true authority of the kingdom . . . and will make thee as a signet ring; for I have chosen thee, saith the LORD of the hosts. Almost 2500 years ago, Zerubbabel and a small remnant were used by God in a living parable that is really about what is happening now. Many people continue to say, "It isn't time," but the time is when the Lord says.

Let us pray:

Lord, we want to know, we want to hear from your mouth when the time to believe is, so that you'll wake up our spirit to edify your true house, in order to encounter the fullness of your glory. Amen.

Chapter Fifteen

The Prophet Haggai on Placing the Right Foundation

The book of the prophet Haggai contains additional features. Old Testament examples, shadows, and figures show spiritual and prophetic lessons of what will come in the New Testament. Some say the Old Testament should be interpreted in the light of the New Testament. This has been the norm through the centuries since the Reformation, but it isn't always valid.

Parts of the New Testament cannot be interpreted without understanding the significance of the shadows, examples, living parables, and symbols of the Old Testament. For example, Revelation bases its terminology, signs, and symbols in examples that have been defined in most of the books of the Bible. The book of Daniel and the book of Zechariah are key to understanding the symbols in Revelation.

The book of Haggai only has two chapters and is considered one of the "minor prophets." It isn't a minor prophecy; it's one of the most fundamental prophecies in the Scriptures. It deals with rebuilding the bases, the foundation of the house of God in the time of Haggai, Zechariah, Ezra, Nehemiah, Zerubbabel, Joshua, etc. If we can understand it, we recognize the figure, example, and shadow of the true restoration of God's house, which is us.

These prophecies can be interpreted however the Spirit of God desires. He can apply them to the individual, to the Jewish nation, or to the Christian church in a certain period. They can also refer to the believers at the end of the church age, to the day of the Lord. The day of the Lord is the central theme in this prophecy because according to Revelation 19:10, the testimony of Jesus is the spirit of prophecy.

Many people seek God because they want him to fix their lives. The

Lord Jesus has not denied himself to people who have cried out to him during past centuries with that purpose in mind.

However, what is central in God's heart is not that we seek the Lord Jesus for our own benefit, but that we desist from our own things and enter into his life because complete victory is found only in him. He that has the Son has life; and he that does not have the Son of God does not have life (1 John 5:12). Thinking of eternity, what is the use of having the Lord fix a physical or economic problem if we haven't found his life?

Jesus is willing to find us wherever we are. The Lord visited the sinners; he entered houses and ate with people who were contaminated and unclean. However, even though he was criticized for that, the Lord didn't leave those people in that state. Contact with him cleansed that which was unclean. During Jesus's visit to Zacchaeus's house, Zacchaeus repented, not with words only but also with deeds. He said to the Lord, Behold, Lord, the half of my goods I give to the poor; and if I have taken any thing from any man by false accusation, I restore him fourfold. In that instant the Lord replied, This day saving health is come to this house (Luke 19: 8–9).

Haggai is also an example of the Lord Jesus. Jesus was probably born on a feast day, most likely on the Feast of Trumpets, on the first day of the seventh month. For the Jews, the agricultural year (based on when the children of Israel left Egypt) had its own calendar, and God's sacred year began on the seventh month of that calendar.

This is normal for the Lord because he always prepares one thing to bring about another. Scripture speaks of certain things prepared from the foundation of the world: of the book of life from the foundation of the world (Revelation 17:8), of a Lamb that was slain from the foundation of the world (Revelation 13:8). The word "foundation" is the central part of the book of the prophet Haggai because God declared it was time to place the foundation of the true house.

Two lines in Scripture speak of the foundation: one of the earth, and the other of the world. They aren't the same. Scripture says the meek shall inherit the earth (Matthew 5:5). It also says this world will end (Revelation 11:15), and even the elements will burn; this world will vanish.

The word "world" refers to a way of doing things (a world system initiated by Satan, based on lies that lead to death); the word "earth" comes from the root of "God's original purpose for humanity." Scripture says the first creation resulted in frustration due to Adam's sin, but a second Adam is not of the earth (not earthly like the first Adam). The

second Adam is the Lord of heaven and the beginning of the new creation.[155] Jesus's kingdom is not of this world, and this present world will
be destroyed.

God promises new heavens and a new earth where righteousness
dwells (2 Peter 3:13). The true foundation is Jesus Christ. He is also the
cornerstone who was rejected by the builders and has been rejected by the
great human organizations (and organizers) ever since (Psalm 118:22).
But Scripture is clear in saying there is no blessing until the foundation
is placed.

The blessing occurs from the moment in which the Lord decrees and
we respond individually and corporately to lay the right foundation.

> [Therefore,] *whosoever hears these words of mine and does them, I
> will liken him unto a prudent man, who built his house upon
> the rock. (Matthew 7:24)*

The Lord Jesus is the right foundation in any of our lives (or corporate
gatherings) so that we can have a house that is built on a safe foundation.
In order for this to be the case, however, we must do what he says. This
is only possible if we by the Spirit put to death the deeds of the flesh
(Romans 8:13).

The difference between Matthew's account in chapter 7 and Luke's
in chapter 6 is that while Matthew mentions the man who built upon
the sand, Luke speaks of someone who built upon the earth (and earth
is linked to man, to Adam) "without a foundation," and when the storm
comes, when the winds blow, when the rivers rise, the house will be destroyed. "House" means "work," "family," "congregation," "denomination,"
or whatever we do. The one who built his house upon the rock is the one
who hears the words of the Lord and does them.

Lucifer and Iniquity

It's obvious that this story begins from before the foundation of this world.
What is the foundation of this world? The foundation of this world that
we have (which is in enmity with God) is the way in which this world
does things. According to James 4:4, to be friends with this world is to
be enemies with God because the foundation of the world is based on a
lie. Lucifer, one of the cherubim, was perfect until iniquity was found in
him.[156] Iniquity is "sin that is hidden" and is disguised as something else.

---

155 1 Corinthians 15: 45–47; 2 Peter 3
156 Isaiah 14:12; Ezekiel 28:14–19

Lucifer wanted to destroy Adam and Eve, but he didn't want to do it head-on; so, he introduced the lie, and with the deception of the lie, he sowed death. As a result, Adam had to choose between Eve and his friendship with the Lord. Scripture says Adam entered into rebellion while Eve was deceived.[157]

The serpent's original problem had to do with iniquity – sin that is hidden so that it is not readily known from where it came or what it is (in reality it has to do with our own way versus God's way, lies versus truth). This is why the lie relates to darkness because it's the opposite of the light of the truth. The devil is the father of lies and is a murderer from the beginning (of his rebellion).[158] His lie caused the death of the human race, making it enter into the "shadows" of death. He obtained the empire of death; he became the jailor of the jail (called Sheol in Hebrew and Hades in Greek, mistakenly translated as hell in most English Bibles) where the first death kills the body, but doesn't kill the soul.

Scripture says that a second death (a lake of eternal fire) has been prepared for the devil and all his angels (Matthew 25:41). Furthermore, it says that we need not fear those who can kill the body (the first death) because they cannot kill the soul (Matthew 10:28). We should fear the One who can destroy both the body and the soul in hell, the lake of fire, which is the second death.[159]

Death was very fearsome when the devil had the keys, but the Lord Jesus overcame him with his death and resurrection, and now he has the keys to Hades and death[160] The Lord Jesus led captivity captive. He took his own, ascended on high, and received gifts for men (Psalm 68:18; Ephesians 4:5–13).

If we take up this line in Ephesians 4, it says that there is only one faith and one baptism; then it says that because he overcame, he gave some to be apostles, others prophets, others evangelists, other pastors and teachers. It isn't speaking of two types of people: the clergy and the laity. It's saying that with what the Lord did, he purchased and redeemed everyone and everything, and he has the right to command and to gift people like us to do what he wants.

---

157 Romans 5:14; 1 Timothy 2:14

158 John 8:44

159 And Hades and death were cast into the lake of fire. This is the second death. And whosoever was not found written in the book of life was cast into the lake of fire. (Revelation 20:14–15)

160 And he that lives and was dead; and; behold, I am alive for evermore, Amen, and have the keys of Hades and of death. (Revelation 1:18)

The Lord has the right to proclaim the true gospel of the kingdom of God, which is different from the kingdoms of this world, and he can do it through the people he chooses. He has the ability and the right to wake up the spirit of any of us so we can teach others, so we can take care of others, if that is what he wants.

We must bear in mind that the Lord Jesus is the true apostle, the prophet, the evangelist, the pastor, and the teacher; now he gives us the opportunity to become his brothers as part of the body of Christ. In Matthew 28:7, the angel said: And go quickly and tell his disciples that he is risen from the dead; and, behold, he goes before you into Galilee; there ye shall see him; behold, I have told you.

When the Lord, however, appeared to the woman, he didn't say, "Go and tell my disciples." He said, go tell my brothers that they may go into Galilee, and there they shall see me (Matthew 28:10). With his death and resurrection, the Lord Jesus made it possible for us to be part of his family (the Lord Jesus Christ's family) instead of being in Adam's family.

Let us pray:

Lord Jesus, thank you for making it possible for us to be part of your family and for establishing the true foundation of your church. We seek you for the life that only you can offer. Thank you for not leaving us as we are but, instead, transforming us into your likeness. Because you overcame death, we may also become overcomers in your family. Amen.

CHAPTER SIXTEEN

God's House Restored: Prophecy of Zephaniah and Haggai

Zephaniah, which means "the Lord hides," came and prophesied before God's people were taken captive by the king of Babylon. The kingdom of Babylon was all swept away, but Zephaniah the prophet ends by speaking of a "remnant." In the book of the prophet Haggai, this remnant is called Zerubbabel, or "sprout from Babylon." As mentioned before, Nazareth means "sprout," so the Lord Jesus, being from Nazareth is also a "sprout." (He was the only man born spiritually alive since God breathed the breath of life into Adam.[161])

At that same time, John the Baptist came through the wilderness to prepare the way of the Lord (Isaiah 40). This is part of the same picture of the house of God that will be restored. The Lord Jesus Christ was and is that house because the glory of the presence of the Father dwells in him. He said to his disciples when they asked him to see the Father, He that has seen me has seen the Father.[162]

This doesn't mean the Lord Jesus is the Father. It means the body of Christ, of which he is the head, is a body of many members because he was the temple of God (the fullness of the Godhead[163] dwelled in Jesus

---

161 It is also very interesting to note that Jesus was born of a woman, and Adam was not (the woman was taken out of Adam and designed by God to be a helpmeet for him). This is why Jesus is the only begotten Son of the Father.

162 Philip said unto him, Lord show us the Father, and it will suffice us. Jesus said unto him, Have I been such a long time with you, and yet thou hast not known me, Philip? He that has seen me has seen the Father; and how sayest thou then, Show us the Father? Believest thou not that I am in the Father and the Father in me? The words that I speak unto you I speak not of myself; but the Father that dwells in me, he does the works. Believe me that I am in the Father and the Father in me, or else believe me for the very works' sake. (John 14:8–11)

163 Colossians 2:9

by the Spirit while he was here upon the earth). We are also part of the temple of God if we are in Christ.[164]

King David (another example of Christ) prepared materials for the construction of the temple in the days of Solomon: stones of great value, all his personal fortune, all the spoils they acquired from the enemy, plus all that the people of Israel had freely given in gladness of heart, starting with the elders. This temple was not made with tithes; it was not made by forcing people; it was spontaneous; it was built of free-will offerings (1 Chronicles 29).

In the same way, those who will rule and reign with Christ are a coalition of the willing. When the servant of Abraham went to find Isaac a wife, he chose the most charitable girl of the town, the one willing to travel through the desert to the husband God provided for her. Zephaniah, John the Baptist, David, Rebecca, and many others form pictures of what the Lord will do with a people in this last day.

Just as Zephaniah prophesied, God had his remnant that he kept hidden. To be protected under his wings in the shadow of the Almighty means we take refuge in his life, not in our own. This gives us hope.

Zephaniah 3

[8] *Therefore wait for me, said the LORD, until the day that I rise up to the prey; . . .*

They had to wait seventy years while all the hopes of the people of God disappeared because they were all captive in Babylon. But right there in Babylon, God raised up a remnant. He lifted up Daniel and his companions. They faced the fiery furnace. Daniel had to face the lions' den and many other things. This was a symbol of what the Lord Jesus would face, and it is the same path for any one of us who truly follows the steps of the Lord Jesus. The Lord asks us to wait for him until the day that he will rise up to the prey.

[8] *. . . for my judgment is to gather the Gentiles, that I may assemble the kingdoms to pour upon them my indignation, even all my fierce anger; for all the earth shall be devoured with the fire of my jealousy.*

For those who took over the inheritance of the sons of God, for those who invaded the land of God, he said he was just a little angry at his people and therefore let them proceed, but the enemies of his people sur-

---

164 1 Corinthians 3:16; 2 Corinthians 6:16

passed their mandate, and that is why the Lord dealt with them severely. However, it was through these dealings that the Lord allowed his people to be cleansed. Now the time is coming when the Lord is going to require that things be done his way.

> [9] *For then I will restore to the peoples the pure language . . .*

The pure language is the opposite of the confusion of Babel.

> [9] *. . . that they may all call upon the name of the LORD to serve him with one consent.*
> [10] *From beyond the rivers of Ethiopia my suppliants, even the daughter of my dispersed, shall bring me an offering.*
> [11] *In that day thou shalt not be ashamed for any of thy doings, in which thou hast rebelled against me, for then I will take away out of the midst of thee those that rejoice in thy pride, and thou shalt no longer be haughty because of the mountain of my holiness.*

God confused the language when he saw men making their own kingdom, elevating their own name, and trying to avoid God's judgments with the Tower of Babel. This confusion will go on until God decrees to make it stop. He will restore a pure language, which is another picture of the Lord Jesus because he is the living Word of the living God (John 1:1–14).

It's when he is returned to the place that he deserves that everything else falls in place. Instead of having some people seeking the gifts of the Spirit (instead of the Giver) where, many times, it sounds like the Tower of Babel all over again, there is going to be a people that are truly the Lord's, who not only look for what he gives, but who also truly seek him so that he has the place that rightfully belongs to him, and so that he is truly the foundation. He's looking for a people who don't reject the foundation, who don't reject the cornerstone, but who give him all the honor and glory. But first, God promises to restore the pure language. He's doing this now.

Zephaniah also speaks of rivers and of a poor and humble people.

> [12] *and they shall wait in the name of the LORD.*

He speaks of a remnant of Israel that:

> [13] *. . . shall not do iniquity nor speak lies; neither shall a deceitful tongue be found in their mouth, for they shall be fed and lie down, and no one shall make them afraid.*

This is what God is producing.

> [14] *Sing, O daughter of Zion; shout with joy O Israel; be glad and rejoice with all thy heart, O daughter of Jerusalem.*
> [15] *The LORD has taken away thy judgments; he has cast out thine enemy; the LORD is king of Israel in the midst of thee; thou shalt not see evil any more.*

These promises have not been fulfilled . . . yet. They were partially fulfilled with the first coming of the Lord Jesus. The people of Israel rejected the Lord, and this resulted in the gospel being opened to the Gentiles. God cut off the unbelieving branches of the good olive tree and inserted the believing Gentiles.

In Scripture, the prophet Zechariah doesn't speak of one olive tree, but of two (Zechariah 4:3) because when the God does something good, he likes to multiply it. Joseph was such a good son that Jacob wanted another just like him. That is how Benjamin was born (which is another story). The number two can represent a body or a corporate people. God the Father wants to make the Lord Jesus Christ into a corporate and complete body of Christ.

God the Father was so pleased with the Lord Jesus, he wanted to have more of the same family. The Lord Jesus is the beginning of the new creation, the head of a greater body, and the Firstborn among many brethren. He is also, in another sense, the only begotten Son (born of a woman). For of him and by him and in him are all things.[165]

The Lord left his throne in glory and became a man like us. Jesus Christ, fully man, is now at the right hand of God the Father with all power and authority to mediate this new covenant so we can enter into his nature: the nature of God, the nature of the new man in Christ. The Lord Jesus Christ is not of a weird race, like in mythology when the Greek gods would supposedly marry humans and produce these creatures that were half god and half man. No, the Lord Jesus is a legitimate man, but he is also one hundred percent God. He is God and also man, and not by halves. Scripture says that in the new man, Christ is all and in all (Colossians 3:9–11) so in the new creation, God will be all in all (1 Corinthians 15:28).

Adam's fallen race will end because it's heading toward perdition, while eternal life is in the Lord Jesus Christ. Eternal life is another quality of life, God's life. In the new heavens and the new earth there is no longer any sea of lost or rebellious humanity (Revelation 21:1).

165 Romans 11:36

[16] In that time it shall be said to Jerusalem, Do not fear; and to Zion, Do not let thine hands be slack.
[17] The LORD thy God in the midst of thee is mighty; he will save; he will rejoice over thee with joy; he will rest in his love; he will joy over thee with singing.

The winepress of God's judgment has two possibilities: with song or without song. It has the possibility of life and blessing or the possibility of vengeance.

[18] I will gather those that are weary because of the long time,
. . .

How many are weary because of the long time and the desolation in the house of God?

[18] . . . who are thine, unto whom her confusion was a burden.

Living in Iniquity

When the confusion of Babylon came, many of the people of God did their own thing in God's name. When they finally returned to Jerusalem, their first inclination was that each one should build their own house instead of God's house. In the beginning of the book of Haggai, they were saying, "It isn't time to build the house of God."

[19] Behold, at that time I will undo all that afflict thee; and I will save her that is lame and gather her that was driven out; and I will make them a praise and of good reputation in every land where they have been put to shame.

God will invert things. Everyone has heard of a priest, a pastor, or any person that represented God who got off track. Shame is everywhere, and even worse, some people enter into full rebellion when they say, "Okay, I'm like this. So what?"

Some rob and hide it, while others do it in your face and say, "So what?" Some slip into perversion and conceal it; others sin openly and say, "So what?" This has resulted in many scandals among supposed representatives of God who are so deviant that instead of trying to hide their captivity to sin, they show their rebellion openly.

Once we were in a place where some friends congregated while ignoring iniquities of the group. These things were covered up. When that group finished their meeting, another group united with the same purpose: supposedly in the name of the Lord. This new group (the actual owners of the place) allowed their perversion out in the open. The Lord will change this, not solely for us, but for himself. Scripture says it is for the love of his own name. The Lord wants to draw us in his name, not ours.

> *[20] At that time will I bring you again, even in the time that I gather you; for I will give you as fame and as praise among all peoples of the earth, when I shall return your captives before your eyes, saith the LORD.*

God told his people this before they were taken captive so a small remnant hidden in him would have hope and intercede for the rest of the people like Daniel did. Not only did Daniel intercede for his people, he repented for their sins so the prophecy of God given through Jeremiah (saying that their captivity would last seventy years) would be fulfilled.

Sadly, captivity in the Christian church has lasted many times longer. However, the Lord Jesus is opening the seals that were reserved for the end time. It's time to restore God's temple, which is us.

God sent Haggai with a word in the second year of Kind Darius's reign. Let's review the history that we have covered: the Babylonians took Daniel captive along with his people, God gave him the interpretation of the dream that the king had forgotten, then Daniel began to see visions of what was going to happen. The balancing point in the middle of the book of Daniel is after the great feast of King Nebuchadnezzar's son Belshazzar when the king and his guests began drinking out of the vessels of the temple. Everything came down around their ears in the middle of what may have been the most tremendous feast (turned into a perverted drunken party) in the history of Babylon. A hand came and sculpted on the wall of stone and made the whole place shake, causing the king to remain naked and trembling. They had to bring Daniel in who gave an interpretation similar to: "Look king, your dad realized his mistake through many dealings, but you didn't pay attention to your father's lessons."

There have been many times when some of the human race realized its mistake. The church had a good beginning, but like Belshazzar, many have not been able to learn from history, and what started out good has now, in many places, turned into a tremendous pagan feast with the vessels of the Lord's temple. They are drinking the old wine from Babylon, and not the new wine of the life of Christ; they are getting drunk in Adam's life with the vessels and the gifts of God; they are using the things of God to obtain maximum pleasure in the things of this world, and God is about to bring it all down. In one night, the Medes and Persians diverted the river and entered the city through the empty waterway. God will stop the river of humanism and replace it. This is why he's revealing his Word; God's true Word destroys the kingdoms of this world. Humanistic Babylon is about to be severed from the river of humanism.

Joseph, in Egypt, is another picture of this. Seven years of abundance would be followed by seven years of famine. Seeing it from God's point of view, the seven years of abundance had to be administered with wisdom so they would survive the seven years of famine. Everyone who had animals and lived off them (symbolic of those who lived according to the flesh) had to sell their flocks to Joseph. Those who had their own lands (symbolic of private kingdoms) had to sell them to Joseph in order to survive. Those who thought they owned themselves had to sell themselves to Joseph. Everything ended up in Joseph's hands.

Joseph is a symbol of the Lord Jesus. The famine fast approaching us is described by the prophet Amos as a famine not of food or drink but of hearing the words of the LORD.[166] This is similar to the problem of the foolish virgins of Matthew 25 who ran out of oil.

The time came when all those who were against Daniel wanted to overthrow him by making the king sign a law where only the king could be worshipped for thirty days. King Darius had made a mistake and was very afflicted the night that Daniel got thrown into the lions' den, but he recapacitated and immediately did what had to be done. Just like what happened later to the evil Haman in the account of Esther, Darius threw the corrupt advisors into the lions' den and it didn't go well for them in there.

The devil will end up in the "lions' den." He had the Lord Jesus nailed on a cross, something similar to the experience that Daniel had in the lions' den. It didn't go at all bad for Daniel in the lions' den.

It will not go well for the devil; he will end up for one thousand years in what used to be his own empire of death.[167]

Sudden End-Time Events Will Soon Take Place

As we approach the day of the Lord, the Lamb that was slain is in the heavenly throne room opening the seals of the hidden plans and purposes of

---

166 Behold, the days come, said the Lord GOD, that I will send a famine to the earth, not a famine of bread, nor a thirst for water, but of hearing the words of the LORD: and they shall wander from sea to sea, and from the north even to the east, they shall run to and fro to seek the word of the LORD, and shall not find it. (Amos 8:11–12)

167 Hebrews 2:14–15; Revelation 20:1–3

God (including the title deed to the earth).

We are very close to the fall of "Babylon," which will come suddenly. The waters of humanism that have been nourishing this great religious city of Babylon will stop flowing. There is already a famine, but people are happy drinking the spiritual equivalent to diet cola, which tastes good but doesn't have any nourishment.

Joseph's brothers had to go to Egypt after two years of famine to seek food and avoid starvation. Once two years were fulfilled, Joseph's brothers had a revelation of the presence of Joseph. Joseph only revealed himself to his brothers after having carefully measured their hearts. The Lord has something similar coming.

In another picture, the book of the prophet Haggai begins the first day of the sixth month, when they say it isn't the time and God says it is. And then another prophecy comes on the twenty-fourth day of the sixth month when God begins to awake the spirit of his remnant to come and work in the house of the Lord of the hosts, their God. This represents the prophesied "new thing."[168]

> And *the LORD woke up the spirit of Zerubbabel the son of Shealtiel, governor of Judah and the spirit of Joshua the son of Josedech, the high priest, and the spirit of all the remnant of the people; and they came and worked in the house of the LORD of the hosts, their God, in the twenty-fourth day of the sixth month, in the second year of Darius the king. (Haggai 1:14–15)*

Darius had just gotten through the most traumatic experience of his life when he had to throw Daniel in the lions' den because Daniel's enemies played on the whims of his ego. These kings symbolize us with our free will. We may have also had to go through such an experience because of a whim of ours that puts the Lord's true life in danger (either in us or in someone else). King Darius couldn't sleep that night. He fasted and went to the lions' den early where he obviously made a clear decision to agree with Cyrus. To this effect, he said, "It doesn't matter who says whether or not it's the right time. I am going to return the vessels of the temple of God; I am going to return a remnant to Jerusalem; I am going to order them to once again start the construction of the house of God."

Like today, most of God's people were saying, "It isn't the time." But they didn't know what was going on with the "kings of the Medes" and the "Persians" and "Daniel." Daniel didn't have to scold the king; the king

---

168 Numbers 16:30; Isaiah 42:9; 43:19

knew because God himself woke up the spirit of the king. And in this manner, the work began with Haggai 2:1. In the seventh month, in the twenty-first day of the month, the word of the LORD came by the hand of the prophet Haggai, saying . . .

The twenty-first day of the seventh month is the last day of the Feast of Tabernacles. The Feast of Tabernacles had never been celebrated well in Israel until after the captivity; Ezra and Nehemiah tell that story (Ezra 3:4; Nehemiah 8:17).

The spiritual people of God in our time are going through many situations and trials, as are the people of natural Israel. But a new message is being announced relating to the Feast of Trumpets. The message in this feast is: prepare yourself, afflict your soul, turn your back on your own life, and abstain from your own works because the Day of Reconciliation (when those who do not pay attention could be cut off) is looming fast upon the horizon. This will prepare the people of God for the Feast of Tabernacles.

The Day of Reconciliation is an extremely important event in between the Feast of Trumpets and the Feast of Tabernacles. On the tenth day of the seventh month is Yom Kippur, which is wrongly translated as the Day of Atonement (or expiation). In the original it doesn't say "atonement," it literally says, "the day of reconciliations."

In Scripture, reconciliation is not meeting God halfway, but rather, it means to "become upright as the Lord is upright" so we can be compatible with him. The root of the verb "to reconcile" is in 120 verses, a number that relates to divine order. Divine order is to allow God to place his law in our heart and in our soul so we do what is pleasing to the Lord by nature (Jeremiah 31:33).

The Twelve-Year Discrepancy

As a human race, from Adam's time to ours, we have had almost six thousand years according to what is written in Scripture. For the Lord, a thousand years is as a day and one day as a thousand years. Both the Old and the New Testaments say this (Psalm 90:4; 2 Peter 3:8). There are six days for man to work, and the day of rest comes on the seventh, where each one rests from their own works to only do the will of God. And on the seventh day God finished his work which he had made, and he rested on the seventh day from all his work which he had made (Genesis 2:2).

God worked on the seventh day and finished his work; then he rested. And God blessed the seventh day and sanctified it because in it he had rested from all his work which God created in perfection (Genesis 2:3). "Sanctified" means "set apart for his exclusive use."

The Lord walked, ate, and harvested, and did many miracles on the Sabbath (most religious Jews didn't understand he was the Lord from heaven, and the heavenly Father lived in him), and the seventh day is to do God's will and not man's.

We are now coming into the seventh millennium, called the day of the Lord by the prophets. We have entered into it in one calendar, but we have not quite entered in another. If you calculate, there appears to be a glitch. The most likely explanation is that Adam rebelled after living an unknown number of years in the garden. The earliest indication of the foundation of this present world is when Satan deceived Eve and Adam rebelled against God in order to side with Eve (and with Satan). This is when Satan became the prince of this world. Satan's world is based on lies that lead to sin and death. The original world that God created is based on truth (and Jesus is the truth). It cost Jesus his life to redeem us from the fall. Even so, all of us will eventually die physically, and if we are in Christ, we have the hope participating in the first resurrection.

Unlike Adam, the Lord Jesus went to the temple when he was twelve-years old and publicly declared that he must be about his Father's business. This was an important marker. His obedience to God caused him to return and submit to the imperfect leadership of Mary and Joseph even when they didn't understand it very well, even when he was aware of who his real Father was.

If we locate the Exodus in 1488 B.C., a 1500-year period from the giving of the law may have ended with that unique event when the boy was twelve-years old. Scripture sums up the next eighteen years, saying Jesus increased in wisdom and in age and in grace with God and men (Luke 2:52). When he appeared with John the Baptist at about age thirty in the Jordan River at the beginning of his ministry (after submitting to Mary and Joseph for all that time), the heavenly Father declared, This is my beloved Son, in whom I am well pleased (Matthew 3:17, Mark 1:11; Luke 3:22).

So, if Jesus is the real pattern, then the first twelve years of his life represent the law, and then this eighteen-year period of his life represents what would later be known as the times of the Gentiles,[169] two thousand years of the Gentiles (two prophetic thousand-year days) that are about to be fulfilled. Without trying to trace all the prophecies that refer to

---

169 Luke 21:24

our time, in previous chapters we have highlighted three timelines in the Bible that point to the year 1967. The timeline may also be observed from other angles with slightly different results (see Appendix).

The year 1967 is when the Six-Day War was unleashed; it was the beginning of the Lord allowing a new quality of word to be opened in the church. I also believe that the Yom Kippur War of October, 1973, is also an important prophetic marker.[170]

I think Daniel's prophetic "days" will end approximately at the same time as the end of the church age (the age of grace).[171] This prophecy suggests that the justified corporate people of God will come into the fullness of the blessing of God (the fullness of their inheritance in Christ) and enter into a new day, the day of the Lord, which is the subject and focus of most Bible prophecy.

We are about to go over a threshold into the seventh prophetic day from the foundation of the world,[172] and the details are in God's hands. Since he is not willing that any should perish, he can extend time and grace as he sees fit; but sooner or later, we will cross the line into the day of the Lord, the first resurrection will take place, and Jesus will return. This may not be obvious to many in advance (those who are spiritually asleep will be rudely awakened) but when it happens, it will be unmistakable when the last trumpet sounds (1 Corinthians 15:51–53).

> [For] *if we believe that Jesus died and rose again, even so those who sleep in Jesus will God also bring with him. For this, we*

---

170 The United States, under President Trump, moved the US Embassy to Jerusalem on the seventieth anniversary of the modern nation of Israel on May 14, 2018, and this may also turn out to have prophetic importance.

171 As with many prophecies, there may be more than one valid interpretation. They may be taken at face value a day for a day and also a day for a year. If so, I would expect both results to converge on the same date.

172 If the beginning of the seventh prophetic day is measured from when Adam and Eve fell, then we do not know the exact start date of when they were banished from the garden of Eden. All we know is that they had no children in the garden, that Cain and Abel were born to Adam and Eve after the fall (Genesis 4:1–2). We know they grew to maturity until Cain killed his brother Abel, and that eventually God granted Adam and Eve another son to replace Abel (and to continue the line of Christ), and that Seth was born when Adam was one hundred and thirty years old. We do know, however, that we have definitely entered the seventh millennium from the creation of Adam. This seems to confirm that we have entered the Feast of Trumpets (to be celebrated on the first day of the seventh month of the agricultural calendar, which is the beginning of the new year of the of the sacred calendar). If this is the case, then the next major event on God's prophetic timetable is the fulfillment of the Day of Reconciliation (Yom Kippur).

say unto you by the word of the Lord, that we who are ali-
ve and remain unto the coming of the Lord shall not precede
those who are asleep. For the Lord himself shall descend from
heaven with a shout, with the voice of the archangel, and with
the trumpet of God; and the dead in Christ shall rise first; then
we who are alive and remain shall be caught up together with
them in the clouds, to meet the Lord in the air, and so shall
we ever be with the Lord. Therefore comfort one another with
these words. (1 Thessalonians 4:14–18, emphasis added)

God Inside

What does this have to do with us? It's obvious that the Lord has us in the Feast of Trumpets because of the message that he is announcing. The Feast of Trumpets is an ultimatum: whoever doesn't afflict their soul (turn their back on their own life and cease from their own works) will be cut off from among the people of God in the day of Yom Kippur (the Day of Reconciliation). It's also interesting to note that every fiftieth year, the year of jubilee doesn't begin on the first day of the seventh month (on the Feast of Trumpets); it begins on Yom Kippur, the Day of Reconcilia- tion and is also announced by sounding an alarm with the shofar, the ram's horn trumpet that symbolizes the voice of Jesus Christ. I certainly think that the events leading up to and surrounding the return of our Lord Jesus Christ will be the grandest jubilee of all time.

> Then *shalt thou cause the shofar to sound an alarm on the tenth*
> *day of the seventh month; in the day of the reconciliations sha-*
> *ll ye cause the shofar to sound throughout all your land. And*
> *ye shall sanctify the fiftieth year and proclaim liberty throu-*
> *ghout all the land unto all the inhabitants thereof; it shall be a*
> *jubilee unto you; and ye shall return every one unto his posses-*
> *sion, and ye shall return each one unto his family. (Leviticus*
> *25:9–10)*
>
> For *the Lord himself shall descend from heaven with a shout,*
> *with the voice of the archangel, and with the trumpet of God;*
> *and the dead in Christ shall rise first. (1 Thessalonians 4:16)*

The Feast of Passover and the Feast of Pentecost could be lived in Adam's life (in the flesh) while we also rejoice in the benefits and gifts that God bestows on us. Likewise, today we see those who seek to celebrate the blessings of salvation (Passover) and the power of the Spirit (Pentecost) in Adam's life; they call themselves "carnal Christians," which has to be an oxymoron!

Some people have been invested with the power of God for a predetermined time, Samson style, and there have been similar situations even in modern history. In fact, the endeavors of the "Samsons" of the church are scattered throughout history, but how many of them have had "Delilah" cut their hair, have lost their vision, and would end up grinding for the "Philistines?" Philistia represents death, not life.

After Samson repented, he accomplished more in his death than in his life because God desires the death of the old man (old nature). Samson even made it into Hebrews 11. Those who do wonderful works in the old man, even with God's gifts, don't really qualify for anything. They can say, "Lord, Lord, we prophesied in your name, we cast out demons, we did many wonderful works." But if they weren't clean, the Lord will say, "I never knew you."[173]

God doesn't recognize Adam and Adam's natural sons as true heirs to the kingdom. We've talked about how God clothed himself in Gideon and in Zechariah. It was God inside and Gideon or Zechariah on the outside. (This is different from many other Scriptures where it says the Spirit of God "came upon" someone.) The Lord is looking for witnesses like these now, where his life and his nature are inside; it only looks like us on the outside.[174]

So it was with the Lord Jesus; the Father dwelled inside. Jesus never sinned because he never did his own will. His own intimate friends didn't recognize him after the resurrection; they thought he was a gardener because he was transformed.

Jesus broke through the veil and entered into the presence of God the Father for us. He broke the power of death; he rent the veil that was later sewn up by men, and he continues to be our only entrance to the presence of the Father. Soon there will be a corporate fulfillment with the entire body of Christ. This will be the fulfillment of the Day of Reconciliation

---

173 Many will say to me in that day, Lord, Lord, have we not prophesied in thy name? and in thy name have cast out devils? and in thy name done many wonderful works? And then I will profess unto them, I never knew you; depart from me, ye that work iniquity. (Matthew 7:22–23)

174 And the Spirit of the LORD clothed himself in Gideon, who when he had blown the shofar, Abiezer joined with him. (Judges 6:34)

And the Spirit of God clothed himself in Zechariah, the son of Jehoiada, the priest, who being over the people, said unto them, Thus hath God said, Why do ye transgress the commandments of the LORD? Ye shall not prosper in this; for because ye have forsaken the LORD, he shall also forsake you. (2 Chronicles 24:20)

(Yom Kippur).

The symbolism of so many years with high priests, blood, and scapegoats has made it clear that anyone who tries to enter the holy of holies (representing the realm of the presence of the Father) in their own life will not live. Cherubim embroidered on the veil and a flaming sword reminded the priests of the extreme security measures that God placed on the borders of Eden (and what Eden represents) to make sure Adam and Eve (and their posterity) couldn't return to the Tree of Life in their fallen state (Genesis 3:24).

Where are we going with all of this? We are nearing the end of the Feast of Trumpets; the years of plenty, the years of the fat cows, are about to end (or maybe they have already ended, and the famine for hearing the words of the Lord has already begun).

When Haggai prophesied, God himself woke up the spirit in his people so that they could enter in and do a work that we humans cannot do in our natural state. The work of our human hands in Adam, the work of the hands of Cain when he offered a present obtained by the sweat of his brow (even though he came with the best of his harvest), is rejected by the Lord (Genesis 4:3–7).

In the book of the prophet Haggai, we learn that nothing has worked. They returned to the land and tried to rebuild the city of peace, but it wasn't working for them. Presently, many people are looking everywhere, wanting to return to the glory of the early church (or even to the glory of past revivals), but they cannot find it anywhere.

Haggai 1:11 says the Lord called for a drought upon this land and upon the mountains and upon the wheat and upon the wine and upon the oil and upon that which the earth brings forth and upon the men, and upon the beasts and upon every labour of hands. If we work in our own strength, out of the life we inherited from Adam, even with gifts and revelation from God, there is a curse upon what we try to share; there is a curse over the anointing we try to spread.

There is a curse over the mountains, over our fortresses, and God says he is going to not only make the foundations of the earth shake, he is going to shake the heavens! God is going to expose and do away with the foundations of this world (and of the rebellion of Satan and his followers in the heavens) in order to return everything to the true foundation that he has laid out from before the foundation of this world. This is the plan and purpose of God in the Lord Jesus Christ.

Something Different

Haggai 2

> *⁶ For thus hath the LORD of the hosts said: Yet even once, and I will shake the heavens and the earth and the sea and the dry land;*
>
> *⁷ and I will shake all the Gentiles; and the desire of all the Gentiles shall come: and I will fill this house with glory, said the LORD of the hosts.*
>
> *⁸ The silver is mine, and the gold is mine, said the LORD of the hosts. The glory of this latter house shall be greater than of the former, said the LORD of the hosts, and in this place I will give peace, said the LORD of the hosts.*

The house that they built (which was nothing compared to the one Solomon made) had greater glory because God's true glory was in the human form of the Lord Jesus Christ who eventually entered into that house and made two attempts at cleaning it.

However, after the second attempt, they rejected him and sentenced him to death. What happened next is an example and prophecy of what is coming, because the glory of what the Lord did in the early church is nothing compared to what he will do now in the time of the end.

The life of the Lord was present (in measure) in the disciples and in the church back then, but the life he will pour out now is going to be in fullness. The apostle Paul said that what they had back then was the "earnest" or the down payment of the Spirit (Ephesians 1:11–14), and Joel 2:28–29 said the Lord will pour out his Spirit (in fullness).

When Peter quoted Joel in Acts 2, he said he will pour out of His Spirit, but he was speaking of the outpouring of the Spirit, in part, at Pentecost. Now is the time of fullness (the Feast of Tabernacles).

When the foundation was laid, some cried for the joy of the moment, and others cried because they remembered what had been before, because what they were doing in that moment seemed like nothing. But Scripture says we must not despise the day of small beginnings.[175] What is happening now isn't the model of Pentecost. It's the model of Tabernacles, and that is very different. The age of Pentecost has been similar to what began in the upper room, a big deal, a huge revival, and

---

175 For who has despised the day of small beginnings? for they shall rejoice, and shall see the plummet in the hand of Zerubbabel. Those seven are the eyes of the LORD, which run to and fro through the whole earth. (Zechariah 4:10)

then the glory faded like Moses's face when he returned from the mountain of God (every revival since then seems to have followed the same pattern through the history of the church).

But Tabernacles begins small, like the morning star that has to shine first in our hearts until the day is perfect (Proverbs 4:18). Then the moon (a symbol of Israel and the church) will shine with the light of the sun (Christ) and wane no more; the sun will shine seven-fold, the light of seven days in one (Isaiah 30:26).

God has a small remnant who know the presence of the Lord; he has those who have been hidden in the Lord from before the captivity and whom he has been preparing during the whole tragedy. Now when the time comes, before placing stone upon stone, it says that there is a decisive moment, and this is when the foundation is placed, and the foundation cannot be moved. Look at the foundation:

> ^{And} *when the builders laid the foundation of the temple of the LORD, they set the priests in their apparel with trumpets and the Levites, the sons of Asaph, with cymbals, to praise the LORD, according to the ordinance of David, king of Israel. (Ezra 3:10)*

And we know that true praise is a clean life.

> ^{And} *they sang, praising and giving thanks unto the LORD because he is good, for his mercy endures for ever toward Israel. And all the people shouted with a great shout, praising the LORD, because the foundation of the house of the LORD was laid. But many of the priests and Levites and of the heads of the fathers, who were ancient men that had seen the first house, as the foundation of this house was laid before their eyes, wept with a loud voice while many shouted aloud for joy. (Ezra 3:11–12)*

Some want to restore the glory of the early church; but they know that we are not in anything like that yet. However, others have the vision that God will do something far beyond the previous house. Psalm 104:5 says, who laid the foundations of the earth, that it should not be moved by any age.

The true people of God are his "earth." From the beginning, Scripture talks about a seed (singular) of a woman that will defeat the serpent (crush his head) and lift the curse (which is still present). This promise is messianic.

The key to the prophecy of Haggai is showing how the curse is lifted: the curse came upon the earth because of Adam,[176] the curse that came when man wanted the fruit of the Tree of the Knowledge of Good and Evil, the curse that has continued throughout the religion of men (be it the Jews or the Christian church in its different forms – Catholic, Orthodox, Protestant). Even when on their best behavior, some people have only been willing for God to tell them what is evil while they continue to decide what is good, and this is why we haven't been able to come out from under the curse. They haven't understood.

God will restore us into something better than what Adam was, and had, before the fall. He will restore us to the original, of which Adam was only an image and an example.[177] Adam was a type and a shadow of what was to come later in the last Adam, the Lord of heaven.[178] Before the fall, when Adam walked with God in the garden, even though Adam was innocent, the presence of God was external. Now, God has made provision to place his Spirit inside every believer. This is a quantum leap.

The devil convinced Eve to choose the deadly fruit of the Tree of the Knowledge of Good and Evil so they could be like God. This led us to death, but the Lord Jesus wants us to follow him unto death so we can enter into God's divine nature and become joint heirs with Christ (2 Peter 1).

We are chosen from beforehand in the Lord Jesus who comes from before and is the true pattern. . . . who laid the foundations of the earth, that it should not be moved by any age (Psalm 104:5). The true earth, the people of truth that the God wants, is founded on the Lord Jesus Christ.

> *Therefore thus saith the Lord GOD, Behold, I lay in Zion for a foundation a stone, a tried stone, a precious corner stone, a sure foundation: he that believes shall not make haste.* (Isaiah 28:16)

> *. . . that calls Cyrus, my shepherd, and all that I desire, he shall fulfill, by saying to Jerusalem, Thou shalt be built and to the temple, Thy foundation shall be laid.* (Isaiah 44:28)

Cyrus was a Persian king who didn't know God. Yet he was anointed by the Lord to bring down Babylon, to grant a royal decree for God's remnant to receive the vessels of the temple and return to Jerusalem to

---

176 Genesis 3:17–19
177 Genesis 1:26
178 1 Corinthians 15:45

rebuild the temple and the walls, and to even provide finances, supplies, and materials from the royal treasury.[179] God also woke up the spirit of the kings of the Medes (who were partners with Cyrus) to help enable those who chose to leave Babylon and return to Jerusalem (Jeremiah 51:11). Something similar is taking place today.

> *According to the grace of God which is given unto me, as a wise masterbuilder, I have laid the foundation, and another builds upon it. But let each one see how the building is built. For no one can lay another foundation than that laid, which is Jesus the Christ.* (1 Corinthians 3:10–11)

> *. . . and are built upon the foundation of the apostles and prophets, Jesus Christ himself being the chief cornerstone.* (Ephesians 2:20)

For practically the last two millenniums, individuals have entered upon this foundation, but King David (whose reign is another example for us) never built the temple; he only prepared the materials. We have had a time like this, and now God says he is going to begin something different. Up until now, those who had ministries tried to gather people and keep them going to the meetings. This is a problem because people want to break loose and go their own way. Now God says he will gather a people into his name, which is the same as gathering them into his nature.

God will call his people, and they will follow. He will call us "my people," and we are going to let him be our God and follow him.

Haggai 2

> [15] *And now, I pray you, consider in your heart from this day forth, from before a stone was laid upon a stone in the temple of the LORD:*

The Lord has not yet laid stone upon stone, and the men who have laid stone upon stone without a true word from the Lord will be disappointed because they were not building his temple; they were building another house that will fall.

> [16] *since these things were: when one came to a heap of twenty measures, there were but ten; . . .*

"Measures" is the word for what they used to measure wheat. Twenty is symbolic of gifts and of grace; ten is a symbol of law. Instead of gifts,

---

179 Isaiah 44:28; 45:1

instead of grace, instead of goodness, there is a law that no one has been able to keep, leading to guilt trips, problems, and religion where whoever sins and then attempts to cover their sin with religious activity thinks they are okay.

One of the great errors of our time is when men try to follow the New Testament as if it were law instead of grace. If we try to copy what Jesus and the apostles were doing according to the letter of the Scriptures, we will fail miserably in our own strength, just as the Jews failed when they tried to keep the law of Moses on their own. The only way to please God is in the new man in Christ with the strength, gifts, resources, and grace of the Holy Spirit.

Hope of a Godly Remnant

[16] . . . when one came to the pressfat to draw out fifty vessels out of the press, there were but twenty.

The press is where the wine of life is. When they wanted fifty (Pentecost, the wine of the new life of the new covenant), there were only twenty. The blessing of Pentecost vanished, but God kept giving gifts of his grace throughout this long and sad history while the true life of Christ has been diminishing among much of the organized church. It hasn't increased but hasn't disappeared because God decided to maintain our hope: the hope of a remnant that continues to live by faith.

[17] I smote you with the east wind and with mildew and with hail in all the labours of your hands, . . .

Even with the gifts of God, those who are in Adam are not in the blessing. We are from the earth, and the earth is cursed, and the earth only produces thistles and thorns as a result of the curse that remains as long as man insists on the knowledge of good and evil. The only one who can get us out of the mess that Adam got us into is the Lord Jesus Christ. He came to deliver us from the power of sin and death by leading us toward the death of the old man and into the resurrection power of his life. His death reconciles us with God, but much more, now reconciled, we shall be saved by his life (Romans 5:10).

[18] Consider now in your heart from this day forth, from the twenty-fourth day of the ninth month, . . .

From this verse we see that Haggai's ministry had existed for three months, three weeks, and three days, and many things had happened. When

God entered the scene, he woke up the spirit of all of them and brought them into the formation of his true house. The true foundation was laid, and symbolically this divides the history of man in two: the days of the curse under Adam versus the days of the blessing under the fullness of the life of Christ, not just as individuals but as a corporate people chosen by God in the earth.

> [18] *. . . even from the day that the foundation of the LORD'S temple was laid, put your heart into it.*

Haggai didn't preach like the preachers of today who ask for tithes and offerings. No, this is what the Lord had Haggai preach this after waking up the spirit of the remnant: The silver is mine, and the gold is mine, said the LORD of the hosts (v. 8). The Spirit of God must come and wake up our spirit so we can repent from our dead works and God can do his work in and through us. This is why the present (or grain offering), representing the work of our hands, was never accepted in the Old Testament without a blood sacrifice. The work must be done in his life not in ours.

This was highlighted for 1500 years, and even so, few have understood. We will never understand if the Lord doesn't wake up our spirit. John the Baptist baptized in water and many of us can do the same, but only the Lord Jesus can baptize into the Holy Spirit and fire (Matthew 3:11). He can use us just as he used Haggai, Zephaniah, Zechariah, and so many others.

What does God want from us? He only wants our heart; he wants to transform it and write his laws on it. He wants to place the name (or nature) of the Father, the Son, and of the Holy Spirit into our hearts and into our souls because this way there won't be any more problems, because we will have his feelings and his thoughts. Then we will have the resources of the Spirit of God to win this great war against the flesh, the world, and the devil. Then by the Spirit we will be able to put to death the deeds of the flesh (Romans 8:13).

> [19] *Is not the seed yet in the barn? . . .*

Who is the barn? The Lord is. He wants us to be the tithes and the firstfruits so we can be taken into the granary, which is himself. The Lord will produce bread for the starving and seed to sow. The seed is yet in the barn, but when we are in his hands, we will soon be used by God wherever he desires. God will begin the blessing as soon as the foundation is laid.

This has been obtainable at an individual level; maybe it has been obtained in little groups. But we are very close to the time when God is going to decree it on a grand scale that has never been seen before in all the earth.

This great feast of Babylon is going to come down, and a new thing that is pure and clean will rise. And God is going to reveal his work to many who have had a similar trajectory to Cyrus and Darius. He's going to reveal what has really been done; he's going to remind us of the problem with the lions' den and the responsibility that we all have concerning the true body of Christ; and he's going to wake up the spirit of his people (and even of some who don't know him) to return the vessels and the gifts of God again to where they belong.

This is what God is going to do on the earth, where the work of our hands will no longer be according to our whims but ordained by him. There will be blessing if the true foundation is in place because the Lord Jesus broke the curse. He is the beginning of the new creation, and in the new creation there is no longer any curse. The life of Lord Jesus represents good ground where no thistles or thorns can grow that crowd out the message, where what is planted can produce thirty, sixty, or one hundred-fold, and he desires to place his life in us (in fullness).

> [19] *Is not the seed yet in the barn? Not even the vine, nor the fig tree, nor the pomegranate, nor the olive tree, has blossomed yet, but from this day will I bless you.*

This is where the curse ends. The difference between the blessing and the curse is huge. We cannot imagine what the true blessing is like because we have spent far too long struggling and kicking trying to get free of Adam's problem without success.

> [20] *And the word of the LORD came the second time unto Haggai in the twenty-fourth day of the month, saying,*

When the Lord repeats something a second time, it means that what he's saying is firm.[180]

> [21] *Speak to Zerubbabel, governor of Judah, . . .*

Zerubbabel represents a sprout from Babylon. Judah are the people in charge of God's praise here on the earth.

> [21] *. . . saying, I cause the heavens and the earth to shake,*

---

180 And that the dream came unto Pharaoh twice, it is because the thing is established by God, and God will shortly bring it to pass. (Genesis 41:32)

When God places the true foundation, what is bound here on the earth is bound in heaven, and what is loosed on the earth is loosed in heaven.[181] What does God want us to do? He wants us to bind the life in the flesh in Adam and loose the life in the Spirit in Christ, and the heavens and the earth will shake!

> [22] *and I will overthrow the throne of the kingdoms, and I will destroy the strength of the kingdom of the Gentiles, . . .*

This is the kingdom of the unconverted, those who are not circumcised in their hearts

> [22] *. . . and I will overthrow the chariot and those that ride in them;*

God will overthrow the humanistic religious, political, and economic machinery and those who depend on man's machinery.

> [22] *. . . and the horses and their riders shall come down, each one by the sword of his brother.*

Those who are carnal and humanistic will fall. As in the days of Gideon, they will do themselves in.

> [23] *In that day, said the LORD of the hosts, I will take thee, O Zerubbabel, my slave, the son of Shealtiel, said the LORD, and will make thee as a signet ring [like Mordecai]; for I have chosen thee, saith the LORD of the hosts.*

The Lord will soon take this remnant that has come out of the systems of men and has been walking in a spiritual desert with many trials, tribulations, and unmet needs. They have been confused at times and have found themselves repeatedly saying, "It isn't the time."

God is about to tell many of them, "It is the time, and I have chosen you."

Paul told Timothy that he needed to be ready in season and out of season because if it isn't time for others, it may be time for us (2 Timothy 4:2). The time is when the Lord says and not when we think.

When it was time in Haggai's days, some entered in, but others had to be separated because they were polluted and didn't have a clean trajectory.[182] Now we are in the priesthood of all believers, but God will

---

181 Matthew 16:19

182 And of the sons of the priests: the sons of Habaiah, the sons of Koz, the sons of Barzillai; who took a wife of the daughters of Barzillai, the Gileadite, and was called after their name. These sought their register among those that were reckoned by

separate those who are clean from those who are unclean, those who are in Christ from those who are in Adam (the wheat from the tares).

Joshua, Zerubbabel, Ezra, Nehemiah, and others were blessed, but Sanballat and Tobiah, among others, had to be taken out because they mocked the remnant of Israel.[183] There are many who say they are of the church of God; they say the church is their mother, but if God the Father doesn't recognize them as his sons, they are not clean.

Unlike the other feasts, in the Feast of Tabernacles, God doesn't accept us in the life of Adam (our own life), even with ministries and gifts that he has given us. What God has given to the slaves or servants (of sin and of the flesh) will eventually to return to him in the year of liberty (of jubilee), but what God has given to his sons (who are under his correction and discipline) remains theirs, as part of their inheritance forever. Eventually those who are the slaves of sin and of the flesh will be separated from those who are not (John 8:34–35).

> *Thus hath the Lord GOD said: If the prince gives a gift of his inheritance unto any of his sons, it shall be theirs; the possession thereof shall be by inheritance. But if he gives a gift of his inheritance to one of his slaves, then it shall be his until the year of liberty; when it shall return to the prince; but his inheritance shall be his sons' for them."* (Ezekiel 46:16–17)

This is the time when the true sons of God will shine (Daniel 12:3). Those who have received God's discipline, those who have washed their garments in the blood of the Lamb (which is his life), those that teach righteousness to the multitude, shall shine as the stars in perpetual eternity.

Let us pray:

Father, we have been under the curse caused by Adam for so long, and now we await the blessing in Jesus Christ. We ask for the fullness of the power of your Holy Spirit to win this great war against the flesh, the world, and the devil. Then by your Spirit we will be able to put to death the deeds of the flesh and experience a grand celebration in your presence along with the remnant of your children. Amen.

---

genealogy, but they were not found; therefore, they were, as polluted, put from priesthood. (Ezra 2:61–62) (This is also found in Nehemiah 7:64.)

183 Nehemiah 2:10; 2:19; 4:3; 4:7; 6:1–2; 6:14

CHAPTER SEVENTEEN

City of Truth and Mountain of Holiness: Zechariah's Prophecy

The book of the prophet Haggai ends, and the book of Zechariah the prophet begins.

Zechariah 1

¹ In the eighth month, in the second year of Darius, the word of the LORD came unto the prophet Zechariah . . .

This message overlaps with Haggai, and it is a prophecy full of detail that can keep on going indefinitely because it doesn't have a limit.

Here is something very interesting a few chapters later.

Zechariah 8

³ Thus hath the LORD said, I will restore Zion and will dwell in the midst of Jerusalem; and Jerusalem shall be called City of truth . . .

When he dwells in the midst, this will be the historic fulfillment of the Feast of Tabernacles. The corrupt seed of this world will wrinkle up and fail, and only the true seed will remain, which is the Lord Jesus Christ. He is the light, the truth, the life, and everything new will be based upon him.

³ . . . and the mountain of the LORD of the hosts, the mountain of holiness.

This refers to the people who are separated exclusively for his use. On the other hand, the foundations of the mountains of this present world system will be swept away. All the mountains, all the powers, all the people who use God's name for other purposes, will come to nothing because they were based on lies.

> *⁴ Thus hath the LORD of the hosts said; Old men and old wo-*
> *men shall yet dwell there in the streets of Jerusalem, and each*
> *one with his staff in his hand for the multitude of days.*

The "staff" is a symbol of discipline and righteousness. The mention of old men and old women means that now it will be possible to come to maturity in Christ.

> *⁵ And the streets of the city shall be full of boys and girls who*
> *shall play in them.*

We are talking about a thousand years of God's chosen people reigning with Christ and of the new generations that will arise (Revelation 20:4–6), even though some of this literally happened beginning with the restoration under Ezra and Nehemiah, and it is also literally happening now.

> *⁶ Thus saith the LORD of the hosts, If this should appear di-*
> *fficult in the eyes of the remnant of this people in these days,*
> *should it also be difficult in my eyes? saith the LORD of the*
> *hosts.*
> *⁷ Thus hath the LORD of the hosts said; Behold, I will save my*
> *people of the land of the east and of the land where the sun*
> *sets;*
> *⁸ and I will bring them, and they shall dwell in the midst of Je-*
> *rusalem; and they shall be my people, and I will be their God,*
> *in truth and in righteousness.*

Just as the natural Jews have come to the natural Jerusalem and are in a great conflict with some of their neighbors, the church is also in a great conflict (between the old nature of Adam and the new nature of Christ). This conflict is not over, but we know who will win in the end.

When this is accomplished, there will only be one people of God; there will be no more divisions; there will be one sheepfold and one shepherd.[184] This isn't going to be done by us attempting to accommodate everyone; it's going to be done in the Lord's life because his life, with his nature, produces the fruit that he desires to see come forth in us.

> *⁹ Thus hath the LORD of the hosts said, Let your hands be*
> *strong, ye that hear in these days these words by the mouth of*
> *the prophets, from the day that the foundation of the house of*
> *the LORD of the hosts was laid, that the temple might be built.*

---

184 Ezekiel 34:23; John 10:16

> [10] *For before these days there was no hire for man, nor any hire for beast; neither was there any peace to him that went out or came in because of the affliction: for I set all men each one against his neighbor.*

This is the present state of the natural nation of Israel and of much of the church because neither one has been able to break free from the curse God pronounced upon the ground because of Adam, which applies to all those who remain in Adam.[185]

> [11] *But now I will not do unto the residue of this people as in the former days [as in the six-thousand-year days of man, which are now ending] said the LORD of the hosts.*
> [12] *For the seed of peace shall remain; the vine shall give her fruit, and the ground shall give her fruit, and the heavens shall give their dew; and I will cause the remnant of this people to possess all this.*

The vine will give her fruit (Jesus is the vine, and we are the branches) when everything is on this foundation, when the cornerstone that was rejected is in its proper place. When the life of Christ flows unhindered, the earth will give her fruit, the true fruit of the Spirit. Then the heavens shall give their dew; God's blessing will fall, and the meek shall inherit the earth (Matthew 5:5). This has to do with Zerubbabel, the sprout from Babylon, the clean body of Christ.

> [13] *And it shall come to pass that as ye were a curse among the Gentiles, O house of Judah and house of Israel; so will I save you that ye might be a blessing; fear not, but let your hands be strong.*
> [14] *For thus hath the LORD of the hosts said, As I thought to punish you when your fathers provoked me to wrath, said the LORD of the hosts, and I did not repent:*
> [15] *so again have I thought in these days to do well unto Jerusalem and to the house of Judah; do not fear.*
> [16] *These are the things that ye shall do: . . .*

Only in Christ

What does God want? He wants to circumcise our hearts, cut the control of the flesh, and bring us under his control by the Holy Spirit. Our hearts

---

185 Genesis 3:17–19

have to do with our goals and motivation and desires. He wants to bring the life of the "old man" filled with wrong desires to a complete end by the Spirit. This requires our full cooperation.

> [16] *. . . Speak each one the truth to his neighbor; execute the judgment of truth and peace in your gates;*
> [17] *and let none of you imagine evil in your hearts against his neighbour; and love no false oath: for all these are things that I hate, said the LORD.*

The Lord wants to place his goals and motivation and desires in our hearts.

> [18] *And the word of the LORD of the hosts came unto me, saying,*
> [19] *Thus hath the LORD of the hosts said, The fast of the fourth month and the fast of the fifth and the fast of the seventh and the fast of the tenth shall be to the house of Judah joy and gladness and cheerful feasts; therefore love the truth and peace.*

God is going to restore unto us (his people) the years that caterpillar, the locust, the cankerworm, and the palmerworm have eaten – God's great army that did away with all the green, with all the attempts of his people to be prospered in the life of Adam. He's going to replace all that was lost in Adam with the fullness of the blessing in Christ.[186]

> [20] *Thus hath the LORD of the hosts said, It shall yet come to pass that there shall come people and the inhabitants of many cities*
> [21] *and the inhabitants of one city shall go to another saying, Let us go to pray before the LORD . . .*

Where is the Lord? He dwells in the realm represented by the holy of holies. How can we enter this realm? Only in the life of the Lamb of God, not in our own life. This is the realm of answered prayers; this is the realm of the throne of the Father, and he will respond if we enter his presence in the life of Jesus as bona fide members of the body of Christ, if we ask in the name of Jesus. The name of Jesus has to do with the nature of Jesus, according to the desires of Jesus and not according to our fleshly desires in the nature of fallen Adam. Those whose hearts are not circumcised will repeatedly ask with wrong motives.[187]

---

186 Joel 2:23–27
187 Ye ask and receive not because ye ask amiss, that ye may consume it upon your plea-

> ²¹ *. . . Let us go to pray before the LORD and to seek the LORD*
> *of the hosts. And the other will respond: I will go also.*
> ²² *And many peoples and strong nations shall come to seek the*
> *LORD of the hosts in Jerusalem . . .*

In the city of peace . . . God says that peace is where he puts peace, and this is where we should put our heart. He says he will place his peace in the place where the true foundation has been laid. He says if we are born from above, the heavenly Jerusalem is the mother of us all (Galatians 4:26).

> ²³ *. . . In those days it shall come to pass that ten men of all the*
> *languages of the Gentiles shall take hold of the robe of him that*
> *is a Jew, . . .*

In Spanish, this word "Jew" is translated as varón Judío. In other words, it refers to a Jew that is born free. There is only one Jew, born of a woman, that has ever been born free, and it is the Lord Jesus Christ.

> ²³ *. . . saying, We will go with you, for we have heard that God*
> *is with you.*

"God with us," Emanuel, is the name of the Lord. "God with us" is the Feast of Tabernacles. After placing the true foundation, there is no limit to what can be built, and so it shall be for all eternity.

We are in the historic moment when God is about to declare the blessing. We cannot predict all the details regarding the future, but we do know we are in the Feast of Trumpets, and the Day of Reconciliation (Yom Kippur) is about to arrive in its historic fulfillment, just as Passover and Pentecost have both been historically fulfilled (with the death of the Lord Jesus Christ for us and with the outpouring of the Holy Spirit beginning on the day of Pentecost).

In the living parables of Daniel, Haggai, and Zechariah, it came in the second year of Darius. For Joseph, it came in the second year of drought. It's at the door for us. Only God knows how much time is left. In that day, one shall be taken, and the other left (Matthew 24:40; Luke 17:34).

As in the days of Noah, some will be hidden in his life (Jesus is our ark of salvation), and others will be taken and swept away by the judgment that is coming. Judgment in the days of Noah was symbolically upon the earth (the dry land realm of the people of God), not upon life

---

sures. Ye adulterers and adulteresses, know ye not that the friendship of the world is enmity with God? Whosoever therefore that desires to be a friend of the world, makes himself the enemy of God. (James 4:3–4)

in the realm represented by the sea (symbolically the realm of pagan nations; the sea of lost humanity). Scripture says that the judgment that is coming will begin from the house of the Lord (1 Peter 4:17).

This judgment comes to clean a "holy place" where many gifts are being exercised by a priesthood (of all believers) that in the majority of cases is not clean. They have prepared a tremendous Babylonian feast.

The only ones who will be protected and preserved beyond any doubt is a remnant called "Daniel." In the feast, Belshazzar offered Daniel to be the third ruler in the kingdom, but after that night ended, Daniel was placed first in Darius's kingdom. The Lord will not act as our bodyguard in what is coming; he will not be our co-pilot. If we want to walk in the new day, he must be the head of the entire body of Christ. In the new day, this foundation is what he requires. And he wants to take us on from there in order to consistently do the will of our heavenly Father here on earth, even as his will in done in heaven (Matthew 6:10).

Let us pray:

Lord, I ask that we will be able to understand the true foundation, that we will long for the restoration of this foundation in your people with the same longing that Daniel, Haggai, Zechariah, Zerubbabel, and Joshua had.

Lord, I ask that we will be able to find refuge in you in the midst of the shortage and hunger that is coming upon the world, upon the great Babylon. That we will be able to be like the priests in the time of Joseph and Pharaoh, who had their sustenance secured because they were linked in the right place. Allow us, Lord, to be found awake by your Spirit, so that as part of that great morning star, you can use us to help wake up others before the day arrives and you cut off all those who are corrupt within those who call themselves the people of God. Allow us, Lord, to be among those who have found our existence in you so that we can be secure upon the true foundation, so that the day that is coming doesn't destroy us, so that the day that is coming only affirms us more in your purposes. Allow us, Lord, to enter behind the veil into the fullness of your life and find in the presence of the Father, our dwelling place. Keep us so that we may remain standing in the face of everything that is coming upon the earth. Amen.

Appendix

Simple Timeline According to Scripture

(Anno Mundi, or AM, from the creation of Adam)

Simple calculation of the birth year of the patriarchs of Genesis chapters 5 and 11:

1)   Adam (AM 0)
2)   Seth (AM 130)
3)   Enos (AM 235)
4)   Cainan (AM 325)
5)   Mahalaleel (AM 395)
6)   Jared (AM 460)
7)   Enoch (AM 622)
8)   Methuselah (AM 687)
9)   Lamech (AM 874)
10)   Noah (AM 1056) [188]
11)   Shem, Ham, Japheth – triplets – (AM 1556)
12)   Arphaxad (AM 1656)
13)   Salah (AM 1691)
14)   Eber (AM 1721)
15)   Peleg (AM 1755)
16)   Reu (AM 1785)
17)   Serug (AM 1817)
18)   Nahor (AM 1847)
19)   Terah (AM 1876)

---

188   The great flood took place when Noah was six hundred years, two months, and seventeen days old (Genesis 7:11).

20)   Abram, Nahor, Haran – triplets – (AM 1946)[189]

The Scriptures list the age of the patriarch at the time of the birth of each son, according to the whole number of years at their last birthday without taking into account the day and month they were born (Genesis chapters 5 and 11). Since their birthdays could have been in any of the twelve months of the year we will add an additional six months per instance to average this gap out (or ten additional years for the 20 names listed above).[190]

This puts the birth of Abram at approximately AM 1956. We know that God promised Abram that his seed would be a stranger in a land that is not theirs for four hundred years (Genesis 15:13). We also know that Egypt was the dominant world power through a very extensive area that included most of Mesopotamia (and the land of Canaan). This began over a hundred years before the birth of Abram. Once they left Ur of the Chaldees, it would not take Abram (later Abraham) and his family very long to enter the jurisdiction of Egypt.

The seed of Abraham began with Isaac, born approximately AM 2056, when Abraham was one hundred years old. Thirty-seven years later when he purchased a burial site (for four hundred shekels of silver in Hebron from the sons of Heth) for his wife Sarah, Abraham declared he was a stranger and a sojourner (Genesis 23:4). If AM 2056 is the

---

189   A straightforward interpretation of Genesis 11:26 is that Abram, Nahor, and Haran were triplets (as was evidently the case in Genesis 5:32 with Shem, Ham, and Japheth). Therefore, it follows that Abram left Haran according to Genesis 12:4 at seventy-five years of age and that his father, Terah, remained in Haran, where he died at age 205 (Genesis 11:32). On the surface, this interpretation seems to be contradicted by what Stephen said in Acts 7:4. However, remember that God told Abram to: *Depart out of thy country and from thy nature and from thy father's house unto a land that I will show thee* (Genesis 12:1). A similar situation is described in the NT: *And another of his disciples said unto him, Lord, suffer me first to go and bury my father. But Jesus said unto him, Follow me, and let the dead bury their dead.* (Matthew 8:21–22)

190   For instance, the Scripture simply states that *Adam lived one hundred and thirty years and begat a son in his own likeness, after his image, and called his name Seth* (Genesis 5:1). Therefore we know that Adam was at or past his 130th birthday and had not yet turned 131 when Seth was born. Since the Scripture does not give the precise day or month regarding the age of the patriarch when his son was born we have added six months per patriarch to average this out and fill the gap. Maybe Adam was 130 years and one month old when Seth was born, But Seth could have been one hundred and five and eleven months old when his son, Enos was born and so on. If this was the case, (and I don't think it at all likely for all the patriarchs to have begotten their sons exactly on their birthdays), by taking the birth month into account, Enos would have been born in AM 236 instead of AM 235 according to average probability.

beginning of the four hundred years, this puts the date of the Exodus at approximately AM 2456. However, Scripture states: Now the time that the sons of Israel[191] dwelt in Egypt was four hundred and thirty years. And it came to pass at the end of the four hundred and thirty years, even that same day it came to pass, that all the hosts of the LORD went out from the land of Egypt (Exodus 12:40–41, emphasis added).

Abram was seventy-five years old when he left Haran (Genesis 12:4), and if he and his family left Ur of the Chaldees five years before, this would account for the total time of four hundred and thirty years living as strangers in a land that was not theirs and under the government of Egypt.

Here is how the apostle Paul, under the anointing of the Holy Spirit, summed up the time from the Exodus to King Saul:

> *The God of this people of Israel chose our fathers and exalted the people when they dwelt as strangers in the land of Egypt, and with a high arm he brought them out of it* [AM 2456]. *And for the time of **about forty years**, he suffered their manners in the wilderness* [AM 2496].
>
> *And when he had destroyed seven nations in the land of Canaan, he divided their land to them by lot. And after that he gave unto them judges **about the space of four hundred and fifty years**, until* [including] *Samuel the prophet.*
>
> *And afterward they asked for a king, and God gave unto them Saul the son of Cis, a man of the tribe of Benjamin, **for forty years*** (Acts 13:17–21, emphasis added).

According to this, the time from the Exodus until Samuel anointed Saul was four hundred and ninety years, and the time, more or less, from the beginning of the leadership of Joshua (the first judge) until David came into the kingdom after forty years of Saul was also four hundred and ninety years. Therefore, David took over as king of Judah about AM 2986.[192]

---

191   Israel is actually a name of God that was given to Jacob at Peniel (Genesis 32:27–30), and God took the name Jacob upon himself (Psalm 24:6) prefiguring God's plan of redemption: *For he has made him to be sin for us, who knew no sin, that we might be made the righteousness of God in him* (2 Corinthians 5:21). Therefore, Abraham and Isaac are included in the "sons of Israel" (the sons of God).

192   It is interesting to note that David reigned over Judah for six and a half years until he was made king over all Israel about AM 2993. After that, he took the stronghold of Zion, overcame many enemies, brought back the ark and placed it in the taber-

From the beginning of the reign of David until the Babylonian captivity was another four hundred and ninety years. This may be calculated two ways:

1) The sum of the reigns of all the kings of Judah beginning with David was 481 years[193] (and we can add nine years to compensate for additional months that did not add up to full years,[194] bringing the total up to approximately four hundred and ninety years, or AM 3476).

2) From the following Scripture, it may be deduced that the Babylonian captivity of seventy years was to compensate for four hundred and ninety years of failure to comply with the sabbath years of rest:

> *And they burnt the house of God and broke down the wall of Jerusalem and burnt all its palaces with fire and destroyed all its desirable vessels. And those that escaped from the sword he carried away to Babylon; where they were slaves to him and his sons until the reign of the kingdom of Persia, to fulfil the word of the LORD by the mouth of Jeremiah until the land had fulfilled her sabbaths; for all the time of her desolation she rested until the seventy years were fulfilled [AM 3546].*

> *But in the first year of Cyrus, king of Persia, that the word of the LORD spoken by the mouth of Jeremiah might be accomplished, the LORD stirred up the spirit of Cyrus, king of Persia, that he made a proclamation throughout all his kingdom and put it also in writing, saying, Thus saith Cyrus, king of Persia, The LORD God of the heavens has given me all the kingdoms of the earth; and he has charged me to build him a house in Jerusalem, which is in Judah. Who is there among you of all his people? Let the LORD his God be with him, and let him go up. (2 Chronicles 36:19–23)*

If we take the above Scripture as the trigger for Daniel's prophecy of seventy weeks (of years) then:

---

nacle of David, wrote many powerful and prophetic psalms, and led a great spiritual revival circa AM 3000.

193   This is counting the six years that Joash, the son of Ahaziah, was hidden as a child while evil Queen Athaliah reigned (2 Kings 11:3).

194   There were twenty kings from Solomon's son Rehoboam to Zedekiah. Two of them only reigned three months each. If we add six months for each of the remaining eighteen kings, this gives us the additional nine years. David put Solomon on the throne a few months before he physically died at age seventy, so we will not add six months for him.

Seventy weeks are determined [Heb. cut] upon thy people and upon thy holy city to finish the prevarication and to conclude the sin and to make reconciliation for iniquity and to bring in everlasting righteousness and seal the vision and the prophecy, and to anoint the holy of holies.

Know therefore and understand that from the going forth of the word to cause the people to return and to build Jerusalem unto the Anointed [Heb. Messiah] Prince, there shall be seven weeks, and sixty-two weeks, while the street shall be built again and the wall, even in troublous times. (Daniel 9:24–25)

Many prophecies in Daniel and elsewhere have an application that is one year for each day; this begins with the judgment of God upon the unbelieving generation that would die while wandering in the wilderness for forty years after having disobeyed for forty days (Numbers 14:34).

The seven weeks (or forty-nine days) mentioned above were forty-nine years of rebuilding the temple and the wall of Jerusalem under Ezra and Nehemiah. This brings us to AM 3595. Then there were another sixty-two weeks, representing 434 years in troublesome times, until the beginning of Jesus's ministry in AM 4.029.[195]

And after the sixty-two weeks the Anointed One [Heb. Messiah] shall be killed and shall have nothing: (and the ruling people that shall come shall destroy the city and the sanctuary; whose end shall be as a flood, until at the end of the war it shall be cut off with desolation).

In one week (they are now seventy) he shall confirm the covenant by many: and at the midst of the week he shall cause the sacrifice and the oblation to cease, and because of the many abominations, desolation shall come, even until complete destruction shall be poured out upon the abominable people. (Daniel 9:26–27)

The "midst of the last week" would be Passover of AM 4033 (the cruci-

---

195 If Jesus was born on the Feast of Trumpets in AM 4000 (the first day of the seventh month of the agricultural calendar, which is the first day of the first month of the sacred calendar and occurred on the day of the new moon), then this is more or less the equivalent of our first of October, 2 BC (assuming there is no year 0 BC or AD and that from 1 BC to 1 AD is one year). According to Luke 3:23, Jesus began his ministry when he was about thirty years of age (or sometime after the beginning of October, AD 29).

fixion), and the end of the week would be in the fall of AM 4036 (near the time when the Holy Spirit was poured out upon the house of Cornelius, Saul of Tarsus was converted on the Damascus road, and the opportunity of the gospel opened up for the Gentiles – even while the disobedience of the Jewish nation intensified until Jerusalem and the temple were completely destroyed by AM 4070. Jesus's once-and-for-all sacrifice and oblation ended animal sacrifice in the temple forever.

It seems quite possible (even probable) that the prophecy of the seventy weeks of Daniel (and in particular the last week) along with what Jesus said in Matthew 24, Mark 13, and Luke 21 all have dual meaning with an application to the destruction of Judea and Jerusalem after the end of the approximately 1500-year age of the law,[196] along with an end-time application to the approximate 2000-year age of grace[197] prior to the day of the Lord and the second coming. If this is so, then we are coming up on some very important 2000-year anniversaries that are likely to be prophetically significant.[198]

After the house of David had reigned over Judah four hundred and ninety years, God intervened and caused the seventy accumulated years of rest (that no one had seen fit to implement every seventh year as instructed by God[199]) to be fulfilled during the Babylonian captivity. Something similar may happen regarding other prophetic requirements

196   Did the age of the law begin with the giving of the Ten Commandments on Mount Sinai? Or was it when each Israelite received their inheritance in the promised land? Did it end with the destruction of the temple? Were there some transitions and overlaps? According to the above timeline, there would have been a 1500-year period of time, more or less, from when Joshua distributed the inheritance to the tribes of Israel, including Judah, circa AM 2500 until Jesus was born about AM 4000 (or, if the seventy years of Babylonian captivity are not to be counted this period of 1500 years would have ended in 70 A.D. with the destruction of Jerusalem and the temple).

197   When did the age of grace begin? When Jesus was born? When Jesus was twelve and spent three days in the temple? At Jesus's death and resurrection? When the Holy Spirit was poured out on the early church when the day of Pentecost was fully come? When the gospel was made available to the Gentiles? It certainly appears that the age of grace is coming to an end, and the day of the Lord is near.

198   According to this timeline, the two thousandth anniversary of the beginning of Jesus's ministry would be early October of AD 2029 (AM 6029). As we get closer and closer to the end of the age, the first day of the seventh month (beginning on the new moon), the Feast of Trumpets (Rosh Hashanah), and the tenth day of the seventh month, the Day of Reconciliation (Yom Kippur), bear watching (every year) as possible anniversaries when God might do something unique in fulfilment of prophecy. Remember that a year of Jubilee actually begins on Yom Kippur (Leviticus 25:9).

199   Exodus 23:10–11

(such as the seventieth week of Daniel) that were not completely fulfilled due to human deficiency, unbelief, and rebellion. If the seventieth week of Daniel is to be repeated (and this is a big if), then a possible date for it to end would be at the end of the age of grace (which should be about 2000 years long).

For the sake of curiosity, if we calculated the two thousandth anniversary of the beginning of Jesus's ministry using this timeline, it would be in the fall of AD 2029 (AM 6029). Scripture, however, is very clear the exact day and hour of the Second Coming (and the end of the age of grace) is known only to the Father (Matthew 24:36) although we are all expected to be aware of the times and the seasons (1 Thessalonians 5:1).I consider this timeline, as spelled out here, to have a margin of error given the fact that the vast majority of the information provided in Scripture is rounded to the nearest year. We also need to keep in mind that according to Scripture, the second coming will occur at a time when most are not expecting it. Therefore, we are repeatedly admonished to be ready at all times.

At the time of the destruction of Jerusalem and the temple in AD 70, those who were in tune with the Holy Spirit remembered the words of Jesus and were not trapped in the devastation surrounding the end of the age of the law. This will also be the case regarding the coming day of the Lord and the end of the world as we know it under the dominion of Satan.

Jesus put it like this:

Luke 21

[24] *And they shall fall by the edge of the sword and shall be led away captive into all nations, and Jerusalem shall be trodden down of the Gentiles until the times of the Gentiles are fulfilled.*

What are the times of the Gentiles? Does this have to do with the end of the age of the church? with the end of the age of grace? In the natural realm, the city of Jerusalem is back in the hands of the Jews after historic prophetic events in 1948, 1967, and 1973. Since 2018, the city has been gaining more and more international stature and recognition as the capital of Israel.

[25] *Then there shall be signs in the sun and in the moon and in*

the stars, and upon the earth distress of nations, with perplexity; the sea and the waves roaring;

I think we can agree that this is also happening.

26 men's hearts failing them for fear and for looking after those things which are coming on the earth; for the powers of heaven shall be shaken.

This is what we can expect in the near future.

27 And then they shall see the Son of man coming in a cloud with power and great glory.
28 And when these things begin to come to pass, then look up and lift up your heads, for your redemption draws near.

Meet the Author

At the age of four, while his family was living in Minneapolis, Minnesota, Russell Stendal prayed and asked God to call his parents, Chad and Pat, to be missionaries. God answered that prayer and within just a few years the whole family was on the mission field in Colombia, South America. He became an accomplished jungle pilot and married a beautiful Colombian lady named Marina. They have four children, Lisa, Alethia, Russell Jr., and Dylan, plus six grandchildren.

When Russell was 27 years old, Marxist guerrillas of the FARC kidnapped him for 142 days. The story of his kidnapping is told in the book he wrote titled Rescue the Captors. His reason for the title is because he realized that his captors were more captive than he was. There was a possibility he would be released, but most of his kidnappers were young people who had been taken from their families, given a weapon, and taught to kill. They had little hope of survival.

To reach all the actors of the armed conflict, including his former captors, Russell established a radio ministry to air programs into the dangerous war stricken areas of Colombia with messages of peace and hope. He has also written more than 50 books in English and Spanish.

In 2017, he was awarded the Shahbaz Bhatti Freedom Award, (given to Pope Francis the year before) for his tireless efforts towards spreading peace and reconciliation in Colombia (in the context of promoting religious freedom). Russell travels extensively as a guest speaker in conventions around the world. His speaking is unique in that he is very sensitive to the Lord's voice and does not hesitate to deliver the message imparted to him, no matter how uncomfortable that may be to him or to others. Most of the books he has published were transcribed directly from the radio messages he has preached in Spanish and beamed into virtually all of the war torn areas of the countryside.

Russell is the editor of the Jubilee Bible translation that has been published in English and in Spanish. Well over a million copies of this Bible have been donated and distributed into the most needy areas of Colombia and Venezuela.

Made in the USA
Monee, IL
07 July 2026